Development Communication

Reframing the Role of the Media

Edited by

Thomas L. McPhail

⟨W⟩WILEY-BLACKWELL

A John Wiley & Sons, Ltd., Publication

This edition first published 2009
© 2009 Blackwell Publishing Ltd

Blackwell Publishing was acquired by John Wiley & Sons in February 2007. Blackwell's publishing program has been merged with Wiley's global Scientific, Technical, and Medical business to form Wiley-Blackwell.

Registered Office
John Wiley & Sons Ltd, The Atrium, Southern Gate, Chichester, West Sussex, PO19 8SQ, United Kingdom

Editorial Offices
350 Main Street, Malden, MA 02148-5020, USA
9600 Garsington Road, Oxford, OX4 2DQ, UK
The Atrium, Southern Gate, Chichester, West Sussex, PO19 8SQ, UK

For details of our global editorial offices, for customer services, and for information about how to apply for permission to reuse the copyright material in this book please see our website at www.wiley.com/wiley-blackwell.

The right of Thomas L. McPhail to be identified as the author of the editorial material in this work has been asserted in accordance with the Copyright, Designs and Patents Act 1988.

Wiley also publishes its books in a variety of electronic formats. Some content that appears in print may not be available in electronic books.

Designations used by companies to distinguish their products are often claimed as trademarks. All brand names and product names used in this book are trade names, service marks, trademarks or registered trademarks of their respective owners. The publisher is not associated with any product or vendor mentioned in this book. This publication is designed to provide accurate and authoritative information in regard to the subject matter covered. It is sold on the understanding that the publisher is not engaged in rendering professional services. If professional advice or other expert assistance is required, the services of a competent professional should be sought.

Library of Congress Cataloging-in-Publication Data

McPhail, Thomas L.
    Development communication : reframing the role of the media / Thomas L. McPhail.
        p. cm.
    Includes bibliographical references and index.
    ISBN 978-1-4051-8795-4 (hardcover : alk. paper)—ISBN 978-1-4051-8794-7 (pbk. : alk. paper)
    1. Communication—Social aspects.   2. Mass media—Developing countries.
    3. Telecommunication—Developing countries.   I. Title.
    HM1206.M3873 2009
    302.2309172′4—dc22
                                    2008055223

A catalogue record for this book is available from the British Library.

Set in 10.5 on 13 pt ITC Century by SNP Best-set Typesetter Ltd., Hong Kong
Printed and bound in Malaysia by Vivar Printing Sdn Bhd

01   2009

Contents

Tables and Figures

Tables

Figure

Notes on Contributors

Satarupa Dasgupta is a documentary film maker, editor, and journalist. Previously, she has worked with NGOs in Calcutta, India and is a world authority on the Sonagachi project. She is currently completing her doctoral studies at Temple University where she worked on a Robert Wood Johnson funded project dealing with tobacco corporations.

Renée Houston is an Associate Professor of Communication Studies at the University of Puget Sound. Her research and teaching interests include systems theory, and information and communication technologies. Her most recent research examines the intersection of public and organizational policy on women, the working poor, and the homeless. This work is used to inform a broader systems analysis of homelessness for local government and state-wide efforts. Her work includes book chapters and journal articles some of which have appeared in *Communication Theory, Management Communication Quarterly, International Journal of Learning*, and *World Futures*.

Michele H. Jackson is an Associate Professor and Chair of the Department of Communication at the University of Colorado at Boulder. Jackson is founder and director of the ASSETT program, which develops initiatives to use technology to support teaching and learning for CU's College of Arts & Sciences. She has long ago come to terms with the fact that digital communication technologies tend not to stick around for very long in any one form, even when they seemed like good ideas at the time. For the past several years, she has focused on: design of applications to motivate collaboration; interrogating the social function of determinism in organizations and groups; and theorizing how we socially construct communication within a technologically induced context of indeterminacy and change.

Thomas L. McPhail is a Professor of Media Studies and a Fellow in the Center for International Studies at the University of Missouri-St. Louis. In 1981 he published with Sage a now classic work, *Electronic Colonialism* with an Introduction by Everett Rogers. For several years he was associated with the Canadian Commission for UNESCO and worked at UNESCO in Paris in the late 1970s. Currently he serves as a media analyst for several media outlets across North America and is working on a third edition of *Global Communication: Theories, Stakeholders, and Trends* (Oxford: Wiley-Blackwell).

Luz Estella Porras is an Adjunct Instructor at the School of Journalism and Communication, University of Oregon, where she recently received her PhD. She is interested in communication for social change particularly in Latin America. Her dissertation, an ethnographic study of the practice of development communication in Colombia, explores the limitations of modernization-related practices and the opportunity of aesthetic and embodiment resources for participatory communication. Previously Dr Porras taught at Universidad Autónoma de Bucaramanga in Colombia and worked as a practitioner with women's organizations and as a scriptwriter of educational media materials. At Oregon her teaching includes development communication, diversity and media, and mass media and society.

Mitchell F. Rice is a Professor of Political Science at Texas A&M University and a Fellow of the National Academy of Public Administration, Washington, DC. He has written extensively in the areas of public policy, multiculturalism, and cultural competency issues. His most recent book, *Diversity and Public Administration: Theory, Issues, and Perspectives* (Armonk, NY: ME Sharpe Publishers, 2005), received the Best Book Award for 2005 from the Section on Personnel Administrations and Labor Relations of the American Society for Public Administration. He has been a Ford Foundation Post Doctoral Fellow, a Rockefeller Foundation

Post Doctoral Fellow, and an American Council on Education Fellow.

H. Leslie Steeves is Professor and Associate Dean for Graduate Affairs and Research at the School of Journalism and Communication, University of Oregon. Her PhD is from the University of Wisconsin-Madison. Her research examines media representations of gender and ethnicity, and communication in developing countries, especially sub-Saharan Africa. She has published many articles in these areas, as well as a book: *Gender Violence and the Press: The St. Kizito Story* (Athens, OH: Ohio University Monographs in International Studies, 1997). She is co-author (with Srinivas Melkote) of *Communication for Development in the Third World: Theory and Practice for Empowerment, 2nd edn* (New Delhi: Sage, 2001). She has had two Fulbright grants for teaching and research in Africa, and she directs an annual study abroad program in Ghana.

Eva Szalvai is an Assistant Professor of International Business at Colby-Sawyer College. She recently earned her PhD in International Communication from Bowling Green State University, OH. Being a multidisciplinary researcher, she also holds an MSc degree in Economics from Hungary, and MA degree in Arts Administration from the University of Akron. Prior to her academic career, she accumulated over 20 years of international business experience while living in several countries. She has also developed several international projects with non-profit organizations. Relying on her cosmopolitan identity, her praxis-based critical research lies within the fields of globalization, sustainable development, media convergence, and value creation. In particular, she is interested in the forms of international relations that are culturally less biased (participatory communication, action research) and the non-hegemonic processes of globalization.

Preface

This book is about the state of development communication. As such it deals with the history, highlights major trends and theories, looks at various players, ranging from academics, to foundations, to non-government organizations, and finally spells out some of the more current and perhaps positive elements in the sector. A difficult aspect of this journey is about whose language, or frames, one is going to apply. There are two broad streams of discourse.

The one was promoted after World War II by a collection of development communication specialists who sought to create both an industry and a body of knowledge. They came at development with a Western nations', northern hemisphere, and industrialized lens, which focused on economic goals and indicators. Almost an "if only they could act and be like us" mantra. Yet success was always just around the next corner, which seldom came.

The other stream, which emerged in the late 1960s and had a strong basis in Latin America, looked at the failures of the other stream, and as part of their criticisms, sought to move out of the economic frame and unitary goal of development and replace it with more of a "made in the southern hemisphere" approach. It also had somewhat of a neo-Marxist slant. Basically this approach wanted to turn the imported approach on its head. The top-down approach was sacked and a bottom-up approach was pushed. In addition, the economic determinism gospel was demoted and other aspects were pushed to the front of the line. Culture, language, women, environmental issues, small steps or projects, the role of technology, and grass-roots participation were added to the development communication lexicon.

So this book is about both streams. And it requires some understanding about how did we get to where we are now. What may the future of development communication look like down the road? Or, will the elusive corner ever be reached? And how, by whom and on whose dime, yen, peso, or euro?

I would to share how I came to be a student of development communication. During the 1970s I engaged in two seminal activities. The one was being a member of the Canadian Commission for the United Nations Education, Science, and Cultural Organization (UNESCO) during the turbulent New World Information and Communication Order (NWICO) era. This turbulent era eventually caused both the USA and Great Britain to withdraw from UNESCO. The second was an actual consulting phase with UNESCO at their headquarters in Paris in the late 1970s. UNESCO is viewed by many poor nations as their agency within the United Nations' system of specialized agencies. While at UNESCO I became familiar with leading academics from the southern hemisphere dealing with both the theory and practice of development communication. It became apparent and a familiar story that many of the academic critics, like Luis Ramiro Beltran of Bolivia, were educated at some of the best North American universities. Their writings had to be taken seriously. They were not a bunch of neo-Marxist extremists as some of their critics, like Henry Kissinger, contended. I also worked with Marshall McLuhan at the University of Toronto, Sean MacBride and his commission members in Paris, and Everett Rogers who became a friend as well as colleague. In fact, Rogers wrote the *Foreword* to my book *Electronic Colonialism* (London: Sage Library of Social Research, 1981). This book provides comprehensive details about the extended saga of UNESCO and the NWICO debates, the MacBride Commission of 1979, which had the formal title of the International Commission for the Study of Communication Problems, and the growing role of the International Telecommunication Union (ITU) in development telecommunication matters. This role for the ITU was to peak with the World Summit on the Information Society (2003–2005) (WSIS). WSIS unexpectedly became a battle ground over the future of the global control of the Internet. Many from Europe and the Third World expressed grave reservations about the USA's hegemonic control of the Internet through the California-based Internet Corporation for the Assignment of Names and Numbers (ICANN). ICANN was tightly controlled by the White House and failed to appreciate the strength of the grievances against the ethnocentric American perspective. Some of this debate, along with the background to the WSIS, appears in my book, *Global Communication: Theories, Stakeholders, and Trends* (Oxford: Blackwell Publishers, 2006).

I want to thank the authors of the commissioned chapters. They were selected on the basis of their academic reputations in this area and writings about key aspects of the current development communication scene. They are Satarupa Dasgupta, Renée Houston, Michele H. Jackson, Luz Estella Porras, Mitchell F. Rice, H. Leslie Steeves, and Eva Szalvai. In addition, I want to thank my students who survived parts of the manuscript and the researchers who assisted me from time to time. They are Mauro Mueller, Kerry Marks, Krisdon Manecke, Ryan McPhail, and Taylor Pietz. Any mistakes are obviously mine.

Thomas L. McPhail
St. Louis, Missouri

1

Introduction to Development Communication

Thomas L. McPhail

The time of white missionaries telling people of color how to lead their lives must come to an end. (New York Times, November 5, 2007, p. 1)

Introduction

There have now been over six decades of theory, research, foreign aid, and various paradigms and strategies covering initiatives in development communication. These have been carried out by academics, social workers, clergy, non-governmental organizations (NGOs), foreign-aid from industrialized nations, and specialized agencies of the United Nations (UN). Yet the frustration and situation in the southern hemisphere[1] continues to worsen. Violence is up and security is declining, the numbers of displaced people is increasing, assistance is stagnant, foreign aid has more conditions attached to it, human rights violations are ignored, a free press is rare, military and other corrupt regimes ignore kidnapping, rape, and murder is far too common; even basics like housing, shoes, schooling, water, or medicine are frequently hard to find. In addition, women tend to be marginalized or ignored in many underdeveloped regions. The history of early development media projects had no mention of women's roles or how they might benefit.

Another parallel stream of action has been apparent when one examines proselytizing in the southern hemisphere or less developed countries (LDCs) among religious groups including Catholics, Mormons, evangelical Protestants, and others. They sought converts to Christianity but at the same time they also tried to tell locals, many poor rural peasants, how to lead their lives. An interesting part of these theology-driven interventions gave rise to what is called Liberation as well as Prosperity Theologies, which are covered later in this chapter.

In many ways this preaching was similar to northern hemisphere aid projects which were doing the same things. They also were telling the poor how to live their lives, raise families, and how to get ahead economically at the same time. The road to development was to follow the processes in place in industrialized nations, plus reject, change, or abandon traditional ways of doing things. Yet despite the efforts of thousands of researchers, aid workers, and clergy along with billions of dollars in aid, the situation and people in the southern hemisphere and poor regions of the world are in many ways worse off today than they were at the end of World War II. Expert Ernest Wilson in 2006 points out that "more than eighty countries have a lower per capita income today than a decade ago" (Wilson 2006, 8).

World War II is the point when major aid, interventions, and the beginnings of modernization planning and schemes commenced. The plans and hopes of economic and cultural elites based in the northern hemisphere failed to materialize in the southern hemisphere as promised. At first it was the churches promising a better life both here and the hereafter. Then a wave of NGOs, foreign aid agencies, and academics took up the cause. The cause or goal was to improve the lives and lot of inhabitants of the peripheral regions of the world. Yet the lives of many in the southern hemisphere either remained unchanged, or in some cases, their situations – economic, health, housing, education, media access – became worse. After more than six decades of modernization, the southern hemisphere is still facing economic, cultural, and social challenges. This distinct lack of progress has led to a movement to replace rather than replicate the mistakes, theories, and practices of the past. There is now a broad-based movement challenging academic-, political-based leadership, NGOs, development theory, practices, motives, roles, paradigms as well as agendas and methodologies.

Why this came about, what is changing, and how, is what this book is about. We will begin by defining development communication and recounting how the history of the modernization era and theory began, along with highlighting the leading early theorists and their works. We will also note some of their assumptions and successes as well as failures.

Development communication is the process of intervening in a systematic or strategic manner with either media (print, radio, telephony, video, and the Internet), or education (training, literacy, schooling) for the purpose of positive social change. The change could be economic, personal, as in spiritual, social, cultural, or political.

The book will look at the changing area and focus of development communication. This area has focused on Third World issues and how modernization has essentially failed to deliver change in developing nations or regions. The lack of telephone service, illiteracy, few indigenous media successes, and lack of connectivity and the costs of the Internet all come into play. In some regions the spread of HIV/AIDS has both hurt the work-force as well as diverting and absorbing millions in foreign aid. After more than six decades of development the Third World or peripheral nations still lack access to modern telecommunications and mass media. This core text will address the history, major approaches or theories, the role of NGOs, and the paradigm shift currently underway.

It is this shift from an economic preoccupation to a broader and more inclusive approach that makes this book unique. The key aspect is that for decades the old paradigm had an economic focus or lens whereas the new focus is on practices and policy matters with a social or cultural lens. One of the emerging roles is how are media and telecom systems promoting democracy as well as broader quality of life/environment issues. Part of the change is also a bottom-up or grass-roots approach rather than top-down decision making that has dominated the field since the end of World War II.

Over the past decades some objections to globalization have also emerged. Not all see the same benefits from the global economy. The benefits of globalization are not evenly shared by all. Compounding this criticism is the post Cold War fear of the United States becoming a hegemonic power and defining aid, paradigms and international policies to suit its own goals and economic purposes, and not necessarily taking into account the interests of receiving nations. For example, since 2000 the area of family planning, contraception, abortion, and the role of women in society has become a particularly sensitive area, particularly in terms of US foreign assistance efforts. Yet over the same period there has been a significant increase in feminist scholarship dealing with the media. Other factors include what is now being referred to as coercive democracy. This is where the US is combining its post Cold War military power with its hegemonic economic power to set conditions on foreign aid or international treaties that at times further cripple weak nations or regions. The bulk of the benefits go to Western nations, their farmers, and corporations, while the poor in the Third World see little improvement. As a result "development media for whom" is a critical issue; this aspect will be expanded upon in the following chapters.

History

A convenient starting point is with President Harry Truman's Inaugural Address of January 20, 1949.[2] Referring to the end of World War II, Truman states "Since the end of hostilities, the United States has invested its substance and its energy in a great constructive effort to restore peace, stability, and freedom to the world" (Truman 1949, 3). Following this he went on to show enormous support and praise for the United Nations and its specialized agencies but it was really the fourth point in his address that dealt directly with expanding US foreign aid to poor nations. Truman stated "Fourth, we must embark on a bold new program for making the benefits of our scientific advances and industrial progress available for the improvement and growth of underdeveloped areas" (Truman 1949, 4). Soon the US Congress established a Technical Cooperation Administration unit to implement the major new Point Four initiative. In 1954 the unit became integrated into the US Department of State.

With funds from this new unit began a series of assistance projects and experiments, many with a communication or media, primarily radio, focus. President Truman understood the larger issues and picture:

> More than half the people of the world are living in conditions approaching misery . . . Their economic life is primitive and stagnant. Their poverty is a handicap and a threat to them and to more prosper-

ous areas. For the first time in history, humanity possesses the knowledge and the skill to relieve the suffering of these people. (Truman 1949, 5)

So began the long trek of the application of foreign assistance, values, and ideas to the southern hemisphere. And with the expanding role and fear of Communism and the Cold War era which followed, the funds for spreading both democracy and hope were unabated. For example, it is estimated by the John Templeton Foundation that aid to Africa alone during this period exceeded $600 billion. As will be detailed later American Foundations, such as Ford and Rockefeller, not only supplied substantial money but they also packaged projects involving American academics going to less developed regions to oversee projects and collect data as well. Several other industrialized nations, such as Canada, France, Germany, Great Britain, Japan, the Nordic countries, also contributed substantial amounts to a long list of projects. Currently the world's foreign aid total is in excess of $100 billion annually. It comes from a broad range of industrialized nations, now including China. So money was not the basic problem.

It is important to note that US foreign policy during this era can be summed up in two words: Stop Communism. This phenomenon framed external efforts by the US and other industrialized nations. It was good versus evil, or freedom versus communism. There were no compromises or middle ground in this fight. When foreign leaders looted aid projects, many looked the other way as long as the leaders were stridently anti-communist. This tension lasted until the fall of the Berlin Wall in 1989, which was perceived as the symbolic ending of the Soviet-led Marxist movement across the Warsaw Pact countries.

The structural problem was in the application or uses of the vast sums of money. More will be said later about how a collective effort to promote development communication essentially failed but at this point it is important to keep in mind that most of the foreign aid dollars went directly to governments in the southern hemisphere. In turn because a substantial number of these governments were military or authoritarian in nature, this resulted in the looting of aid funds where the poor saw little or none of the aid or sought-after benefits. Corruption and authoritarian regimes have been a constant drain on funds designed to aid the poor, particularly women in rural and remote areas.

A good yet sad example is President Suharto of Indonesia. His 30 year authoritarian rule was marked by two trends that are fairly typical across a number of poor nations. The first was a massive death toll, in his case estimates of more than one-half million killed, as part of violent anti-communists purges. The second was his looting of foreign aid funds from almost every aid project undertaken in Indonesia. He, his family, the military, and their friends siphoned off more than $1.5 billion in aid over three decades. The money was destined for the poor. Similar stories and actions took place in Africa, Asia, and Latin America, particularly in Peru, Chile and Argentina during the same period.

Theoretical Issues: Modernization

The questions of aid, to whom, how much, methodologies, and the role of communication within these broader policy questions has a long history as well. Development communication, particularly radio, was viewed as being central to improving the economic and social lot of the poor in the southern hemisphere. Theorists like Daniel Lerner, Wilbur Schramm, Paul Deutschmann, Walter Rostow, Everett Rogers, Luis Beltran, Michel Foucault, along with other scholars, as well as agencies such as the Ford and Carnegie Foundations, UNESCO, and the UN's Department of Economic Affairs looked at development issues, some cautiously, some critically, and others creatively.

Five early books tend to stand out because to some extent they began the theory of development communication and spelled out foundation or basic concerns and paradigms. They all fall within the modernization school or camp. In 1958 Daniel Lerner wrote his now classic *The Passing of Traditional Society*, which focused on the role of media in conveying actions and models needed to allow economic gains by those in mostly agrarian societies. He gathered data in six Middle East countries about local and international media. Information from the media, particularly radio, aided locals in learning new ideas and practices.

The economic path to modernization, which the poor nations needed to follow, was detailed in a 1960 book by Walter Rostow titled, *The Stages of Economic Growth: A Non-Communist Manifesto.* The economic road that had to be travelled in order to move up on the modernization ladder of success consisted of five stages. They were: stage one with a traditional society, then on to establishing the preconditions for takeoff, such as political stability, to sustained economic growth, to a maturity stage and finally, the fifth and highest stage, which is modernization as witnessed by mass consumption and high rates of GDP. To move from a traditional society (stage one) to a modern one (stage five) required new attitudes, new work habits, progressive economic models, supportive public polices and all of these were to be conveyed by the application of various mass media messages. To move across the five stages required a strong change ethic; societies would have to leave behind old behaviors and traditions and then adopt new rhetoric, industrialized behaviors, and attitudes which reflected western values. While a media marker of traditional societies was illiteracy, the media hallmark of modernity is the widespread application of information technologies and media platforms of all types.

In 1968 Paul Deutschmann, Ellingsworth Huber, and John McNelly produced *Communication and Social Change in Latin America: Introducing New Technology.* This work had been scheduled to come out much earlier but Deutschmann died in 1963. This left his other researchers to complete the analysis of data from 14 Latin America countries involving over 300 interviews. Solidly in the social science tradition, the study dealt with community leaders, mass media and how they should contribute to economic success. A year later, in a UNESCO publication, Prodipto Roy, Fred Waisanen, and Everett Rogers produced a report titled *The Impact of Communication on Rural Development.* It was a report on two different nations, India and Costa Rica. It examined radio and literacy along with the important emerging role of opinion leaders which Rogers pursued in his classic *The Diffusion of Innovations* in 1962. This book focused on how opinion leaders were influential in the adoption process concerning new and better work habits among the rural poor, particularly farmers.

In 1964 Wilbur Schramm with assistance from UNESCO, published an important book, *Mass Media and National Development.* It reflected what others were saying: namely that mass media would lead directly to economic improvement across poorer regions of the world. Traditional ways of doing things, particularly in the agriculture sector, were looked at negatively and modern methods were viewed as saving and eventually uplifting the poor. And these new approaches were to be communicated most effectively to large audiences via the mass media. That same year seeking a wider audience Schramm published a similar text with Stanford University Press titled *Mass Media and National Development: The Role of Information in Developing Countries*. This work served to influence and guide a generation of North American academics, graduate students, aid officials, and foundation officers. Modernization theory linked with an economic perspective was the dominant paradigm for decades.

During the same period a political scientist Lucien Pye edited an important volume, *Communication and Political Development* (1963). Pye and others saw the communication process as a major factor for any successful movement toward a democratic society. Within the discipline of political science there were a number of theorists who tried to spell out new models or theories advancing the democratic nation-state as a goal. They frequently included how their ideas could benefit the Third World. A sample journal piece from this era is Seymour Lipset's 1959 article "Some Social Requisites of Democracy: Economic Development and Political Legitimacy." It is a clear example of the academic mentality during this era.

Thus modernization theory took hold and carried with it an element of economic determinism along with a parallel drive to expand democratic concepts and practices, such as the importance of voting behavior. Although the theories all recognized, to varying degrees, the role and importance of communication, they came from a number of social science disciplines. Sociologists, economists, anthropologists, political scientists, psychologists, social workers, media scholars, and others touched on aspects of modernization approaches. Many also took ideas and strategies from developed, industrialized nations and applied them with some fine tuning to the southern hemisphere. But the long range goal was similar. To make the inhabitants of poorer nations in the South more like the wealthier peoples of the North. This cut across major life-style practices, such as communication and media habits, income, politics, culture, religion, and in some cases, language. Indigenous ways were dismissed, marginalized, ridiculed, or ignored.[3] Thus the push-back wave of criticism could have been predicted. The critique of modernization theory, studies, and practices came from a variety of scholars and nations. The critics were not only concerned with what the researchers and aid officials on the ground were doing, but they had concerns about the Western-based elites pushing a system of social science research that was not value free. The drive to collect data and come up with empirical findings dominated much of the published research on the poorer regions of the world during the initial decades. Other alternative research strategies, paradigms, or methods found few takers among Western-based scholarly books or journal editors.

A summary of 224 studies in 1989 that reviewed the connection between communication and national development over the previous three decades reported that:

> Criticisms leveled at the paradigm . . . contained certain Western assumptions and values about the process of development . . . Yet, based on some of the results presented from the metaresearch . . . it seems fair to say that the impact of the debate has not been to radically alter the way scholars carry out their research. Rather, it seems the field has continued on the tradition of the modernization paradigm. (Fair 1989, 144)

She adds that the passing of the dominant paradigm, that is linear modernization approaches, was still in play among both academics and NGOs alike and the passing phenomena was overstated according to her analysis and study.

The Critics

The following is an overview of early critics, who formed the basis for a broader theoretical movement under the umbrella of "cultural imperialism." This theory is discussed in detail in Chapter 2.

The criticisms began slowly since the entire world was undergoing a major redefinition of power, status, and place after World War II.

Europe had to be rebuilt, the British were in disarray, and the US had become a world power and player with victories over the Japanese, the Germans and Italians. Truman gave them some support in terms of crafting a new and relevant foreign policy but it was always skewed toward containing communism first and development second. One clear American policy on the international level was a commitment to a free flow of information. All industrialized nations fell in line and endorsed this major and fundamental premise.

But what the Western nations saw as free flow was soon to be viewed with suspicion by the receiving nations in the southern hemisphere. They were becoming the receivers of information that was in fact a one-way flow. The free-flow mantra essentially masked the dominance of the former colonial masters and now with the addition of the might and marketing of the US, matters only became worse. There was no reciprocity in terms of information or media flows. It was a structural imbalance that suited the foreign policy needs and communications corporations of the industrialized nations. The entire matter was to blow up within UNESCO during a contentious debate about the New World Information and Communication Order (NWICO) in the 1970s and into the 1980s as well. By the middle of the 1980s both the US, under President Ronald Reagan, and the British, under Prime Minister Margaret Thatcher, withdrew from UNESCO in protest over NWICO; both have since returned.

As a result of two streams of dissent, challenging the actions, motives, and dismal results became more mainstream around the globe. The one stream was Herbert Schiller's works outlining cultural imperialism, together with an articulate number of followers, and the second stream was the NWICO debates and their fallout. Collectively the critics had opened a Pandora's Box which is still in play even today. We will examine in Chapter 3 UNESCO's current involvement with a global cultural matter involving language and protection of domestic or indigenous media systems. It seeks to counter the homogenization of culture – which more and more means mass-produced American popular culture.

A good example of what others perceive as a cultural tsunami is the 2008 release of an Indiana Jones sequel. The first movie was released in 1981 solely in the US market on slightly more than 1,000 screens; in contrast the new version was released on a global scale on over 15,000 screens. The first weekend alone saw revenue of over $150 million and the majority of that was from screens outside the US. Hollywood has gone global and its blockbusters will open in theaters around the globe at an increasing rate and at the same time. How indigenous film makers in developing countries can compete is a major task and problem because of this globalization phenomenon.

Another example of the rise of critics can be traced to Latin America and a movement labeled liberation theology. It also reflects the deep division between significant groups concerning values cutting across culture, economics, and religion.

Liberation Theology

Liberation theology has had three fairly distinct phases and was originally connected to the Catholic Church but now has expanded in concept and practice to other religions as well. The first phase started in 1891 with the publication of the encyclical *Rerum Novarum*. It called for greater social justice and the end to exploitation of workers. The second phase began in the 1950s and tended to be concentrated in Latin America among priests and nuns promoting both land reform and social justice. The third phase began in the 1980s and spread to other religions, particularly evangelical Protestants, promoting a prosperity theology. This included micro-banking and church-based money handling sessions for the poor.

First phase and the encyclical Rerum Novarum

In 1891 Pope Leo XIII issued a progressive church document that called for better treatment of the working classes, social justice, tolerance for unions and other associations of workers, and the spreading of the benefits of the industrial revolution beyond owners and management. Two significant development communication experiments emerged, one in Europe and another in North America.

In Europe the major outcome was in England although other experiments have been reported in Sweden and Spain as well. The English movement was led by the literary giant G. K. Chesterton.

He wrote essays, magazine articles, and made public speeches calling for social justice, aid for the poor, and land reform which he called Distributism. It called for broad-based ownership of land and for current land owners to share their holdings with long-time employees. Since the British Royal family is the largest land owner in Great Britain, they worked aggressively against Distributism. Yet Chesterton took the Pope's encyclical of 1891 as his goal and mandate to aid the poor, including political action. His ideas created a large number of followers based on his communication skills and journalistic talents.

But the Distribution Movement failed in the end for three reasons. First the Movement's charismatic leader Chesterton died in 1936 with no powerful successor, second, the Great Depression changed the economic landscape drastically, and third, World War II broke out across Europe in the late 1930s and all resources went into military enterprises, thus concern for land reform took a dive. Collectively the Distribution Movement became a failed development communication experiment.

Antigonish Movement and adult extension education

This development communication movement was based at the St. Francis Xavier University in Eastern Canada, in the city of Antigonish, Nova Scotia. The main leader was Father Coady who again took the Pope's 1891 document as a challenge to aid and educate the poor. Coady wanted to aid and educate farmers, miners, and fishermen across Atlantic Canada. Coady and others from the university set up meetings of workers, home-based study clubs, and a six week leadership program through the Extension Department at St. Francis Xavier. The clubs had pamphlets, newsletters, and newspaper materials. By the late 1930s there were over 100 study clubs with in excess of 1,000 participants. Coady, as a great orator and with politically savvy, led the movement to eventually call for workers' unions so that they would not be exploited, and opened a large number of credit unions, particularly in small towns and fishing villages. Following Coady's death in 1959 the university established the Father Coady International Institute to continue the work of promoting development communication materials and training, particularly public speaking, to aid the poor. Close to 5,000 development practioners from over 100 southern hemisphere countries have attended workshops and seminars at the Institute since its inception.

Second phase

This second phase was primarily associated with the Catholic Church in South America.[4] It began in the mid 1950s and sought to extend the teachings of the Church to include Jesus Christ as liberator of the oppressed in this life as well as their savior in the after life. It had a left of center tilt and many American-trained Jesuits and other progressive clergy championed this theology across South America. The mission was to add social justice, human rights, decent wages, decent working conditions, and land reform to the goals and deeds of the Church. Also if the only way to obtain the much sought after goals of social justice meant that followers had to become politically active, then so be it. This was until the powerful Latin American Cardinals of the Catholic Church, most of whom were friends with wealthy land owners, ruling elites, and military leaders began to view the movement as a grass-roots movement that could grow to become powerful enough even to challenge their authority and that of their elite and often authoritarian friends. With powerful Cardinals and others labeling the Liberation Movement as Marxist, socialist, or communist inspired, it was not long before the Vatican and recent Popes laid down their law to stop the unsanctioned movement of liberation theology on behalf of the poor.

Encouraging political activism among the poor and trying to change and improve their living conditions by challenging the ruling classes for justice was perceived as a threat to Church leadership and structures as well as the political establishment. The fact that some of the brilliant local priests across Brazil, Peru, Columbia, and elsewhere started to write about the beauty of liberation theology in the context of the Catholic Worker Movement and Marxism only served to galvanize the resentment of the Cardinals and other leaders as well. As a result the Vatican slapped an intervention against sermons, meetings, conferences, with the draconian threat of excommunication for clergy promoting liberation theology.

Yet today there still is a significant following for liberation theology across South America. It is gaining adherents as the pace of the feminist movement (covered in Chapter 8 where liberation theology is expanded upon) continues to grow as well. Some of the underground support for this feminist cause is coming from Catholic nuns who are disenchanted and differ with their local Bishops and Cardinals on the helping the poor issue.[5]

Third phase and prosperity theology

Finally, there is a related religious-based movement called "prosperity theology" in the southern hemisphere. Pentecostal congregations are being told that being poor across generations is not God's will or plan. Becoming more economically better off and self-sufficient was the new religious ethic and Sunday mantra. Now some Catholics families, who have been Catholics for centuries, are converting to Protestantism in the hope that doing well in this life will await them. They are tired of the failure of the Catholic Church to improve their lives economically over generations and where poverty, not prosperity, was their constant companion.

This third phase still sees several Catholic priests and nuns supporting liberation theology in an underground environment so as to not be expelled from their religious order or be forced to leave Latin America. They still follow Pope Leo XIII's call for social action and justice. Basically they are a collection of rogue Catholic ambassadors who use the goals of *Rerum Novarum* to set their road map for social change. They use small group communication in local homes along with Internet blogs to get their message of liberation theology out while circumventing the Church hierarchy who still curry the favor of authoritarian elites and large land owners.

Finally, religion was just one of the many values that European colonizers brought with them as they sought new territories around the globe. The colonizers also made certain that huge imbalances of power were directed in their favor. Colonial administrators from Europe ran mini fiefdoms to the detriment of local ways and traditions, including language and historical customs. When the administrators returned to Europe they returned not only very wealthy but with crates of looted precious cultural artifacts as well. Many who returned to Europe also left those in charge with enormous land holdings, which their descendants still control today.

Conclusion

This chapter examined the historical roots of development communication. Focusing on post World War II activities, the major starting point was when President Truman pointed to the serious need to assist less fortunate nations with some type of US assistance and foreign aid. Soon thereafter academics and foundations began searching for theories, models, and practices that would support as well as enhance modernization initiatives. There was a strong current of economic determinism throughout aid efforts undertaken by a number of industrialized nations. Yet despite a significant body of new literature produced by some of the best social scientists plus ample project funding there were scant gains across the Third World. Some isolated gains were seen as education, health, and agrarian practices improved in the southern hemisphere. But for all the time, effort, and money invested the results looked bleak. The top-down, often authoritarian tone of churches, academics, and politicians alike left a bad taste among the growing army of the poor. To some extent the poor rebelled and wanted to take back their identity, culture, history, and life-styles. Replacing colonial masters with new bureaucratic aid managers was a thorny issue, based on distrust and failed promises of positive change. Some signs of globalization were occurring in the southern hemisphere but the benefits were clearly stacked in favor of the rich nations.

All this has led to a situation in the field of development communication for a better or new paradigm, model, or theory. That is what the following chapters are about. The book takes an interdisciplinary perspective and seeks to enhance the discourse about how, where, and why media of all types may be utilized or applied for the benefit of the inhabitants of the Third World. The materials focus more on a bottom-up approach, looking at culture and identity as key aspects which have to be respected as well as enhanced. The social change will not be top-down favoring donor groups or nations. The book seeks to promote a rethinking or reconceptualization of development communication which takes into account current best practices as well as avoiding the mistakes of the past. The goal is to add to the debate about development and communication in an insightful and constructive manner.

The Balance of the Book

The second chapter builds on the earlier modernization theory. The top-down approach and Western notions of economic change failed to deliver. Thus this chapter takes up three main lines of theory building which dominated the development communication field for several decades. The three approaches are: cultural imperialism, participatory communication, and entertainment-education. There are overlapping issues but collectively they have been the main theoretical and research avenues seeking to replace, modify, or revise modernization theory.

The third chapter takes a look at the broad activities of the United Nations (UN) and its specialized agencies, such as the United Nations Educational, Scientific, and Cultural Organization (UNESCO). A major portion of this chapter is dedicated to examining the UN Development Programme (UNDP), along with the UN's Human Development Report. The Report seeks to build an index which is broader than approaches which focus on income or GDP. This chapter also details major UN commissions, task forces, and forums which look at aspects of the development scene.

The fourth chapter highlights transnational advocacy voices, either NGOs or programs sponsored by governments, such a Canada's progressive International Development Research Centre (IDRC). It will also detail the history and role of major American foundations which have a long involvement with modernization initiatives.

The fifth chapter examines the International Network for Cultural Diversity (INCD). This group's main thrust is to counter the homogenizing of world cultures by commercial interests at the expense of indigenous artists, musicians, languages, and ultimately cultures. Future attempts by the World Trade Organization (WTO) to commodify culture as a commercial good are outlined along with UNESCO's Convention on the Protection and Promotion of the

Diversity of Cultural Expressions. This is indeed the same UNESCO which housed the NWICO debates in the 1970s onward.

The sixth chapter begins a series of five chapters written by selected experts. This chapter looks at research on information and communication technologies. The chapter also proposes alternative ways of looking at development communication.

The seventh chapter also looks at information and communications technologies and what structural and economic barriers exist in terms of perpetuating the digital divide.

The eighth chapter attempts to redefine development communication by adding newer dimensions, such as feminism and spirituality. The authors make a case for a stronger voice and role for women in the development sector.

The ninth chapter is a "case study" of participatory communication theory and practice. It focuses on a successful community-based intervention among sex workers in Calcutta. It started in 1991 as the Sonagachi Project which sought to reduce the spread of HIV/AIDS. It may serve as a model for other attempts to utilize development communication strategies for positive social change.

The tenth chapter is another "case study" and outlines the innovative work of the George Soros Foundation. It is a case study involving widespread gypsy clans across Europe and how a promising alternative development communication paradigm, called interlocalization may emerge.

The eleventh chapter is the summary, conclusions and directions piece. It pulls together both the externally written chapters and the earlier chapters to determine the extent to which the field of development communication is changing. This chapter provides advice for practioners, academics, researchers, NGOs, and government enterprises alike.

Notes

1   The terminology for this book will consist of varying terms in the literature when describing those nations or regions which are poor. Most are located in the southern hemisphere and they are also referred to as less developed countries (LDCs), or peripheral nations/regions in terms of world system theory categories. The northern hemisphere is where

most of the industrialized, high technology, or developed nations are located. They are often referred to as industrialized nations or Western nations. In terms of world system theory they are core nations. As a group they are the 30 nations belonging to the Paris-based strategic planning body of the Organization for Economic Cooperation and Development (OECD). It is a think tank for the wealthy nations of the world.

2   Truman, H. *Inaugural Address of January 20, 1949.* Washington DC. Government Printing Office.

3   A sad but far too common tale of how far the mostly European coloniz-ers went in their assimilation attempts is the case of the British in Australia. After taking their lands throughout most of the nineteenth century, beginning around 1900 the British administrators via the Australian parliament, with the cooperation of the Anglican Church missions, began removing Aboriginal children from their parents and culture. They were placed with Australians of Anglo-Saxon descent. The purpose was to obliterate the Aboriginal way of life. Their history, customs, dress, family, and language had to go. The goal was, over time, to make them more like the white European settlers. This massive assimilation strategy lasted for decades and ruined many lives and families. It was not until the mid 1990s that the Australian government initiated a national inquiry into the child removal scheme. The inquiry resulted in 54 recommendations, including reparations as well as a broadcasting service for Aboriginals across Australia. The assimilation failed.

In Quebec, Canada, similar attempts to eradicate the French language also failed and to this day the British Royal family is not welcomed in Quebec. The growth and current strength of a separatist political party across Quebec is a direct result of the anti-French bias of the British colonizers.

4   The role of the Latin America-based clergy advocating liberation and change for the poor is not without its consequences, sometimes includ-ing death. Consider the impact of the training that takes place at the US-sponsored School of the Americas at Fort Benning, Georgia. This facility is specifically designed to train Latin American military officers and foot soldiers to become efficient terrorists and who have, upon their return from training in the USA, been implicated in torture, intimidation, and death. Usual targets are clergy, particularly Jesuits, social workers, journalists, academics; human rights advocates, or union organizers. Many protests have taken place outside the facility at Fort Benning but so far the US Pentagon's only response has been to change the name to the Western Hemisphere Institute for Security Cooperation.

Graduates of the Institute play a leadership role among military and para-military death squads across Latin America. Initially they sought out communists but more recently they have focused on leftists or liberals which mean that political opponents advocating social and economic justice are frequent targets. They have also been taught to label or brand opponents as terrorists as well.

Finally, a priest posted for years to the Vatican related the following during the 2008 IAMCR conference in Sweden. I enquired why the Vatican banished Liberation Theology writings and activists. He claimed that in the 1970s US vice-president Nelson Rockefeller travelled to Latin America to meet with political and military leaders, as well as wealthy land owners about the growth and threat of communism in the region. They collectively pointed to social activist priests as aiding the poor, including seeking agrarian reform, under the philosophical umbrella of Liberation Theology. Upon his return to the US, Rockefeller directed the American ambassador to the Vatican, the CIA, and the Secretary of State to convince the Pope and other senior Cardinals that these priests represented a threat to private land ownership and were communist sympathizers and needed to be silenced. The Jesuit Order resisted the most but Latin American Cardinals wanted them silenced as well. Ultimately they were threatened with trusteeship if they did not disavow Liberation Theology as the Pope insisted because of the intense American pressure, plus the rich Catholic land owners feared populist movements claiming their family lands across Latin America.

5 Many of the poorer nations were colonies of European nations. These colonizers brought substantial values with them. For example, they all, to varying degrees, took religion with them. The Spanish, Portuguese, and French took the Catholic religion, including priests on their fleets. For example, even today Brazil is the largest Catholic nation in the world and they also speak Portuguese while the rest of South America speaks Spanish. For these three, on behalf of the royal families in Spain, Portugal, and France, their first goal was to establish the Roman Catholic Church in the conquered lands and second to establish commercial ties. The commercial trade was essentially one way; namely raw materials from the colonies to the European homeland.

By contrast, the consummate colonizer Great Britain reversed the goals. Specifically, to their many colonies the first goal was commerce; the second was Christianity. For the British, the official religion is the Church of England, headed by their reigning monarch. Around the globe this denomination is also known as the Anglican or Episcopalian religion. The current head of the religion is the Queen of England.

The vastness of the European race for colonies and international prestige is detailed in the work of Filipe Fernandez-Armesto titled *Pathfinders: A Global History of Exploration* (2006). For example, he states "Explores were vectors: they carried culture with them" (Fernandez-Armesto 2006, 17). He outlines the strong influence of the Catholic Church among the explorers, particularly the Spanish. He also details the origins of globalization. Frequently these explorers tried to replace existing symbols and traditional ways of doing things with European practices, including language (Lee 2002).

2

Major Theories Following Modernization

Thomas L. McPhail

Introduction

This chapter examines three major theoretical schools reflecting significant changes in the development communication field. Following the criticism and almost total abandonment of modernization theory, scholars sought other more relevant approaches to development communication. The resulting three major theoretical paradigms are first, cultural imperialism, second, participatory communication, and third, entertainment-education. The major aspects of each are outlined as well as their implications for current trends, or activities in the field.

It should be noted that there are other theories about development communication as well. Some are from rural sociology, social marketing, economic grounded theories, neo-Marxist theories, the empowerment paradigm, and some from the health sciences, relating particularly to HIV/AIDS research in the southern hemisphere. The latter looks at how communication strategies may be applied in campaigns promoting safe sex practices to reduce the tragic spread of HIV/AIDS.

But to detail all of the preceding theories, as well as others, would be to write another book. The other theories have merit within their disciplines but this book is attempting to take an interdisciplinary approach and cannot cover everything.

The following trifecta of leading theories gives the broader landscape of what has emerged or occurred in the field over the past few decades. These theories emerged because modernization-based initiatives were failing to produce the positive economic and social changes that were predicted. The linear and top-down approach was discredited by most scholars as well as practitioners.

Cultural Imperialism

Cultural imperialism theory proposes that a dominant sociopolitical group influences and shapes the culture of weaker groups, or nations, through mass media and other practices and institutions. In application, the former group of dominant nations is often referring to the United States and other Western, democratic powers while poorer southern hemisphere nations comprise the later. Cultural imperialism of one group by another frequently carries the assumption of capitalistic intent where mass media is used as a propaganda tool in the effort to control and influence the target population for the economic and political benefit of the dominant powers.

This theory emerged from the Neo-Marxist school of philosophy, fueled by the parallel evolution of the United States into a world superpower. The development of cultural imperialism theory benefited advancement in the understanding of cultural interaction and the importance of the media within the broad mix of aid and commercial efforts. This theoretical school also heightened concerns about the negative or dysfunctional consequences of attempting to transfer foreign modes of knowing how to do things. This cut across economic systems and practices, cultural images, religious beliefs, and political practices, such as voting behavior. The unstated presumption that core nations knew best how to do things did not sit well with some academics and locals in remote villages or farms around the world.

To some extent the intellectual heritage of cultural imperialism finds its roots in Marxism theory. In the mid 1800s Karl Heinrich Marx and Frederick Engel published *The Communist Manifesto*. It was a pamphlet detailing their theory of the social emergence of the working class and the resulting conflicts among the social ranks. They declared that the rise of industrial capitalism in society would lead to a large working class and oscillating economic cycles where the workers would suffer most and the capitalist economic elites would be shielded from fiscal harm. Furthermore, inequalities would emerge between the ruling and working classes which would combine with periodic recessions to create a large amount of dissatisfaction among the working class. In order to combat hardships imposed upon them, the working class would naturally form organizations, such as unions, to fight for their rights. The emergence of unions throughout a society would eventually result in a revolution where society and government would be managed in a socialist manner. Eventually such a society would evolve into a communist nation without the formal structures of class and ruling economic elite. Everyone would be equal and share equitably in the economic benefits of the industrial state. In order to explain why such revolutions did *not* occur across Europe, precisely where they had been forecasted to occur, Antonio Gramsci formulated his theory of cultural hegemony. Gramsci, an Italian communist in a fascist nation, put forth the notion that the dominating class mitigates class conflict by controlling the culture of the working class through such social institutions as education, religion, and the mass media, particularly through profit-driven, private ownership. He claimed that the media were used to suppress dissent and promote the ruling economic elites. The leftist and influential Frankfurt School also picked up on some of the Marxist themes in their writings as well beginning in the 1930s.

In the aftermath of World War II, the US and the Union of Soviet Socialist Republics (USSR) emerged as the two key world power brokers. The once powerful British Empire was no longer a major player. Much of President Truman's Inaugural Address, discussed in Chapter 1, was a reflection of this new global dichotomy. The dichotomy would dominate Truman's foreign policy concerns. His successors inherited the issue as well until the implosion of communism in 1989. The symbolic fall of the Berlin Wall was the end point of the matter begun by Joseph Stalin at the close of World War II.

With the advent of the Cold War, ideas related to Marxism, socialism, communism, or leftist ideology became not only taboo, but downright treasonous according to US Senator Joe McCarthy and a cadre of others. The concept of selling capitalism, democracy, and market forces as a way of life to nations around the world vulnerable to communism became a mission both in the US and across Europe. Actively constructing social systems within foreign states which position them to function within capitalist and democratic frameworks became a virtually unquestioned American stated goal. Neo-liberalism was the policy mantra of industrialized nations. The US and the UK were the cheerleaders.

For decades US foreign policy could be summed up in two words: Stop Communism. Foreign aid money flowed into development projects around the globe to counter USSR inroads and successes, such as the launching of the Sputnik satellite in October, 1957. Some of the money flowed through the newly created Central Intelligence Agency (CIA) which began after World War II.

When the Cold War ended with the collapse of the USSR, the US became even more powerful; The US dwarfed every other nation or region in both military and economic influence and authority. Today, for example, Rupert Murdock with his News Corporation Empire and the Disney Empire are models of capitalism driving media conglomerates that cultural imperialist's dread.

Against this general background of capitalism, Herbert Schiller and a few others began publishing a series of articles, essays, and eventually books outlining the foundation for a theory of cultural imperialism. It rested on three key ideas: first, in a free market the economically powerful will become more powerful while the poor will get poorer, second, further concentration of media ownership will influence and reduce the variety, plurality, and type of messages in the media, and third, media technology is a social tool, created and used for sociopolitical means and economic ends. Schiller in his now classic work titled *Communication and Cultural Domination* states that:

> In this sense, the concept of cultural imperialism today best describes the sum of the processes by which a society is brought into the modern world system and how its dominating stratum is attracted, pressured, forced, and sometimes bribed into shaping social institutions to correspond to, or even promote, the values and structures of the dominating center of the system. (Schiller 1976, 9)

Schiller contends that within core nations, particularly the US, communication conglomerates dominate the global stage of mass communications. American media giants, such as Time-Warner, Disney, Viacom, and News Corporation overshadow all other nation states (only SONY of Japan and Bertelsmann of Germany are in the global conglomerate league). Collectively they have formed an oligopoly of cultural industries. With the ever expanding global free trade and market-driven economies, the economic and media elite will expand their control as well as profits. Within this line of reasoning, power, privatization, deregulation, and liberalization of markets requires the promotion of free enterprise globally, primarily through the World Trade Organization (WTO), over which corporate America has considerable influence.

The increasing power of communication industries is further enhanced by mergers and consolidations, such as the takeover of the *Wall Street Journal* by Rupert Murdock's News Corporation in 2008. The few giants that remain in control of global media will produce media products in line with their culturally determined – capitalist and free trade – values. The primary concern of any corporation is market share and increased profits. In such pursuits, communication corporations develop and promote those information technologies that support their global goals. They employ new communication technologies in a manner to increase market share and ultimately earn them more money. For example, cable and media conglomerates are seeking to restructure the Internet so that higher speeds would only be available to corporations and select organizations while the general population would be restricted to the slow land on the information superhighway. While those that support such a shift in control contend that prices for Internet service will decrease, it will benefit the corporations and conglomerates that then can control the traffic on the Internet and direct flow to their benefit.

Building upon the foundations of Gramsci's writing about cultural hegemony, Schiller asserted that the core nations, specifically the US, use the media as a sociopolitical tool to warp the cultures of other countries around the world into ones more homogeneously suited to the purpose of capitalist industry – namely profit – which leads to global inequalities and the exploitation of third world countries. In his view, this process is an extension of empire-building which occurred more blatantly before the twentieth century – "the colonial system, disappearing rapidly as a formal apparatus of domination, lives on and flourishes in an intricate web of economic, political and cultural dependencies" (Schiller 1976, 70). The early era of global colonization was dominated by a different global hegemonic power; Great Britain. Even during this era the BBC, Reuters, Cable and Wireless, Marconi Company, and the British film industry benefited by following the expansion of the British Empire.

Colonialism, the active search and settlement of new territory, closely relates to the concept of Imperialism, defined as "the process of empire. It occurs when the dominant interests of one nation bring to bear their military and economic power upon another nation or region in order to expropriate its land, labor, capital, natural resources and markets" (Parenti 2006, 48). Neo-colonialism, the process by which "the colonial relationships of the past were maintained through forms subtler than forceful military control" (Elasmar and Bennett 2003, 12), involves the economic and cultural settlement of other nations. Under this definition, the expansion of global industries and global media conglomerations would fall under the category of empire building. One can think of cultural imperialism as an overarching theory including the following two notions which represent further refinements: Electronic Colonialism and Media Imperialism.[1]

Electronic colonialism theory refers to the reliance, created by mostly American communication technologies, which subsequently impact global markets and cultures (McPhail 1981; 2006). The theory of electronic colonialism is about the spread of popular culture and media systems around the globe by mostly US corporations. *Media imperialism* concerns itself specifically with the domination of the *media* by a select few groups and the impact it has on weaker factions (Boyd-Barrett 1981–2). Both of these theories have their roots in the writings that Schiller stated decades ago.

Participatory Communication

Unlike other mass communication theories which deal with the effects of the few and powerful on the masses via vertical diffusion, the participatory communication approach focuses on the effects of individuals on mass communication with special emphasis placed on the development of the third world. The study of participatory communication emerged in the late 1970s and took prominence in the 1980s; in part, it emerged as a counterbalance to theories

such as cultural imperialism. It was formulated through a discon-
nected group of scholars and practitioners from around the world
searching for something to replace the modernization paradigm
or cultural imperialism approaches. While cultural imperialism
focused on the ability of the powerful to influence cultures and
economies around the world, advocates for participatory communication sought to describe the power of the individual to influence
the world and to find ways to further advocate and enrich such
action with the ultimate goal residing in a utopian scenario of
positive development for all and better inter-cultural understanding.
Brenda Dervin and Robert Huesca, after examining "a rich and
diverse body of theoretical and empirical research" (Dervin and
Huesca 1997, 46) in their meta-analysis, state that participatory
communication "is understood as being at the heart of what it means
to be human, to have an identity, and to possess a sense of belonging vis-à-vis humanity, nature and God" (Dervin and Huesca 1997,
46). They view participation as being central to positive or successful development.

The ever growing development and spread of globalization coupled
with changing technology, especially the Internet, has given new
importance to understanding how grassroots communication can
change the world.

Participatory communication thrives on input from people from
all walks of life and of every socioeconomic sphere. In application
towards the development of nations in the southern hemisphere, this
change of thought is a shift of understanding aimed at not simply
studying indigenous communication from an outside, social scientific, or even imperialist perspective, but instead delving into the
point of view of native people on their own terms, looking at their
culture, and issues that they consider relevant. In doing so, one of
the primary concerns is the language used to describe the people
and cultures of third world countries. Participatory communication
stresses the basic right of all people to be heard, to speak for themselves and not be represented or reworded by another party. This
open approach to communication attempts to facilitate trust and is
aimed at recruiting the participation of the native populations in
third world countries in their own development. Such an approach
to communication requires outside parties to act as co-collaborators
and facilitators, seeking to aid third world nations economically and

diplomatically without dominating the native cultures. In theory, active listening, respect, and trust are needed on both sides for the model of participatory communication to succeed in such an environment.

Participatory communication as a theory

Participatory communication is mostly a self-determining model in that it does not focus on describing conditions that already exist but rather seeks to perpetuate environments, especially within the economic development of third world nations, that encourage the indigenous populations and the intervening parties to communicate in such a fashion. Having a tightly focused objective, literature on participatory communication tends to lean towards evaluation of change implementation with real world projects and examining the effectiveness of inclusion of native citizens in the development of third world countries. The literature also differs in the application of participatory actions as either an end in itself, or as a means to end – whether that be social, cultural, economic, or political in nature.

Three rationales exist for participatory communication: the native population possesses relevant information regarding their own circumstances and are a unique resource without which a development project might fail; the native population has the fundamental human right to contribute to the formation of their own advancement; and inclusion of the native population will draw more support which will in turn facilitate the achievement of common goals. Some credence for this approach can be found within psychological studies conducted at the turn of the century in order to best determine the conditions for increasing productivity in American workers. Results indicated that the more empowered an individual feels about a venture, the more he or she will want to work towards the common goal. The more that individual has contributed to the design and implementation of the project, the more responsible he or she will feel for its outcome.

Participatory theory is closely associated with Paulo Freire's[2] model of communication which consisted of five key concepts: dialogue, conscientization, praxis, transformation, and critical consciousness. *Dialogue* consists of the back and forth communication between those within development organizations and those they serve. *Conscientization* is the acknowledgement, awareness and handling of the inherent power differential and possible disenfranchisement between the organization and the native population. *Praxis* involves the ongoing examination of theory and real world practice. *Transformation* refers to the enlightenment or education of the native population in a way that promotes active consciousness and critical thinking in regards to their situation and/or why certain change implementation is taking place. *Critical consciousness* is the active social and political involvement of the beneficiaries. According to Freire, the incorporation of the above in the design of a development project would lead to a more democratic form of communication.

In practice, applying participatory communication scenarios to real world projects meets several hurdles. Given the subjective, non-quantifiable terms that describe the participatory communication approach, implementation and evaluation becomes difficult when dealing with concrete practicalities. How much participation should the indigenous population have before a development project can be labeled participatory? How does one facilitate that participation with enough neutrality as to not overly influence the people one wants to participate, thus negating the entire approach? What about education and translation issues? Indigenous people might not be equipped with the skills to participate actively. How easily can the term be manipulated to cover up a venture that is more profit- and power-based than well meaning? Who should hold the ultimate responsibility for a project – the intervening party, the investors, or the stakeholders? There are no definitive answers for these questions. And again, no concrete, quantifiable definitions for participatory communication exist. Here lies the trouble with applying the notion of "theory" to the participatory communications approach. By its nature, participatory communication rejects the analytical, scientific method inherent in Western evaluation methods for an inclusive acceptance of individual opinions. A successful theory, at least within academia, is a proposition that is reliably proven and infinitely testable. Anything else may be a good idea, perhaps based on good theories, but must be rejected as a theory itself. As early the mid-1980s, researchers concluded that "[participatory research] is quite the opposite of what social science research has been meant to be. It is partisan, ideologically biased and explicitly non-neutral" (Tandon 1985, 21). Yet enthusiasm for a participatory approach to communication has not waned.

Implementation needs

To implement a new model of mass communication, media needs to evolve in order to foster or enable democratic communication. Participatory communication relies on the horizontally constructed exchange of information rather than the traditional, vertical dissemination of knowledge from the top down. Recent development in technology, especially regarding the proliferation of the World Wide Web, has allowed for greater horizontal communication, inherent in the approach of participatory communication. Also, one should consider the facts and situation on the ground when attempting to implement a program using a participatory approach. Most likely the powers that be will have conflicting and less altruistic goals than those working to elevate the living conditions of the third world country. Empowered, educated, and questioning populations are not usually held in high regard by tyrants and authoritarian, militaristic regimes. Like most non-profit endeavors, funding will be scarce and creative, cheap solutions are frequently in play. The subjects of the development themselves might seriously resent the presence and meddling of outside organizations, social scientists, clergy, and individuals; moreover, there may be some lack of trust based on historical negative encounters. Educating the populace enough to participate in an effective manner will probably lead to some bleed over of cultural contamination in that they will need to think and communicate like the more powerful, imposing cultures from where the development workers originate in order to get their messages understood. Using translators with indigenous people will most certainly be uncontrollable and will be relying on a third party to interpret individuals, which is against one of the precepts of participatory communication. Further, as of yet there are no effective methods developed to study and thus justify participatory communication to the Western, scientific-minded organizations that will, most likely, be governing the development and providing monetary assistance.

What the concept of participation communication does have is the seeds to understanding the new realities of communication in a global world linked together by the Internet and the possibility for instigation of revolutions by outside parties. When a person can film atrocities in Tibet or national disasters in China that will be seen around the world, they are bypassing vertical limitations to communicate on a horizontal level in a way that has an actual political impact. This of course fights against the existing power structures and countries, such as China, have already moved to censure such dissemination of information. It also empowers people within those countries to speak up and act and when the oppressed gain enough power and tools in order to come forward and speak out against the ruling parties, revolutions are born. This might be even more effective when coupled with negative political, economic, and military sanctions imposed upon repressive regimes for brutality against their own "subjects," especially in retaliation to free speech – a value held in high regard by the West and the United Nations. Of course this approach is a double-edged sword because the high value placed upon free speech is itself a Western concept that would be imposed upon cultures in the third world that might already have conflicting beliefs. It is also a conundrum in that "while existing structures are a substantial impediment to participatory processes, valid, applicable restructuring can occur only through some degree of authentic participation. Therefore, unless policymaking and the social process are themselves participatory, it is unlikely that the result will be a democratic pattern of communication" (Servaes and Arnst 1999, 118).

The Khomani bushmen: Theory vs. reality

The Khomani bushmen in Africa are photographed, filmed, and interviewed by so many people from around the world that they've adapted to consider "[p]erforming for tourists, researchers and photographers [as] one of the few employment opportunities available to some communities" (Tomaselli, McLennan-Dodd, and Shepperson 2005, 25). To them, information exchange is a commodity, one they provide for desperately needed items like food, fresh water, and clothing. This tribe is famous for being represented in documentaries and films such as "The Gods Must Be Crazy." They have seen themselves in these pieces and although they say they do not correlate the projected image with whom they perceive themselves to be, they have adapted to play the part people expect of them in a sort of "cultural tourism" where outsiders can come to feel as if they've experienced native Africa and the Khomani bushmen compete with neighboring tribes to be the most "authentic." Researchers are viewed in the same light as filmmakers – as employers. Payment is expected. Such a relationship alters the Khomani and makes them dependent on the very researchers who are trying to remain a neutral party and figure out ways not to influence them overly or change them.

Khomani bushmen expect immediate payment, with the exchange of information seen as a commodity. Broader implications are little understood and the abstract notion of simply contributing to the advancement of academic knowledge means little when immediate necessities are scarce. They consider anything less than cash payment for stories or information as exploitive and they have little to no trust for outsiders. They do not have a say in what is done with the information they provide, where it goes, how it is interpreted, or how that interpretation will affect them later. They have no experience with the foreign arena of academic research. The interpretation itself distorts the identities of the Khomani bushmen as it attempts to make their concrete concerns and locally distinct lives adapt to fit the mold of a generalized theory. The distortion continues as more foreign academics, who have never experienced the desert existence of the Khomani tribe, attempt to analyze and decipher the research provided without a proper, first hand understanding of the world in which they live. Yet it is this analysis and theory, from academics without immediate experience with the Khomani bushmen, which will inevitably be the used to advise NGOs concerning methods for development and these academics' opinions will be those on which decisions on implementation and funding are based. And while academics and NGOs argue and write for abstract human rights, the practicalities necessary to facilitate those rights are paid little attention. When the strategies taken by the NGOs eventually suffer due at least in part to the mistranslation of abstract theory back into concrete reality, the subjects lowest on the totem pole – the Khomani – suffer the blame. Participatory communication approaches in theory should stop this cycle and empower the Khomani, however the same real-world obstacles that conflict with other communication theories pose the same problem for the more horizontal approach to communication for development.

Finally, as Dervin and Huesca as well as others have noted some of the motivation or call for greater grass-roots participation was a by-product of the debates and background reports surrounding the New World Information and Communication Order (NWICO), which found sanctuary in the halls of UNESCO.[3]

Entertainment-Education

More recently a major movement to combine media and social change has emerged. Many countries are plagued with problems such as disease, particularly HIV/AIDS, hunger, illiteracy, poor family planning, domestic violence, poverty, etc. To combat these major issues several countries have turned to various media to teach the public different ways of conducting themselves in order to bring about the changes that are needed to improve their society. The concept of using media to push for social changes is referred to as entertainment-education (or in some cases labeled "edutainment").

> Entertainment-education is the process of purposely designing and implementing a media message to both entertain and educate, in order to increase audience members' knowledge about an educational issue, create favorable attitudes, and change overt behavior. Entertainment-education seeks to capitalize on the appeal of popular media to show individuals how they can live safer, healthier, and happier lives. (Singhal and Rogers 1999, 12)

This section will describe how the entertainment-education movement came into existence, showcase studies in which this concept has influenced, and give data about the effect this concept has had on the people and environments in which it has been implemented applied.

Key and early works are a 1999 book by Arvind Singhal and the eminent scholar Everett Rogers titled *Entertainment Education:*

A Communication Strategy for Social Change and a 2003 work by the same authors and others called *Entertainment-Education and Social Change: History, Research and Practice*. These books established the intellectual infrastructure for several applied development communication projects in poor nations. Some of the educational objectives are in the areas of health, civil society, environment, family issues including sexuality, or nutrition. It cuts across several areas ranging from children's media to adult cooperative education programs. A sample of these efforts is outlined below.

Background: Canadian Broadcasting Corporation's National "Farm Radio Forum"

From 1941 to 1965, with the motto: "Read. Listen. Discuss. Act" the CBC National "Farm Radio Forum" considered different agriculture-related issues via the CBC radio network. The weekly half hour program would broadcast a discussion on a topic of special interest to farmers and was supported by printed background material. It was a listening discussion project with an educational purpose and it brought together rural people from across Canada.

The program was developed by the CBC and sponsored by the Canadian Association for Adult Education and the Canadian Federation of Agriculture. It represents the first successful entertainment-education media experiment aimed at positive social change. Families and friends would gather together to listen to the radio broadcast and then discuss the issues presented. They were assisted by a small newspaper, *The Farm Forum Guide*, which was sent to every participating farmer. The newspaper outlined the topics to be discussed in the following program and included different sets of questions each farmer had to answer on the subject. Following the Monday night program, the farmers were encouraged to send in their own conclusions about the topics discussed and some of these were reported in the next week's broadcast. This was an early version of an interactive radio program since it allowed its listeners to take part in their education. Beside the educational effect, it also fostered a sense of community across the country and often the discussions lead to self-help community groups that took actions. The successful model of the CBC "Farm Radio Forum" was soon taken overseas. India, Ghana, and France began using Canadian Farm Forum approaches and models in their own programming. The CBC was forced to end the Forum in the 1960s because various community groups began demanding political solutions to a broad range of rural and agricultural problems.

The Archers

In the UK, the BBC picked up a similar idea of the program and started its own educational program called "The Archers." In 1950, the BBC broadcasted five pilot episodes of a new drama series. The soap opera was set in a rural setting following the rural life in the fictional county of Borsetshire. The producer of "The Archers," Godfrey Baseley, had previously worked on agricultural programs. He hoped that the audience would not only listen to the story but also pick up messages that helped England get back on its feet after the War. Britain was still subject to food rationing at that time. "The Archers," the "everyday story of country folk," lost its original, educational, purpose in 1972. Originally it was aimed at a farming audience but with its increasing success it widened its agricultural theme. Since then, the program has dealt with issues like adultery and had a homosexual couple kiss. However, the program still tells its audience about the everyday happenings on a farm and life in the country and in 2001 included a discussion about the foot-and-mouth disease. "The Archers" is now the longest running radio soap opera with more than 15,000 episodes broadcast. Currently it is broadcast on BBC Radio 4 and has a loyal following.

Latin American Experiments

The history of entertainment-education as a strategy using television is inextricably linked with the work of Miguel Sabido. He was a well known writer-producer-director of theater and television in Mexico. More than any other individual, Sabido helped formulate the intellectual basis and successful models for the entertainment-education strategy for television. He sought to use television for educating the poorer people about how to lead better lives. Sabido's work in Mexico directly inspired other entertainment-education efforts worldwide, including the Indian television soap operas, "Hum Log" ("We People") and "Hum Raabi" ("Co-Travelers"); the Tanzanian radio soap opera "Twende na Wakati" ("Let's Go with the Times") and the Indian radio soap opera "Tinka Tinka Sukb" ("Happiness Lies in Small Things"). Sabido's work also inspired Johns Hopkins University's Population Communication Services (JHU/PCS) to re-invent the entertainment education strategy in rock music campaigns promoting sexual responsibility among teenagers in Latin America, the Philippines, and Nigeria, and to implement other entertainment-education projects" (Singhal and Rogers 1999, 47).

> In 1975, the Mexican network Televisa broadcast the first "entertainment-education" soap opera, which was written and produced by Miguel Sabido according to his own theory-based research formula. The soap opera, called "Ven Conmigo" ("Come with Me"), promoted a government-sponsored adult literacy program, and its commercial and social success prompted Televisa to produce, broadcast, and research the audience effects of five other Sabido-designed soaps. Development themes treated in these shows included family planning, women's rights, responsible parenthood, and adolescent sexual education. (Nariman 1993, 15–16)

This provides an insight into how the concept of entertainment-education came about in Mexico. Although Miguel Sabido is credited with developing the foundation upon which this concept is set, it is from this foundation that the concept has been able to penetrate other third world countries and the application of it is usually dependant on what needs are unique to that society. The general idea may be the same, but its application may be different. One example of how needs are taken into consideration when applying this concept would be that of the process of using Telesecundaria in rural parts of Mexico. This was used because of the low number of students in the area plus the lack of teachers.

> Educational television has always been a mainstay of the program throughout its years of operation. Yet, the mode of use of television has evolved and is already in its third generation. At its earlier stages, a regular teacher ("talking head") delivered lectures through a television set installed in classrooms. Books and workbooks were provided

to follow the television program with exercises, revisions, applications and formative evaluations. The second generation improved on the process and created programs with greater variety and more sophisticated production techniques. The third and present generation, which began in 1995, deploys a satellite to beam the program throughout the country and uses a wider range of styles of delivery. Telesecundaria is now an integrated and comprehensive program providing a complete package of distance and in-person support to students and teachers. It puts teachers and students on the screen, brings context and practical uses of the concepts taught and extensively uses images and available clips to illustrate and help students. It enables schools to deliver the same secondary school curriculum offered in traditional schools. (De Moura Castro, Wolff, and Garcia 1999, 48)

Although there has been much of entertainment education on television to showcase, there is even more when one considers radio. In many parts of the world there are some countries that cannot afford to broadcast educational programs each day. For these, radio has been another way in which messages have been transmitted. Radio is certainly not a new medium and in fact has been around a few decades more then television, and so it is no wonder that many societies have turned to this medium, which has stood the test of time, to be reliable and more affordable. In many of these societies one of the major issues which radio, as well as television, is used to address is combating HIV/AIDS. Entertainment education is used to teach the public about an array of other problems as well and different methods to handle these problems, but in third world countries their main edutainment goal is to fight the spread of HIV/AIDS and give people a better understanding about how to conduct their sexual lives.

> The use of [entertainment-education] is increasingly being used in addressing health-related issues ranging from issues such as blood pressure, smoking and vaccine promotion to family planning and HIV/AIDS prevention. The result is a growing volume of media products, especially radio and TV soap operas and similar serial productions produced with the specific goal in mind to educate their audiences. (Tufte 2004, 2)

Our focus will primarily be centered on how less developed countries are affected by media which has a teaching agenda, but it should not go unnoted that in regards to the spread of HIV/AIDS there have been other developed countries that have benefited from this concept as well. This idea can also be classified under something called health literacy. "Health literacy is the degree to which individuals have the capacity to obtain, process, and understand basic health info and services needed to make appropriate health decisions" (Rogers, Ratzan and Payne 2001, 2178). The area of health communication is central to the entertainment-education movement.

African experiment

Perhaps one of the best examples of how entertainment-education works would have to come from Tanzania.

> Tanzania, an East African country of 30 million people, is one of several countries that compose the so-called AIDS Belt, where 2% of the world's population lives but where nearly 50% of the world's AIDS cases are found. The actual number of AIDS cases in Tanzania, according to conservative estimates, approached 450,000 by 1996. HIV infection rates in Tanzania are among the highest in the world. An estimated 1.4 million HIV positive individuals lived in Tanzania in 1996, about 90% of HIV infections in Tanzania result from unprotected heterosexual intercourse. Secondary modes of transmission include prenatal transmission from mother to infant and infected blood supplies during blood transfusions. Homosexual intercourse and intravenous drug use are relatively less important modes of transmission than they are in many developed countries. (Vaughan, Regis, and St. Catherine 2000, 84)

In 1993 a radio soap opera entitled "Twende na Wakati" ("Let's Go with the Times") started in Tanzani. This was primarily created to serve two purposes. One was to inform the population about the different ways to deal with the AIDS problem, and also to inform the public about family planning techniques. In regards to how this radio soap opera affected the public regarding the AIDS issue, Vaughan, Regis, and St. Catherine (2000, 81) state:

> the effects of the radio program in Tanzania include (1) a reduction in the number of sexual partners by both men and women, and (2)

increased condom adoption. The radio soap opera influenced these behavioral variables through certain intervening variables, including (1) self-perception of risk of contracting HIV/AIDS, (2) self-efficacy with respect to preventing HIV/AIDS, (3) interpersonal communication about HIV/AIDS, and (4) identification with, and role modeling of, the primary characters in the radio soap opera.

The characters in the soap opera were designed to have specific effects on the people who tuned in to the production and each circumstance these characters were depicted in was geared to relate to the general population of Tanzania and make them feel like this soap opera was not a fictional story but something that could happen to them.

> Role modeling of characters discussing HIV/AIDS was intended to stimulate interpersonal communication about AIDS by audience individuals. The characters in *Twende na Wakati* were designed to provide negative, transitional, and positive role models for HIV prevention behaviors. Negative characters provide models of the consequences of HIV-risky behaviors. For example, the main negative role model in the storyline, Mkwaju (literally translated as "Walking Stick"), is a highly promiscuous truck driver who does not use condoms and who ultimately becomes sick with AIDS. Our content analysis showed that Mkwaju appeared in 96% of all episodes, frequently depicted in bars or consorting with various women, thus reinforcing the concept of his promiscuity and HIV/AIDS-risky behavior throughout the radio soap opera. (Vaughan, Rogers, Singhal, and Swalehe 2000, 86)

Another major result which came from this popular soap opera in Tanzania was the effect it had on family planning in the country. The government looked to the entertainment-education experiment in the hopes of reducing the escalating birthrate because of a substantial birthrate increase recorded in 1992. "The population of Tanzania was approximately 27.4 million in 1992 . . . nearly four times larger than the 1948 population of 7.7 million. The population growth rate of 3.5 percent implied that the population would double in 20 years" (Rogers, Vaughan, Swalehe, Rao, Svenkerud, and Sood 1999, 194). Since many in Tanzania were already aware of this problem but simply didn't put better practices into place to combat it, "Twende na Wakati" was an excellent model in allowing the audience to view first hand what solution would work to improve the state of their community. "In general, positive, negative, and transitional role models for family planning were perceived as such by the soap opera's listeners. The entertainment-education strategy was effectively implemented in Tanzania by RTD (Radio Tanzania) with this program" (Rogers, Vaughan, Swalehe, Rao, Svenkerud, and Sood 1999, 200).

Another study done using Tanzania and entertainment-education to gain information from this region was done by Everett Rogers and Peter Vaughan (2000). The aims of the study were to develop a stage model of the effects of this experiment in order to implement this method with other communication media and provide a guide that others could follow.

> The authors draw on (1) the hierarchy-of-effects (HOE) model, (2) the stages-of-change (SOC) model, (3) social learning theory (SLT), and (4) the diffusion of innovations (DOI) to synthesize a staged model through which communication messages have effects on individual behavior change by stimulating (1) involvement with media characters and role modeling of their actions, and (2) interpersonal communication. Data from a field experiment in Tanzania on the effects of an entertainment education radio soap opera, Twende na Wakati (Let's Go With the Times), on the adoption of family planning, are analyzed in light of a six-staged model of communication effects. It is found that (1) the model provides a useful framework for understanding the effects of an entertainment education program, and (2) the radio soap opera promoted progress through the stages for family planning adoption in the treatment area in three of the four years of broadcast, and in the comparison area after broadcasts of the radio program began there. (Rogers and Vaughan 2000, 203)

This passage is a prime example of how although entertainment-education through the use of the soap opera in Tanzania was being used for one purpose, the concept can become much more then what it was intended to do and results can be used to serve an array of other things.

Unlike television and entertainment shows in the developed world, countries like Tanzania must be wary about how it receives funding and sponsorship to continue their on air programming. They must be sure that the content these sponsors may wish to push through to their audience through commercials and advertising coincides with what they are doing with their programming, and at the same time they still must maintain an open relationship with the sponsor in order to keep the production successful.

> "The strength of a project which is core-funded by one single international donor (such as Nepal's *Cut Your Coat* (USAID), Tanzania's *Twende na Wakati* (UNFPA) is that it can spend more time on the creative process and all the other myriad tasks of running a media project on the ground. It has more freedom to develop storylines, without worrying about different sponsors for separate topics, it only has to nurture one relationship instead of many, and it has far fewer headaches in terms of reporting schedules and accounting minutiae. The weakness of such a project is that it is vulnerable if, for some reason, it falls out of favor with the donor, or if the donor discontinues funding that country for political reasons. Another weakness is that there is less scope for personal involvement from the (often remote) donor, and consequently less possibility of replication or scale-up of a successful project. (Myers 2002, 12)

The station or program must be mindful that although their message may be of an educational nature, and that they indeed may be affecting change, there still needs to be money involved in order to keep the production going and these third world countries' resources are very limited so donors must be kept happy at all cost.

Just as shown with Tanzania, the concept of using entertainment to teach and to push for positive social changes has also been applied to other communities in the third world and has also been met with such success as well.

> Over a period of 18 months during 1997 and 1998, Population Services International (PSI) carried out a targeted radio campaign in Mozambique to promote behavior change for the prevention of STIs and HIV/AIDS. The campaign consisted of a series of nine radio spots developed to stimulate risk reduction among specific groups identified by the project. Launched first in Portuguese in December 1996, the spots were translated into the ten most common local languages in Mozambique. By the end of the radio campaign in June 1998, the spots had aired over 10,000 times. (Karlyn 2001, 3)

Among those exposed to the radio campaign, 97.2 percent reported intent to change their sexual behavior, compared to 62.8 percent of those not exposed to the campaign. Even though the targeting of specific messages to specific groups was not effective, exposure to the radio campaign appears to have contributed significantly to changes in individual sexual behavior.

Another study was undertaken in Nepal with the use of another radio drama:

> Panel data from a population-based survey in Nepal were collected over three waves, from 1994 to 1999, to evaluate the impact of a radio drama serial among couples of reproductive age. Data from 1,442 women were used to assess changes in couples' family planning decision-making, identify predictors of spousal communication and family planning use in relation to program exposure, and clarify temporal relationships among these variables. (Sharan and Valente 2002, 16)

Yet even another study showing how entertainment education can produce change would be one carried out in St. Lucia.

> An entertainment-education radio soap opera, Apwe Plezi, was broadcast from February 1996 to September 1998 in St. Lucia. The program promoted family planning, HIV prevention and other social development themes . . . Compared with non-listeners, regular listeners were more likely to trust family planning workers (83% vs. 72%) and considered a significantly lower number of children the ideal (2.5 vs. 2.9). Fourteen percent of listeners reported having adopted a family planning method as a result of listening to the program. (Vaughan, Regis and St Catherine 2000, 148)

In today's world the divide between the third world and the developed world is great on many levels. Most issues that plague the third world are almost nonexistent in developed countries and it would seem that as time goes by this problem is getting worse. Using entertainment to bring positive messages and information that could improve less developed communities is one huge step towards lessening this gap. It is very important that the success of these initiatives like the ones mentioned earlier are not down played and are held high for the world to see. "One of the ways to turn around the marginalized status of communication in development efforts is to demonstrate the positive impacts of communication on development initiatives" (Inagaki 2007, 1). We have seen how something as fun as a soap opera can indeed produce change, which can save many lives and improve living conditions, but the work does not stop there. These soap operas were not meant to be the total answer for these problems in which they were introduced, the real work comes from the people who watch them. Seeing that the communities are willing to make the needed changes based on the evidence collected from these case studies shows that with the right opportunities from the developed world these impoverished places can thrive. The soap operas were just a starting point, but from this point it is time to make this a reality production and pick up in real time where the soap operas left off and give the help needed towards bridging the gap between the third world and the developed world.

"Soul City"

HIV/AIDS knows no borders or nationalities. For example, the southern Africa region has the highest HIV infection rates in the world. South Africa has found its own way to educate adults and teenager of the danger of HIV/AIDS. A soap opera with its very own mission called "Soul City" is the first show of its kind on television and radio. The program is a vehicle for social education by the non-governmental organization The Soul City Institute for Health and Development Communication.

"Soul City" examines many health and development issues, imparting information and impacting on social norms, attitudes and practice. It was first broadcast in 1994, in the year of South Africa's transition to democracy and since then, it has constantly ranked among South Africa's three most watched television programs.

"Soul City" is comparable to Britain's BBC radio series "The Archers" when it was first launched in the 1950s with the purpose of informing the British population living in the countryside about modern farming methods. However, unlike its British precursor, "Soul City" has stuck to its original mission of informing about HIV/AIDS, getting the audience to take heed of its implications, by means of entertainment. The program also deals with a variety of other issues ranging from racism and domestic violence to maternal health, alcohol misuse, and household energy conservation.

"Soul City" is produced at a relatively modest cost of $120,000 per episode and does not intend to compete with Hollywood productions. "Soul City" is broadcast on SABC1, the largest-audience public channel in South Africa, and every prime time TV series on this channel is backed-up by daily radio broadcasts in all nine indigenous languages. Some audiences can be reached more effectively with certain kinds of media, with most of the rural South African audiences best reached by radio while the urban audience is best reached by television.

"Soul City"'s budget of approximately $10 million per annum is mostly funded by international donors, led by the European Union, the UK, Ireland, the Netherlands, and Japan, and receives commercial funding from BP and previously from the Old Mutual financial services group. It is also funded in part by the South African health ministry.

"Soul City" reaches more than 16 million viewers and 70 percent of South Africa's youth watches the program. In a country where 76 percent have access to television, by African standards a high proportion, it makes completely sense to reach out to its audience by the means of an educational television program to convey educational information about HIV/AIDS. The venture also had its first spin-off, a separate TV, radio and booklet series aimed at the 8-to-12-year-olds called "Soul Buddyz". This program was a huge success and re-broadcasted four times since its start in 1999. It conveys potentially life-saving messages before they become sexually active. Every episode, the actors come across and solve all kinds of issues and problems that face young South Africans in real life, from love, sex and HIV/AIDS to bullying, racism, abuse, and smoking. Sixty-five percent of children said it was their favorite program. After the first series' huge success, different youth clubs emerged. Like the TV series, the growing network of 2,200 youth clubs countrywide, where children meet to take part in activities based on the themes of the program, celebrates a success.

Related to the TV series is another big program that Soul City Institute is involved in. The Soul City Institute, together with local organizations in eight southern African countries, has initiated another project called the Regional Programme to reduce levels of

HIV and AIDS in the region. The scale of the project is extraordinary and it is the largest prevention communication program in the southern African region. It has researched, developed and distributed 27 different booklets dealing with HIV and AIDS and other related health issues. These books have been developed in English and 13 other indigenous languages. The Regional Programme has also produced 11 radio drama series in 15 languages in 5 countries with a potential audience of 40 million people.

The International Institute for Communication and Development

The International Institute for Communication and Development (IICD) is a non-profit foundation that specializes in information and communication technology (ICT) as a tool for development. The institute focuses on less privileged people by assisting local partner organizations in nine developing countries to make effective use of ICTs on their own. IICD was established by the Netherlands Minister for Development Cooperation in 1996 and has its headquarters in Den Haag.

Currently, IICD is active in Bolivia, Burkina Faso, Ecuador, Ghana, Jamaica, Mali, Tanzania, Uganda, and Zambia and works on improving development in the sectors of education, environment, governance, health and livelihoods (agriculture). Disadvantaged people may be excluded from political processes, be unaware of what is going on, and therefore unable to voice their needs. ICT can help them to access and spread information quickly. IICD creates solutions using modern media such as computers, Internet, email and multimedia and traditional media like radio and television to link local organizations and the international community and enables the community to benefit from ICT. It is an essential factor to address issues concerning poverty, illiteracy, and a general lack of development, such as no public services or electricity. As an example, in Ghana 75 percent of the population have no access to basic telephony and in Zambia only one in 400 people have a personal computer or laptop.

Together with local partners from the public, private, government, and non-profit sector, IICD enables people to improve their living standards and quality of life by using technology as a link to benefits gained via information and communication. Figures show the progress made in Uganda, partially due to IICD. In 2000, just 5 people in every 1,000 had a mobile phone subscription. At the end of 2006 that figure had risen to 95 people per 1,000. Besides, given that most (88 percent) of the population, lives in rural areas, it is no surprise that the ratio of mobile to fixed line phones is 20 : 1. In Ecuador, IICD launched different projects which all use ICT; for example to inform rural communities about pest control and market prices and to repopulate the mangrove swamps with shellfish. With its projects, IICD clearly contributes to the Millennium Development Goals made at the United Nations Millennium Summit in 2000.

IICD receives its core funding from the Dutch Directorate-General for Development Cooperation (DGIS), the UK Department for International Development (DFID) and the Swiss Agency for Development Cooperation (SDC).

Conclusion

This chapter reviewed the three major schools of thought, or theories, which sought to look at development communication with new thinking or directions after modernization theory had failed to deliver the economic or social change that was boldly promised. The three approaches are:

1   *Cultural imperialism theory* – most closely associated with the writings of Herbert Schiller. This theory really questioned the motives and outcomes of aid and projects undertaken by Western nations. It focused on the dysfunctional aspects of applying top-down planning for development projects that ignored the human or cultural consequences of their actions. This theory looked at power and performance issues.
2   *Participatory communication* deals with a different approach. Rejecting the top-down and bureaucratic ways of aid agencies, foundations, academic field work, and NGOs, the new focus was on grass-roots participation. It also considers culture as a major tenant in terms of what needed to be held undamaged. Brazilian

Paulo Freire's works and writings provided a great deal of the rationale for implementation of this school of development.

3 *Entertainment-Education theory* attempts to marry off the ability of media, primarily radio and television, with pro-social scripts to foster positive social change. A number of media examples were discussed. They include the CBC's "Farm Radio Forum," the BBC's "The Archers," South Africa's "Soul City", the International Institute for Communication and Development, the impact of Miguel Sabido in Mexico, and Radio Tanzania's HIV/ AIDS-related health issues programming.

Notes

1 An interesting example of eColonialism theory is a new rage in the UK. The American phenomenon of high-school proms is sweeping England, to the disgust of cultural purists. Having watched party loving teenagers on imported American television shows such as Fox's "The O.C." or MTV's "My Super Sweet Sixteen," and Hollywood movies like "American Pie," British teens are mimicking American proms in growing numbers. They select a prom king and queen, rent stretch limos, or arrive in a Rolls-Royce, rent tuxedos, buy prom dresses, corsages, and the mandatory sneaking liquor into the decorated high-school gym. It is a pop culture craze that is right out of the cultural imperialism school. While the British elders shake their heads, the British youth just want to have fun and follow closely the imported media models and music.

2 Paulo Freire (1921–97) was a Brazilian educator and politician. His seminal work, *Pedagogy of the Oppressed* (1970) established him as a leader in thinking about many aspects of the human condition, particularly in the Third World. As Sharma notes the "essence of Freire's teaching is dialogue" (Freire 1970, 44). Freire impacted adult education, health education, agricultural groups, political strategies and groups, social justice movements, and development communication. He had a significant influence on UNESCO's International Commission for the Study of Communication Problems, also known as the MacBride Commission (1978–9). The final report called for greater participation of the powerless in society. The Canadian representative on the Commission was Marshall McLuhan (1911–80), with whom I taught in the early 1970s. The American representative was the Dean of the School of Journalism at Columbia University. Neither Great Britain nor Brazil had representatives on the 15 member Commission. Finally, Freire

championed interpersonal communication and small group communication rather than focusing on mass communication. For additional reading about this important scholar see Freire's own works, as well as the excellent articles by Manoj Sharma (2006) and Jan Servaes (1995) which aided the description of Freire's work in this chapter; they are listed in the bibliography.

3　The NWICO era and debates are detailed extensively in *Electronic Colonialism* (McPhail 1981). I attended the debates in Paris and elsewhere and wrote the definitive book which also has a Foreword by my late friend Everett Rogers, who figures prominently in development communication literature. At the heart of NWICO is a chasm between the free flow and neoliberal positions of industrial nations, particularly the US, and peripheral nations that want greater, not less, control over both their media and destinies. The latter group sees free flow as a one way flow and that deregulation will simply open their markets to even greater foreign competition with little or no reciprocity. Other aspects of NWICO appear in various parts of the following chapters. In particular, the rhetoric of the World Summit on the Information Society and UNESCO's Convention supporting cultural and linguistic diversity are "back-door" attempts to reignite NWICO.

3

United Nations and Specialized Agencies

Thomas L. McPhail

Introduction

This chapter looks at numerous specialized agencies, conferences, and reports sponsored by the United Nations (UN). The materials deal with the main aspects of both the UN itself and a few of its 16 specialized agencies which have a direct link to development communication. Many aspects of development communication are studied and reviewed from applied, policy, technical, as well as scholarly perspectives across the UN system. Over the decades the UN system has become a major global stakeholder in development communication matters from both theoretical and applied perspectives. This chapter highlights the United Nations Development Programme (UNDP), the Paris-based specialized agency, the United Nations Educational, Scientific, and Cultural Organization (UNESCO), and a trio of Geneva-based players, the United Nations Conference on Trade and Development (UNCTAD), the World Intellectual Property Organization (WIPO), and the International Telecommunication Union (ITU). The latter was central to the World Summit on the Information Society (WSIS), which will be outlined in this chapter and also in Chapter 7.

There is a discussion of the World Social Forum (WSF), which is a movement opposed to neo-liberalism, US hegemony, and the promotion of a capitalist global economy, in Chapter 4. The WSF has a number of UN critics among its membership.

Some other relevant UN activities are the 1995 Beijing Women's Conference, The Literacy Decade 2003–12, promotion of civil society issues, establishing in 2003 an Information and Communication Technologies Task Force, as well as a Permanent Forum on Indigenous Issues. Finally, in a growing number of UN-sponsored meetings the contentious issue of Internet governance has become a high profile matter, much to the chagrin of the US government.

United Nations Development Programme (UNDP): The Role of Development Communication in the World

Inequality among societies has existed for centuries. There will always be a gap between the rich and the poor, yet each year that gap continues to stretch farther and farther. Instead of closing, it is becoming wider. The industrial revolution was the major factor of this trend, allowing the spread of material wealth and natural resources to be had by a small group of powerful European nations, and later the United States, Japan, and a few others. To combat the inequality among countries, the United Nations created the United Nations Development Programme (UNDP) in 1965. The aim was to reduce poverty across the globe, and also to promote development. According to Abdul Basit Haqqani, former Pakistani Ambassador and member of the UN Information and Communications Task Force (ICT), who is quoted in the introduction of the ICT Task Force Series 3 *The Role of Information and Communication Technologies in Global Development*: "Development . . . is a multidimensional exercise that seeks to transform society by addressing the entire complex of interwoven strands, [and] living impulses, which are part of an organic whole" (Haqqani 2005, xi).

In other words, the process of development communication involves the utilization of multiple communication tools and media to achieve behavior change in order to improve quality of life. It requires a mass of people in poverty and with low literacy rates to be not only informed but also motivated to accept new ideas/skills that are brought to them. Skills are learned at a much quicker rate than what these people may be accustomed to normally (Quebral 2006, 102).

This section examines topics, ranging from a brief history and overview of the UNDP, to their role in the process of development communication. The *Human Development Report*, an annual publication of the UNDP, will also be examined.

Problems within the UNDP and development communication will be addressed, as there are critics who believe that development communication is nothing but a way of promoting western capitalism and foreign values. Others believe that development communication is a solution, but that it is not being implemented effectively. They argue that importing capitalism into peripheral nations does not necessarily equal capitalist development. In the eyes of core nations and the UN, however, it is seen as a method of empowering individuals and groups towards prosperity and success. This applies in urban and rural areas alike.

Because development communication expanded as a result of the UNDP, it is best first to look at the UNDP. The UNDP came about from the merging of two UN organizations. They were the Expanded Programme of Technical Assistance and the United Nations Special Fund. In 1965, the general assembly of the UN made the UNDP's existence official. The UNDP is a critical component to the UN; much of the UNs' work is devoted towards development, and the UN considers development a central mandate in promoting social and economic progress. The UNDP is able to fund their work through support from major capitalist countries such as the United States,[1] Germany, and Great Britain. In return, these funding nations expect certain economic returns for their contributions, such as meeting a quota when it comes to selecting "experts" that are hired or equipment purchases that are made for projects. For example, Germany would expect the UNDP to purchase some agreed upon amount of computers from them, in exchange for their donations or Japan would expect that trucks purchased for select aid missions would be Japanese vehicles. This concept is known as "tied-aid."[2]

While fighting poverty had long been seen as the overall goal of UNDP, the members of the UN decided to form Millennium Development Goals in 1990 at the world summit meeting. The goals came about from the previously created *Millennium Declaration*, which currently remains the UNDP's flagship publication towards defining international agenda. It ranks countries based upon data gathered about topics, such as literacy and life expectancy. The Millennium Development Goals (MDG) are refined versions of all the important criteria of the declaration which relate to development communication. There are eight goals, and each was made to be achieved by the year 2015. The success of these goals depends on their ability to be measured quantitatively. Progress is seen as a result of enriching people's lives by accomplishing the following:

1   Eradicate extreme poverty and hunger.
2   Achieve universal primary education.
3   Promote gender equality and empower women.
4   Reduce child mortality.
5   Improve maternal health.
6   Combat HIV, AIDS, and other diseases.
7   Ensure environmental sustainability.
8   Create a global partnership for development.

It is important to note that goals relating to human rights and good governance are not included as part of MDG. The reason for this is because according to the UNDP Secretary-General Ban Ki-Moon, the results of the Millennium Development Goals are thus far mixed. There are fewer people each year living on less than one dollar per day, by examining statistics taken from the 1990, 1999, and 2004 reports. In 2004 there were 980 million people, while in 1990 there were 1.25 billion. This is seen as a substantial gain for the MDG project, although progress is not moving along quite as quickly as they hoped for. At the current rate of poverty reduction, it is expected that by 2015 there will still be 380 million people who exist upon no more than a dollar each day. Kofi Annan quoted in the 2005 *Human Development Report*: "The Millennium Development Goals can be met by 2015 – but only if all involved break with [the mindset of] business as usual and dramatically accelerate and scale up action now" (United Nations Development Programme 2005, 5).

Other than development communication and the MDG, the UNDP focuses efforts on combating HIV and AIDS, the improvement of the environment and energy sources in third world nations, gender equality, as well as protection of human rights. With the advent of global warming and natural disaster, the UNDP also strives towards crisis prevention and recovery through the creation of a bureau designed specifically towards those events. Much like the millennium goals, most of what UNDP works on is referred to as "projects," each with specific timeframes/deadlines in mind. The execution of these projects rests upon coordination among the 130 country offices of the UNDP.

The MDG project has created controversy for the UNDP, causing them to come under direct criticism from many scholars and bloggers. It is not just because the goals are not being reached, but rather the question of the ability to accurately measure the goals themselves. Some argue that much of the data presented on the MDG come from estimation and surveys, rather than hard evidence, and that there are differing data sets and definitions across nations.

A major problem has created a mindset where, if the UNDP does not achieve what it set out to accomplish by 2015, there will be many direct criticisms of the United Nations. This includes criticism from journalists and also those who oppose foreign aid. To those who oppose government funding of several projects, it would be an excuse to not contribute any more funds due to a lack of progress.

Despite criticism directed at the UNDP, it does have its merits. In January 2005, Condoleezza Rice spoke to the US Senate about the tragedy which occurred in the Indian Ocean. She stated, "The tsunami was a wonderful opportunity for us" (Murphy 2006, 3). Some may have seen this as an insensitive remark, but it serves as a reminder that national disaster can help bridge the gap between enemy nations. In this case, the tsunami affected the lives of many Middle Eastern people, especially those in Indonesia. The crisis enabled the United States, through their aid, to gain better footing with some of the people they feared most.

The term "development" or "development communication" seems to take on a slightly different meaning depending on which scholar or person you ask to define it. However, at its core, the process of development is the action of empowering people to be able to communicate more effectively with one another, in order to improve the lives of not just themselves but the nation they live in. There are many facets to development. Some have suggested it is conquering the digital divide, while others have suggested that it is simply the MDG that needs to be achieved. At a 2004 meeting of the bilateral and multilateral development agencies, a conclusion was agreed upon, in that:

> Communication is fundamental to helping people change the societies in which they live, particularly communication strategies which

both inform and amplify the voices of those with most at stake and which address the structural impediments to achieving these goals. However, such strategies remain a low priority on development agendas, undermining [the] achievement of the Millennium Development Goals. (United Nations Development Programme 2006, 11)

As mentioned previously, material needs are an important aspect towards modernizing these peripheral nations, however they should not dominate the goals of an organization such as the UNDP. Participation and willingness in adopting these so called "Western" values and modernization should come while respecting ethical expectations of citizens. First overcoming that obstruction and getting citizens motivated to learn will permit greater achievement of material needs. After all, one cannot simply use a computer or learn to grow crops effectively without prior instruction. This instruction must come first. Then and only then should the UNDP focus on material needs such as wiring the country for Internet, or distributing laptops to children. Education is a priority and should focus on instilling the values of health and knowledge to people in third world countries. This way, development can occur in a way that promotes life first and foremost, and then technology. Doing so in this manner will allow for adequate time towards attaining economic prosperity.

In conclusion, the deadline of 2015 for the MDGs is still a way off. Some of the goals can be met. The task lies in preserving the culture and languages of those in the southern hemisphere while simultaneously getting certain habits, particularly relating to education and work, and prior dysfunctional beliefs to change in order to create a better future.

United Nations Educational, Scientific and Cultural Organization (UNESCO): The LDC's Hope for a Voice

This specialized UN agency was founded in 1945, shortly after the end of World War II, with the aim of building peace in the minds of women and men. The initial focus was on education. For example, in 1948 it recommended making primary education public, free, compulsory, and universal. Now based in Paris, it has 193 members and over time it has developed five thematic areas. They are education, natural sciences, social and human sciences, culture, and communication and information. They also have special themes which include a number of issues, many of which apply to development communication. Examples are eradication of poverty, basic literacy, promoting cultural diversity, empowering people through access to information and knowledge, and indigenous peoples. UNESCO has official connection with 310 NGOs.[3]

Historically UNESCO has become involved in contentious issues and controversy. The major one was their support for a New World Information and Communication Order (NWICO) which, by the mid 1980s, led to both the UK and the USA leaving UNESCO, taking with them their annual monetary dues. The UK returned in 1997 and the USA in 2003. More details are provided later on this matter.

Today UNESCO seeks to promote universal agreements on ethical issues, such as building human capacities in a number of areas. It promotes projects aimed at creating sustainable development, education for all, alleviation of poverty, and respect for cultural and linguistic diversity. More is detailed about the latter issue, including a UNESCO Universal Declaration on Cultural Diversity, in the next chapter.

In 1975 UNESCO with the UN established the United Nations University in Japan. Recently UNESCO has begun to produce for the parent UN system an annual progress report about the Least Developed Countries. In the fifth annual report in 2007 there is detailed reporting on three educational goals, all of which have a southern hemisphere focus. They are: First, "Ensuring that by 2015 all children, particularly girls, children in difficult circumstances those belonging to ethnic minorities, have access to and complete free and compulsory primary education of good quality" (UNESCO 2007, 2). This is Millennium Development Goal (MDG) number 2 discussed previously. Second, "achieving a 50 per cent improvement in levels of adult literacy by 2015" (UNESCO 2007, 4). Third, "achieving gender equality in education by 2015" (UNESCO 2007, 7). This is MDG goal number 3.

Culture

The cultural division of UNESCO set its goal to protect the cultural and natural good in the world, which have universal value. It designates projects and places of cultural and scientific significance. The agency is the most important international instrument for the international community to protect their cultural and natural heritage.

World heritage

The UNESCO members commit themselves to preserve and maintain cultural and natural good. The UNESCO created a record of the cultural and natural heritage, which are listed as World Heritage sites and are divided into cultural, natural, or mixed properties. The UNESCO "seeks to encourage the identification, protection and preservation of cultural and natural heritage around the world considered to be of outstanding value to humanity." These goals of UNESCO were embodied in an international treaty adopted by the Organization in 1972. The World Heritage list currently comprises 851 sites worldwide. Places as precious and distinctive as the Great Barrier Reef in Australia, The Great Wall in China, the Historic Sanctuary of Machu Picchu in Peru, Galápagos Islands of Ecuador, The Acropolis in Athens, Greece, the Serengeti National Park in Tanzania, or the largest pre-Columbian city, the Pre-Hispanic City of Teotihuacan in Mexico, to name just a few, are part of the world's heritage.

One of the agency's mandates is to become aware of new global threats that could affect the heritage and to ensure the preservation of its sites and monuments. The agency describes its role as "reflecting the natural and cultural wealth that belongs to all of humanity, World Heritage sites and monuments constitute crucial landmarks for our world. They symbolize the consciousness of States and peoples of the significance of these places and reflect their attachment to collective ownership and to the transmission of this heritage to future generations."

The World Heritage Fund is intended to support restoration projects at world heritage sites. The fund consists of contributions of the member states and donations. Each state pays an annual general percent of its contributions to UNESCO in the fund which provides the modest amount of $4 million per year to support activities requested by States Parties in need of international assistance.

The World Heritage list is a success story. An entry of a site on the World Heritage list is often associated with prestige and the importance has grown strongly in recent years, especially for tourism marketing. UNESCO recognized several years ago that a thematic and geographical imbalance threatened. To prevent this, the agency developed a strategy for a representative and credible world heritage list and in this context it encourages historic categories on the World Heritage list which are underrepresented – such as cultural landscapes or industrial monuments. To avoid a rapid growth of the list, the UNESCO annually allows a maximum of only 45 new objects on the World Heritage list. In addition, each country now can only register two nominations per year.

Another important mission of UNESCO is to ensure space for and freedom of expression to the entire world's cultures which should help to avoid segregation and prevent conflict. Cultural dialogue becomes more and more important in a globally growing and intertwined world. Thus, it is a factor to maintain peace and world unity.

One of UNESCO's main goals is the promotion of cultural diversity which is covered in detail in Chapter 4.

Communication and information

UNESCO's Communication and Information Sector (CI) was established in its present form in 1990 and promotes the free flow of ideas by word and image. The sector provides the secretariats for two intergovernmental programmes: the International Programme for the Development of Communication (IPDC) and the Information for All Programme (IFAP).

The benefits of knowledge and technology are not available to the large majority of the world's population. The main objective for UNESCO is to build a knowledge society based on the sharing of knowledge and incorporating all the socio-cultural and ethical dimensions of sustainable development. Some of its priorities in this field include empowering people through access to information and knowledge with special emphasis on freedom of expression, promoting communication development, and advancing the use of ICTs for education, science, and culture. Moreover, the organization's aim is to facilitate universal access to information and knowledge and to prevent an expansion of the knowledge gap.

Differences in access to information and knowledge mainly affect developing nations and disadvantaged communities, but within these societies there are also significant disparities. Women find themselves, in most cases, excluded from equal social and economic opportunities and in terms of the benefits offered by ICTs. UNESCO's actions focus on providing all the people with the skills and abilities to use information in their professional and personal lives through media education and information literacy programs. Some of its projects are aimed at gender, others at people with disabilities. UNESCO also uses different strategies to foster equitable access to information and knowledge as awareness-raising about the importance of information literacy at all levels of the education process and training teachers to sensitize them to the importance of information literacy. Further, one of its focuses is the battle against HIV/AIDS through a preventive education and raising awareness among the public in making best use of communication resources.

IPDC

International Programme for the Development of Communication (IPDC) is a forum intended to strengthen the communication and mass media in developing countries. IPDC was launched as a result of the MacBride report. In 1977, UNESCO set up the International Commission for the Study of Communication Problems, also known as MacBride Commission. It had the task to deliver a report investigating communication in mass media and news in view of emerging technologies and to propose a plan to diminish problems. The report *Many Voices, One World*, presented in 1980, identified unequal access to information, communication technologies, and media concentration. It was greeted with great support from Third World nations; however, it also aroused controversy and bitter opposition by the US and the UK. They viewed the report as an attempt to curb freedom of the press and both countries withdrew from UNESCO in the mid 1980s. Both have since returned.

IPDC also stimulates the development of, and access to, diverse content, promotes freedom of expression, press freedom and access to information and its projects encourage the free flow of ideas by images and words by promoting universal access to ICTs, and supporting independence, pluralism of the media, democracy, peace, and tolerance. Moreover it furthers cultural diversity in the media. IPDC intends to give a voice to the voiceless and focuses on developing human resources in media.

IPDC programs aim to modernize independent news agencies, broadcast, and radio stations by enhancing the training of their staff and by purchasing new equipment as in Chad, Senegal, Peru and many other developing countries. A program in Guatemala trained journalists in freedom of expression and indigenous rights, briefing them on the issues of discrimination. IPDC also funded a community radio for women of South Cameroon, supported the establishment of the first women's radio station in Cambodia, and upgraded the scope and range of broadcasting services that are available to radio and TV audiences in Mongolia. IPDC also promoted the folk music of Nepalese musicians; to protect and develop the disappearing Nepalese culture.

Recent approved projects include training for female journalists in Mauritania, promoting investigative journalism in Bangladesh, and broadening the gender vision in Mexican and Central American Media. Over the past 27 years, IPDC supported over 1,100 projects in 139 developing countries and countries in transition.

United Nations Conference on Trade and Development (UNCTAD): Focus on Least Developed Countries

The United Nations Conference on Trade and Development (UNCTAD) is a permanent intergovernmental agency and was established in 1964. Headquartered in Geneva, its mandate is to advise the UN by studying global trade patterns, investment, and a broad range of development issues. It is headed by a Secretary-General and to date they have all come from developing countries. There are 193 member countries. UNCTAD's website states:

> UNCTAD has progressively evolved into an authoritative knowledge-based institution whose work aims to help shape current policy debates and thinking on development, with a particular focus on ensuring that domestic policies and international action are mutually supportive to bring about sustainable development.

In general the aim is to restructure the global economy so that the poorer nations have a say and role in setting trade rules. They seek to reframe the debate about the global economy and economic system in an equitable fashion. Many see the past debates as being dominated by concerns about multinational corporations, the World Bank, the International Monetary Fund, and more recently with expanded bilateral and multilateral free trade agreements, particularly those involving and favoring the United States.

UNCTAD's work is across several areas, and communication aspects of development are prevalent. The 2007–8 major *Information Economy Report – Science and Technology for Development: The New Paradigm of ICT* is a good example. This report looks at the "digital divide" between the rich versus poor nations. It details Internet usage, broadband infrastructure where 36 nations have penetration rates of less than 1 percent, and the increased usage of mobile phones across the southern hemisphere. Other aspects look at e-commerce, e-banking, capacity building, technology transfer, and indigenous training for ICT users.

In 2000 UNCTAD began an annual *Least Developed Countries Report*. The focus is on the hundreds of millions who try to exist on less than a dollar per day. It details positive examples of progress across several sectors. Also, concern is raised about the further liberalization and privatization of telecommunication systems which could result in increased marginalization. Another recent activity is the creation of an international blog site "Ideas for Development." The blog seeks open discussion from experts or the general public about matters issues, or models which may advance or contribute to the overall goal of positive development.

World Intellectual Property Organization (WIPO)

The WIPO was established as a specialized agency of the UN system in 1967. It seeks to develop a fair intellectual property (IP) system. It sees IP as being central for economic, social, and cultural developments around the world. The mission is to promote the effective application and protection of IP worldwide. The five strategic goals of WIPO are: 1) promote a culture of IP; 2) integrate IP into national policies; 3) develop international IP standards and laws; 4) assure quality services in international IP protection systems; and 5) increase the efficiency of WIPO's management. These goals have formed the core or central tasks of WIPO almost since its inception but recently WIPO have added a development agenda to their activities.

In 2007 WIPO created a Committee on Development and Intellectual Property. The group was created as a response to concerns raised by Brazil, Argentina, and other southern hemisphere nations. A major part of the development agenda is to reduce the digital divide. It is also interesting to note that when the committee meets over 100 nations attend along with close to 40 NGOs.

To date the committee has mapped out five areas of concern. They are: 1) technical assistance and capacity building; 2) norm-setting along with public policy and public domain issues; 3) technology transfer, information and communication technology, as well as access to knowledge; 4) assessment and evaluation; and 5) governance. WIPO is seeking to move beyond high-tech issues dominated by industrial nations and become more broadly based in its concerns and efforts.

International Telecommunication Union (ITU)

The ITU, another specialized agency of the United Nations, was founded in Paris in 1865 as the International Telegraph Union. It is based in Geneva, Switzerland, and its membership includes 191 Member States and more than 700 Sector Members and Associates. It is the primary global telecommunication agency and is divided intro three core sectors: radiocommunication (ITU-R); standardization (ITU-T); and development (ITU-D).

The agency's mission is to enable the growth and continued development of telecommunications and information networks and to facilitate universal access for everyone. The ITU creates infrastructure to deliver telecommunications services worldwide, manages the radio-frequency spectrum and satellite orbits, and supports countries' development of telecommunication. ITU provides, for example, technical, financial, and human resources to reduce the so called digital divide, which is one of its key priorities. There is a widening gap between people who have access to digital and information technology caused by society changes. Developing countries, especially, find themselves at a global disadvantage re these resources. Issues regarding the Internet are cyber security, spam, and cybercrime which are other critical concerns of the ITU.

In 1984, the Maitland Commission, lead by Sir Donald Maitland, highlighted the "missing link" in developing countries and internationally between the development of telecommunications and overall economic and social development. Historically the ITU was a group of engineers cooperating on cross-border technical standards. Little concern about social or human impact issues was ever mentioned. The Maitland Report changed the culture within the ITU forever. The report concluded that "telecommunications services in many developing countries are poor or indifferent. In many remote areas there is no service at all" (Maitland 1984, 65). The report made some startling comparisons. Three-quarters of the world's population lives in countries with fewer than 10 telephones per 100 people. Since then, the ultimate mission of ITU is to provide every human being an easy and affordable reach of information and communication. The Maitland Report pledged to bring telephone services within easy reach of all humankind by the early part of the twenty-first century. The agency even upgraded its commitment to development in 1992 when it established ITU-D.

World Summit on the Information Society (WSIS)

The ITU was the lead organizing agency for the World Summit on the Information Society (WSIS) conferences, which were held in two phases and in two very different nations. The first phase of the WSIS summit took place in December 2003 in Geneva and the second and final phase was held in Tunis in November 2005. The Tunis phase was marked by anti free press activities on behalf of the authoritarian leadership. The main goal of the WSIS conferences was to reduce the so-called global digital divide between the rich and poor countries and diminish developing countries' reduced opportunities by spreading access to information technology, especially to the Internet.

At the Geneva phase, a Plan of Action set out the goals to be achieved by 2015 to ensure that all of the world's population has access to television and radio services and to ensure that more than half the world's inhabitants have access to ICTs.

An issue that emerged at the first conference in Geneva was governance of the Internet and the dominant role of the US in policy making. The summit failed to agree on the future of Internet governance and a working group was formed to come up with ideas and report at the second phase meeting in Tunisia. The matter threatened to derail the second conference since the Internet Corporation for Assigned Names and Numbers (ICANN) is based in California and many nations demanded independence for the corporation and removal of US hegemony over the Internet. To prevent a major blow-up and after intense lobbying by the US, the members agreed finally not to get involved in the technical operations of ICANN. Keeping US hegemony over ICT is motivated by the drive for monopoly profits at the expense of the underdeveloped countries. Following the conference in Tunis and to raise further global awareness of society changes brought by the Internet and new technologies, the United Nations General Assembly proclaimed May 17 as World Information Society Day.

Some of the present obstacles, with which the ITU sees itself confronted, include the repairing of technology in developing countries which requires trained technicians and the training of computer users on how to find information on the Internet. Language barriers present another major hurdle for the information society and the development of ICT, mostly seen in the African continent with its thousands of local languages. The information presented online might not be in the user's native language and therefore has to be translated or the users have to be educated in a language in which information is widely available online. Moreover, access, not only to computers, but also to handheld devices and portable technologies (i.e., cell phones), digital cameras and other technologies present obstacles to be overcome.

Conclusion

This chapter examined the significant role of the UN system as it impacts development communication issues, polices, and practices. The primary agency is the UNDP which serves as the vehicle for much of the UN's work in this sector. It promotes the Millennium Goals and a number of annual reports which contain global data on communication and media matters.

The next agency was the Paris based UNESCO. It has historically been focused on education but moved into the communication area during the 1970s with its support of the contentious NWICO movement. Since then it has tried to focus more on cultural and non-media matters. (UNESCO is currently promoting an international convention concerning cultural diversity and that entire matter is covered in detail in Chapter 5.) Some discussion of the highly praised but poorly funded IPDC was also outlined

UNCTAD, a Geneva-based intergovernmental agency was also mentioned. It has the daunting task of spreading the benefits of the evolving global economy to the southern hemisphere. It is more open than many UN efforts but in the final analysis the South is still in dire economic and social states.

The WIPO has added development to its agenda and this deals more with intellectual property matters and less with traditional media, such as radio or television. The dual goals of reducing the digital divide and narrowing the global knowledge gap are driving its current agenda.

The final agency was the ITU. Historically it was a technical forum looking at trans-national telecommunication systems from an engineering perspective. Today it takes into account a number of non technical aspects of telecommunication developments, such as economic, social, or cultural matters. The ITU's sponsorship of the WSIS is a clear indication that broad social as well as economic issues will stay part of the ITU's evolving mandate. The WSIS found itself with an unexpected major problem, namely US governance and control of the Internet. Many LDCs fear that the US will only promote selfish policies at the expense of other nations.

Notes

1 The UNDP is not without its critics. In 2008 the US requested an investigation of UNDP activities in North Korea. A number of irregularities were cited. The most glaring problem was the siphoning of UNDP project funds by the North Korean government, particularly authoritarian leader Kim Jong-il and his family. Since the US donates about $250 million a year to UNDP, there were serious reservations about the UNDP's lax oversight and failure to correct the North Korean situation as well as other fiscal problems in a number of UNDP projects.

2 "Tied-aid" is normally used in the context of the activities of the several agencies of the UN. It occurs when donor groups or nations attach specific conditions to their financial donations. For decades almost all Western governments have committed money to development communication projects with strings attached. Examples are Canada donating a radio system to a Third World nation under the condition that Canadian engineers are hired to set up the stations, or a Nordic country will fund a new project only if Nordic specialists run the project for the first year.

But there is another more subtle aspect of tied-aid as well. This is where Western-based foundations provide funding for projects in peripheral nations with the condition that the recipients follow fairly well defined social science methods. For example, theory, statistics, data collection, analysis, paradigms or research issues and strategies that reflect the donor's conception of both the problem as well as the solution have to be agreed upon for funding. Indigenous practices are taboo and do not receive attention or funding. The core-based foundations set the research agenda. Currently the issue of assessment is the new mantra to be included in all contracts for development aid. This forces researchers to seek quick results rather than long-term or best results in order to keep the Foundation donors and their accountants happy.

3   UNESCO is also active with a Convention on the Protection and Promotion of the Diversity of Cultural Expressions. The Convention seeks to protect public broadcasters around the world by keeping the WTO agreements from including cultural/audio-visual industries. It is discussed in detail in Chapter 5. Some may want to refer to it now.

4

The Roles of Non-Governmental Organizations (NGOs)

Thomas L. McPhail

Introduction

This chapter looks at various aspects of the NGO phenomenon in terms of their impact on development communication. The roles of the NGOs are varied and they have been involved in a serious manner since the end of World War II. To a very large extent, development communication fieldwork is carried out by NGOs. Despite their sound research and attempts to assist the less fortunate, some of their actions, motives, and funding sources have come in for criticism. This chapter takes a broad look at the NGO phenomenon. The actions of the United Nations are detailed since that organization established a structure that created a legitimate role and place for NGOs. In addition, there are a few currently active NGOs that deserve special attention, such as the Communication for Social Change Consortium and Canada's IDRC; they will be discussed in more detail toward the end of the chapter.

The Rise of the NGO

NGO is short for Non-Governmental Organization. Just what exactly are Non-Governmental Organizations, and what are their purposes? The idea of NGOs has been around since the 1800s, but officially entered the mainstream as a result of the United Nations in 1945 when they became a way to differentiate between participation rights for intergovernmental, specialized agencies and international, private ones. The Human Rights Charter of 1948 established the need to work towards sustaining peace and improving the quality of life for humans globally, which meant that NGOs were needed in order to fulfill these tasks. NGOs are private organizations run by two groups, professional staff and volunteers. Combined they act towards some common, humanitarian purpose. The Red Cross, the World Social Forum, and the International Network for Cultural Diversity are good examples of NGOs.

Today, the task of development is run by many diverse NGOs. Many peripheral nations these days are too poor to improve the quality of life on their own. They also may have corrupt or military governments who have little intention of improving the quality of life for their citizens. The UN has long recognized the limitations of these nations as vehicles of progressive change, and has placed the task on the shoulders of the private sector through NGOs. The UN and its agencies realized that they needed to go beyond the capabilities, as well as the willingness of nations and free markets, in order to improve communications, combat poverty and promote human rights. According to John Farrington and Anthony Bebbington,

> The excesses of state inefficiency, repression, and corruption require a rethinking among those who have previously assumed that social-ism, or at least social development, would be achieved through public sector actions. On the other hand, nor have profit minded actors in the market shown much willingness to eradicate poverty, empower the poor, or even to invest productively in the wake of neo-liberal economic programs. (Farrington and Bebbington 1993, 2)

Compared to 50 years ago, a dramatically increasing number of NGOs are stepping in to help peripheral regions. In today's world, the term "development" does not just encompass human rights. "Development" is such a vast entity these days that it also relates to democratization, stimulating economic growth within a country, or utilizing media for a variety of causes. It should be noted that even the goal of spreading democracy has stirred some controversy over the idea of cultural, military, or economic imperialism by some core nations.

There are only a few criteria to becoming a NGO. The organiza-tion needs to simply abide by these rules. They are as follows: remain independent from government control, non-profit seeking, non-criminal, and not seeking to challenge governments on issues of control/power. (A NGO cannot enforce or become a political party of any sort.) NGOs can vary in size, from small grassroots movements to juggernauts such as the Red Cross/Crescent, which is currently the largest NGO. This chapter will analyze NGOs, their history, and their roles in development communication in peripheral nations. While NGOs may strive towards this goal, there has been criticism that NGOs have actually been worsening conditions in peripheral nations because of how they interact with local governments. Johanna Kalb states:

> While initially heralded as the "magic bullet" for development, NGOs have come under increasing criticism for their failure to deliver "development" as promised. NGOs have been accused of perpetuating colonial dependencies, infringing on the sovereignty of developing nations, and co-opting and corrupting real community organizations. (Kalb 2006, 299)

The latter refers to either not using locals as resources or requiring them to abandon their historical methods for donor-mandated practices.

Before delving into some NGOs' history, one should know that NGOs may be classified into four different categories. They are as follows:

1 *Charitable orientation NGO*: This type of NGO often involves a top-down paternalistic effort with little participation by beneficiaries. It includes NGOs with activities directed toward meeting the needs of the poor, such as distribution of food, clothing or medicine; provision of housing, transport, and schools. These NGOs may also undertake relief activities during a natural or man-made disaster.

2 *Service orientation NGO*: This type of NGO deals with activities such as the provision of health, family planning or education services in which the program is designed by the NGO and people are expected to participate in its implementation and in receiving the service.

3 *Participatory orientation NGO*: These NGOs are characterized by self-help projects where local people are involved particularly

in the execution of a project by contributing funding, natural resources, and voluntary labor.

4 *Empowering orientation NGO*: This type of NGO aims to help poor people develop a clearer understanding of the social, political and economic factors affecting their lives, and to strengthen their awareness of their own potential power to control their lives. Sometimes, these groups develop spontaneously around a problem or an issue. Empowering orientation NGOs are considered to be the most important in terms of promoting development and reducing the digital divide in peripheral nations.

It is also important to note that each of these types of NGO can vary in size and by how organized and committed their operations are. They also share some of the same objectives. According to John M. Shandra:

> Nongovernmental organizations seek to change the practices of governments and multilateral institutions, which often involves lobbying government and multilateral agency officials . . . Thus, international Non-Governmental Organizations are in a position of pointing out embarrassing failures and hypocrisies of nations, which puts pressure on governments to adapt behaviors to international norms. (Shandra 2007, 666)

Or expel the foreign do-gooders. Shandra also goes on discuss that NGOs may sometimes be more biased towards one particular cause than the overall goal of improving the quality of life in peripheral nations. For example, efforts to reduce deforestation in Latin America have resulted in NGOs taking such extreme measures as prohibiting all individuals from setting foot on the very land they're trying to protect, in essence removing locals from their homes if they happen to be unfortunate enough to live in those areas. Interestingly enough, the number of NGOs emphasizing environmental or green efforts has increased from two in 1953 to hundreds now, making environmental concerns the second largest domain for NGOs. The largest sector being those involved in human rights.

Some of the criticism of NGOs, which will be discussed later, stems from the fact that while NGOs often have similar goals, acting in the interest of the public, they can differ depending upon how powerful they are, and who runs them, and which public they actually serve. Therefore, the agenda of some NGOs can be influenced by white middle class individuals if they dominate the upper ranks of a particular NGO. What occurs as a result of this? It removes the opinions and needs of local citizens from community projects, and the NGO assumes everything for those individuals.

The relationship between the UN and NGOs has been sketchy, at best, for the past 60 years. With each new decade it seems there is some new controversy brought up between the two. The early years of the UN showed NGOs closely aligned with the United Nations Economic and Social Council (ECOSOC). In 1948, there were officially 41 consultative groups that were assigned to consult with ECOSOC. Statistics in 1998 reveal the number of organizations as over 1,500, each with varying degrees of input and success (Simmons 1998, 83).

The early years of NGOs' interaction with the UN saw a focus on social and humanitarian concerns. It did not take long, however for initial opposition to NGOs to surface. Initially, the USSR and several third world nations were against NGOs. As their numbers grew in terms of the UN General Assembly, they began to voice their opinion more. This would eventually lead to a major review of NGOs in 1968–9. The issues at hand were:

1 Western domination of NGOs in Consultation status;
2 the extent of government influence on NGOs;
3 the expanding numbers of NGOs; and
4 criticisms of governments by human rights NGOs.

Basically there was a concern or suspicion that a growing number of NGOs were simply surrogates for Western imperialist ends and that a new form of colonization was taking place.

The result of this review caused a dramatic shift in power in the United Nations. It also further politicized the UN–NGO relationship by creating more tension. The most controversial issue was that of Western domination of NGOs in Consultation status. Basically, only the largest and most powerful NGOs (resonating from core nations) were being given the ability to consult with the UN as a result of Resolution 1296. Resolution 1296 placed many rules and restrictions upon how an NGO could gain consultation status with the UN

General Assembly. An example of a deterrent for many smaller or new NGOs was that Resolution 1296 forced all NGOs to have an official headquarters and executive officer in order to consult. Thus, many argued that alternative methods should be sought to create opportunities for non-global NGOs to participate in a meaningful way with the United Nations (Otto 1996, 114). Basically the old model of grass-roots volunteers was replaced by a cadre of professional and elite NGOs, a two tier system.

Another problem arising is that many governments are establishing their own NGOs, or so called "GONGOs" (Government Organized Non-Governmental Organizations). They then abuse the UN system of accreditation in order to promote their own NGO to having consultative status. Upon reaching this status, they will be able to spread their own propaganda favoring their government at UN conferences and meetings.

As European researcher Kerstin Martens says:

> These recent developments in the NGO scene have prompted well-respected internationally operating NGOs such as Amnesty International, Human Rights Watch, and the International Federation of Human Rights Leagues to fear loss of their reputation as credible sources of information and as trustworthy associates. For example, human rights NGOs can make oral and written statements during the annual six-week sessions of the Commission on Human Rights and present short reports on the human rights situation in a particular country. In recent years, however, more and more GONGOs seek to take the floor first in order to give an account of the "wonderful" human rights situation in nations well known for human rights violations. Such statements not only reduce the available time for more legitimate human rights NGOs, but also undermine the system of NGO accreditation at the United Nations as a whole. In particular, some Chinese and Iranian organizations have been suspected of being government-organized. (Martens 2003, 8–9)

Another criticism of NGOs deals with how they manage their money to fund projects. In Bosnia, there was some controversy over NGO advertising. The money spent on advertising was used to promote actual NGO programs to potential donors, so in essence the advertising money was being spent to help raise more money for the NGOs in Bosnia. Those who opposed this funding claimed that it was condescending, in that the money should have been spent solely on reconstruction efforts. In Rwanda and Ethiopia, money was spent on building new roads and camps for local citizens. However, it is said that the enemies of those citizens took advantage of these roads at the expense of NGOs (Simmons 1998, 88).

Despite all of the internal conflict between NGOs and the UN, the intentions of NGOs are always clear. They are the organizations that bring light to crises around the world, when the global media refuses to. Clifford Bob notes that there are five arguments pertaining to this topic. "First, winning NGO support is neither easy nor automatic but instead competitive and uncertain" (Bob 2005, 4). When competitors fail to get NGO support, they often direct their energy elsewhere, or in most cases, die out. "Second, the development and retention of support are best conceived not as philanthropic gestures but as exchanges based on the relative power of each party to the transaction" (Bob 2005, 5). NGOs may see two desperate movements, and choose one over the other based simply on the fact that the one they chose matched their requirements more than the movement that does not receive aid. One cannot assume that an NGO will simply choose the "neediest" group, because they do not. As mentioned earlier, NGOs can work for different causes, and will place priority on certain causes or regions over others.

"Third, competition for NGO intervention occurs in a context of economic, political, and organizational inequality that systematically advantages some challengers over others" (Bob 2005, 5). To clarify, some movements with more resources at hand get out their message that they are in need of help, and they are the ones who will get noticed by NGOs first, and are more likely to be assisted. Having causes with media-savvy advisors increases the likelihood of funding. Catching the attention of CNN or the BBC will propel a situation to the front of the donor queue.

"Fourth, despite these structural biases, the choices of insurgents – how they market themselves – matter" (Bob 2005, 5). How rebellious movements, such as the Chiapas, market themselves really does matter. Raising international awareness and enhancing their appeal to NGOs are the best strategies for insurgents to gain overseas support and funding.

Fifth, "because of this market dynamic, the effects of assistance are more ambiguous than is often acknowledged" (Bob 2005, 6).

Scholars and journalists are often quick to idolize NGOs as organizations that can fulfill the requests of any struggling nation, as long as a free airline ticket is part of the response. When an NGO steps in to give aid, their needs and agendas are considered top priority, not whatever local movement that requested the help. Sometimes the intent and actions of an NGO can be radically different than what particular aid seekers had in mind, in effect alienating them from their true cause. Clifford Bob notes that members of a particular movement "tempted into attention-grabbing tactics or extreme stances, may find distant stalwarts absent or helpless at moments of gravest peril" (Bob 2005, 6).

In conclusion, NGOs have good intentions but they are not without controversy. Several do work with the UN to carefully monitor developing countries and developed countries alike, in order to help prevent the possibility of crisis or to help heal the damage caused by major upheavals. Unfortunately, these good intentions are lost in the sea of problems that some NGOs face these days. It is in the opinion of expert Ian Anderson that a recurring theme present in the criticism of NGOs today is "the need for them to be more thorough, rigorous, and objective in evaluating their work, and the need to publish evaluation results as an essential component of NGO transparency" (Anderson 2000, 449). This is because there is a nagging feeling that NGOs tend to represent less of a global public opinion and more-so segments of the global population that are sensitive to issues of dependency (Frau-Meigs 2004, 106).

The need to publish evaluation results is more important than ever, and a key for NGOs towards gaining the attention of the mass media. Outside of events such as the World Summit on the Information Society, the efforts of NGOs go largely unnoticed. But there is hope for NGOs, however. As technology increases and globalization spreads with each passing day, the communication efforts of NGOs increases dramatically. This along with the increasing number of NGOs coming into existence each year is certainly a positive sign that goals of development, democratization, and improving the quality of life for millions around the world can still be attainable. And NGOs cannot survive without a communication strategy.

Big Three

The three biggest, oldest, and most well known NGOs in the US are The Carnegie Foundation, The Ford Foundation, and The Rockefeller Foundation.[1] They all have participated in development communication work.[2]

The Carnegie Foundation for the Advancement of Teaching was founded by Andrew Carnegie in 1905. Achievements include development of the Teachers Insurance and Annuity Association (TIAA), publication of the Flexner Report on medical education, creation of the Carnegie Unit, founding of the Educational Testing Service, and establishment of the Carnegie Classification of Institutions of Higher Education. While the Carnegie Foundation is an organization mainly focused on the US, it is still important when reviewing leading NGO/INGOs. The Foundation is focused on education from as early as kindergarten up until the end of college. It also works with teachers to improve their skills and expand on their knowledge to ensure a better education. It is important to look at the Carnegie Foundation because many people learning in the US today will become future leaders and philanthropists.

The Ford Foundation is a little bit younger than the Carnegie Foundation but it is also noteworthy. Founded in 1936 by Edsel Ford (son of Henry Ford) with the initial plan to donate funds to other promising organizations, it soon grew to become much larger than its original mandate. Edsel and Henry both died within 10 years of the foundation's birth forcing Edsel's son Henry Ford II to take control. The new head of the foundation once remarked during the 1950s "this is a turning point in the Ford Foundation" (Berghahn 1999, 402). The Foundation's current mission is to "Strengthen democratic values, reduce poverty and injustice, promote international cooperation, and advance human achievement." The Ford Foundation today is headquartered in New York City and supports programs in over 50 countries.

The Ford Foundation was an early supporter of public broadcasting in the US. And in 1969 it was instrumental in providing support for the Children's Television Workshop which went on to create "Sesame Street." But the Foundation has attracted critics for collaborating with the CIA to promote American political positions abroad under the guise of philanthropy.[3]

The Rockefeller Foundation was founded between the previous two in 1913 by John D. Rockefeller in New York State. The Foundation's mission is to "promote the well-being of mankind throughout the world." Unlike the previous two organizations, one of the Rockefeller Foundation's main focuses now is on health care which is not only an important issue in the US but it is also one of the leading issues in the third world, particularly with HIV/AIDS. Along with health care, this organization is also currently exploring the Green Revolution.

But the Foundation's history is also not without controversy. Indonesia is a nation in Southeast Asia. It is the world's fourth most populated country with over 230 million people, a majority of whom are Muslim. The Japanese invasion during World War II ended the then Dutch colonial rule and pushed the Indonesian independence movement. Two days after Japan surrendered in 1945, Sukarno, who was an influential nationalist leader, declared independence and was appointed president. The once democratic leader quickly moved towards authoritarianism. In 1952 former US Secretary of State Dean Rusk became president of the Rockefeller Foundation. Rusk's first order of business was to push US interests by training and funding opposing forces which could one day overthrow Sukarno. Along with the Rockefeller Foundation, the Ford Foundation also had strong interests about the future of Indonesia. "The Ford Foundation, in the common belief that the modernization of Indonesia, and the rest of the third world, would follow the pattern of western industrial development, initiated the teaching of English (and other important European languages) on the assumption that development required western knowledge" (Parmar 2002, 18). All of the efforts put forth by Western influence were done, if not remove Sukarno from power, then to train the future leaders of the nation and prepare them for a time when the nationalist leader was no longer in power. In keeping with their beliefs in how their foundation should work, the Ford Foundation with aid from others such as the Rockefeller Foundation moved forward to set up more programs based on US beliefs. In the 1950s these foundations along with several universities such as MIT, Harvard, and Cornell set up an area of Indonesian studies with scholars as its driving force. Later came the Modern Indonesia Project as well as several grants to bring Indonesia's top social scientists to the US to train and study. These leading NGOs were well on their way to bringing Western ideologies to the Asian region. During a time when several US universities were integrating an American schooling system into Indonesia and setting up several economics courses "President Sukarno complained that the young Indonesians were not learning anything about Marx and only about Schumpeter and Keynes, the Berkeley team placed the word "socialist" in a number of economics courses' titles at Jakarta, without altering the course content" (Parmar 2002, 19). It was clear that the order the American NGOs had brought to Indonesia was not just an attempt to achieve their mission as a foundation, but it also became a goal to remove the President of Indonesia.

World Social Forum (WSF)

We now turn to the World Social Forum (WSF). It should be noted at the outset that it began as a movement concerned about the asymmetric trends in the globalization of the economy. Basically the failure of modernization theory to advance the lives and occupations of the poor led to a large collective group of dissatisfied people across the globe. These groups, led, in the beginning, by labor unions and environmentalists, sought to rebalance the benefits of the expanding global economy. The World Social Forum meetings are meant to debate ideas, and come up with proposals and effective actions against neo-liberalism.

The forum emerged slowly from different mobilizations, especially from the symbolic actions of the Zapatist movement in Chiapas, Mexico in 1994. Other key events as the protest against the Multilateral Agreement on Investments in 1998 and the mass demonstrations against the World Trade Organization in Seattle in 1999 paved the way for the development of the WSF. The WSF officially formed in January 2001. It met in Brazil for the first three years. Under the slogan "Another world is possible," the meetings attract a huge number of participants, primarily from the left. It has a focus of being anti-globalization and has attracted a number of related issues, complaints, and groups, particularly NGOs. To a large extent the WSF is a symbolic attempt to compete and counter the pro-capitalist and free enterprise zealots and leaders who meet annually during January in Davos, Switzerland. The Davos meeting is to sing the praises of the free enterprise system, free and open market forces, and the advantages of being extremely wealthy. Part of the motivation for establishing the WSF was to attract or counter media reports from Davos. The WSF deliberately sought to counter Davos by meeting in January as well.

Meetings have also been held in India, Venezuela, Mali, Pakistan, and Kenya. The meeting in 2003 focused on the threat of the US to invade Iraq and became the starting point of the largest manifestation for peace in human history. A one off, summer event, was held in the US in 2007. In 2008, in recognition of the growing international series of movements and diversity of the issues being pursued, literally thousands of locally organized events took place under the motto "Global Call for Action" during January. No single global meeting was organized. Future meetings are being planned but two significant and problematic matters have arisen. The first is the growing role and power of NGOs. They have to a large extent hijacked the meetings' agenda in favor of their concerns and issues while the concerns of the poor as well as labor unions have been marginalized. To some extent the NGOs are as bureaucratic, domineering, and bent on assessment as the corporations that dominate and define the global economy. When the poor see that NGO leaders make as much as political and corporate leaders, they view the elites as interchangeable.

The second matter is a broad criticism that the WSF has not accomplished anything of a concrete policy nature. It has become a collection of whiners, talkers, and even anarchists who either do not have a policy agenda, or have widely varying agendas. The end result is that little ever gets done to slow or impact the globalization movement that they originally sought to counter. A permanent and effective world social movement opposed to the economic determinism of globalization has not materialized in spite of the time, talent, and many sessions of the WSF.

Communication for Social Change Consortium (CFSC)

The Communication for Social Change Consortium (CFSC) is an international nonprofit organization based in New Jersey. The Consortium's goal is to build the local capacity of people living in poor and marginalized communities to use communication to improve their lives. It was chartered in June of 2003 and started as a special project of the Rockefeller Foundation in 1997. The network fosters public and private dialogue between the people so they themselves define who they are, their needs, and what they can do in order to improve their own lives. The dialogue is supported by some of the world's leading thinkers and practitioners of communication for development. The Social Change Consortium is currently made up of several hundred scholars, researchers, and practitioners living and working in dozens of countries.

The vision of the organization is to change lives by changing practices. Their set goal for 2015 is fostering the incorporation of CFSC principles into the work of a network of practitioners, as well as most major development initiatives. Another broad goal is ensuring that principles of justice, equity, tolerance, and ownership by affected communities become central to the practice of communication for development. Their projects aspire to a shifting in public values and beliefs that are essential for long-term social changes.

The aids2031 project, for example, looks at the current knowledge about AIDS response to consider future steps. Its goal is to spark new thinking and evidence on AIDS so it can influence the investment and research in the future. It is an initiative that brings together economists, epidemiological, biomedical, social and political scientists to question conventional wisdom, stimulate new research, encourage public debate and uncover new evidence.

The KnowWater project aims to give free of charge information to the world's poor people on water, such as: where it is available; how much it will cost; and information on delivery and distribution, quality, regulation, and social and political concerns that impact its accessibility. The Consortium also published an anthology on a broad variety of views on communication for social change. The book reviews the evolution of communication for social change from the early twentieth century to the present.

The Consortium has different partner organizations among which are many of the UN agencies, and divisions within the World Bank, IADB, and universities.

Canada's IDRC

The International Development Research Centre (IDRC) is a Canadian Crown corporation that works in partnership with researchers from the developing world in their search for the means to build healthier, more equitable, and more prosperous societies. The corporation was created by the Parliament of Canada in 1970 to help developing countries to undertake research and use technology to find long-term solutions to their social, economic, and environmental problems. IDRC is guided by a 21-member, international Board of Governors including members from developing countries, and reports to the Canadian Parliament through the Minister of Foreign Affairs. In 2006–7, IDRC received CA\$135.3 million in funding from the Parliament of Canada. The head office is located in Ottawa and regional offices are in Nairobi, Dakar, Cairo, New Delhi, Singapore, and Montevideo. IDRC's mission is "Empowerment through knowledge."

The corporation funds applied research by researchers in developing countries on the problems they identify as crucial to their communities. Further, IDRC offers expert advice to those researchers and finances the local capacity in developing countries to undertake research. IDRC also funds and administers a training and awards program for young researchers from Canada and developing countries. This funding gives these researchers the opportunity to participate in international development work.

IDRC is committed to advancing the role of information in development. In regards to their Information and Communication Technologies for Development (ICT4D) concentration, IDRC began building databases and information systems. IDRC was one of the first development agencies to see ICTs as a key means to promote development and alleviate poverty. Through some of its programs like Acacia in Africa, and Pan Asia Networking in Asia, IDRC has gained a lot of experience on the impact of ICTs on the lives of people in the developing world.

In Bangladesh, IDRC has worked with Mohammad Yunus, co-winner of the 2006 Nobel Peace Prize and the Grameen Bank he founded, on a number of projects linking the use of ICTs to poverty reduction. The results of this collaboration have included an intranet system boosting communication among the bank's 1,000 branches, mostly in rural areas, an Internet service provider that offered low-cost connectivity to schools, research institutions, and government agencies; and one of Asia's first rural tele-centers, located in Mad-hupur, Tangail district.

IDRC also supports agricultural research in Uganda. It has also supported research on farming and natural resource use in Ugandan cities. In 2005, the capital, Kampala, became one the first five "Focus Cities" in which IDRC is supporting collaboration between local government authorities, research institutions, and community organizations on innovative projects that link poverty alleviation, environmental management, and natural resource use for food, water, and income security.

In Latin America, IDRC set up procedures and standards to manage computer recycling programs based on the Canadian Computers for Schools model. Moreover, IDRC has established two Canadian-led initiatives, Connectivity and Equity in the Americas and Connectivity Africa, to bridge the digital divide.

IDRC also publishes books on issues related to sustainable and equitable development based on their research. Therefore, it contributes to the body of knowledge to foster further understanding of these issues of development.

Conclusion

This chapter focused on three areas. The first was about the role and functions of NGOs, the second dealt with the role and background of US Foundations, and the third was a group of three stakeholders in the development communication scene.[4]

The NGOs were detailed since they have become major conveyors of development communication projects. They work alongside of the UN efforts, or in some cases they are directly contracted to carry out some mission on behalf of a granting agency. The NGOs have grown is size, influence, and professionalism.

The three foundations that were described were Carnegie, Ford, and Rockefeller. Over time they have been influential in what they chose to support or not support. Many of the university-based projects in the southern hemisphere were funded by these foundations. Their connections to both the CIA and ruling elites promoting US foreign policy objectives was mentioned in terms of tainting some of the activities undertaken.

The World Social Forum was outlined since it has a critical role in terms of the actions, or inaction, of the preceding entities, namely the NGOs and Foundations. The WSF seeks to spread the economic as well as social benefits of globalization to disenfranchised groups and regions.

The Communication for Social Change Consortium was detailed as a more recent organization which has a direct development communication focus. The focus is on long-term structural change brought about by the exchange between experts and people who want to change themselves. Positive social change through various media is their goal.

Canada's prestigious International Development Research Centre was reviewed really as a jewel or model for other nations to emulate in terms of development matters. It is big on applied information technology projects around the world. They seek to bridge the digital divide by assisting poorer nations and schools. Canada as a middle power nation has continually sought out progressive and peaceful applications for its foreign aid that has won them respect across the Third World as well as across the entire UN system.

Notes

1   Currently the Bill and Melinda Gates Foundation is by far the largest US Foundation but it is of recent vintage and so far has not been a major player in the development communication sector.

2   An interesting point about the three US Foundations' governing Boards is the fact that several of their members are former political lobbyists,

cabinet members, State Department officials, World Bank executives, as well as other ruling class elites. It is if they have been given a second chance or venue to promote their Cold War or now anti-terrorism mantras. Henry Kissinger is a classic case in point.

3 The close connection among American Foundations, the CIA, and the media has a long history. For example, Tim Weiner an expert on the CIA notes that since the 1950s the CIA "kept in close touch with the men who ran *The New York Times*, *The Washington Post*, and the nation's leading weekly magazines . . . The men who responded to the CIA's call included Henry Luce and his editors at *Time*, *Life*, and *Fortune*; popular magazines such as *Parade*, the *Saturday Review*, and *Reader's Digest*; and the most powerful executives at CBS News" (Weiner 2008, 88). This courting of the media elite as part of the covert CIA propaganda machine continued for decades. And likely continues today.

I also recall being in Paris working at UNESCO in the 1970s and staying at the Paris Hilton where the leading writer for *Time* magazine would meet regularly in the Hilton bar with CIA agents to get the story and slant from them about the NWICO movement, which at that time was evolving across UNESCO meetings and conferences. When I read the coverage in *Time*, which was very hostile to both UNESCO and the UN, it was a duplicate of anti-UNESCO rants that I had with the American delegation, including covert CIA agents among them, at UNESCO. The agents would claim to be reporters from small weekly newspapers in upstate Michigan. When I confronted them about this nonsense, they were quickly sent back to the States. Soon I was persona non grata with the remaining members of the US delegation.

4 The author recognizes that there are other worthy initiatives by various nations but all cannot be covered here. Also there are excellent groups like Nordicom which produce research, newsletters, conferences which have a bearing on the topic of development communication primarily from a Nordic perspective but again that region is not the focus of this book.

5

Differing Views of World Culture

Thomas L. McPhail

Introduction

This chapter looks at three interrelated topics and organizations. The first is a detailed look at an international NGO which is becoming a force within the global development communication debate. It is the International Network for Cultural Diversity (INCD). The second is UNESCO's specific role in promoting an international or global convention on cultural diversity. The convention was adopted by UNESCO in 2005. The third is the World Trade Organization (WTO) which is moving into the development and cultural arenas in direct opposition to, or conflict with, the preceding two organizations.

This dispute is related to development communication because the many poor nations in the southern hemisphere also have the most fragile or unconventional of cultures. As a result, any major structural changes at the global policy and practice levels could adversely impact or even blind-side their cultural heritage, as well as current cultural initiatives. Musicians, artists, and video producers in the southern hemisphere currently lack access to two vital resources. The one is major financing and the other is a global distribution network. If the WTO, as outlined below, prevails then these same disadvantaged cultural artisans will be faced with an additional tsunami of cultural products from post-industrial nations, particularly the US.

International Cultural Networks

A main topic of cultural policy, particularly in developing countries, is the protection and preservation of indigenous cultures, such as national or regional works of art, folklore, music, film, media, and language. In 1998 this goal of protection and preservation of national culture was adopted by the International Network on Cultural Policy (INCP). It brings together culture ministers from several countries. Initially it was set up as an international forum through which culture ministers could exchange views on emerging cultural policy issues and challenges. (The USA does not belong to it; and does not have a federal cabinet level minister or secretary of culture. In contrast, becoming minister of culture is a high ranking cabinet post in most other countries.)

The INCP was born out of an idea to create an informal, international NGO and venue where national ministers responsible for cultural policy and grants could explore new and emerging cultural policy issues, plus consider integrated ways to promote cultural diversity in an increasingly globalized world.

Soon they focused on a major issue of attempting to exclude cultural goods and services from future World Trade Organization (WTO) agreements. In turn they expanded the work and membership and this led to a new international non-government organization (NGO) which was named the International Network for Cultural Diversity (INCD); the INCD seeks to complement and support the INCP's efforts.

The INCD is a global network of artists, painters, musicians, policy-makers, and cultural groups currently consisting of 500 members from 70 countries worldwide. Their basic aims are twofold. First, they are dedicated to counter the homogenizing effects of globalization on world cultures. They have crafted a crucial alliance with UNESCO on this matter. Second, INCD seeks to counter the WTO's movement to include cultural industries, also known as audio-visual industries across Europe, as services in future agreements. The INCD is working to counter attempts to inflict free trade rules across the cultural sector.

Their membership also includes producers, cultural activists, creative industries, and other industry representatives, lobbyists, and several other non-government cultural organizations. Many are from the southern hemisphere.

INCD was formed in 1998 and held its first annual meeting in Greece in 2000. Following meetings have been held in Switzerland, South Africa, Croatia, China, Senegal and Brazil, in parallel with the annual ministerial meeting of the International Network on Cultural Policy. The French, Spanish, and Canadian governments strongly support the protection of cultural diversity and they were the most enthusiastic promoters of INCD.[1] A major goal of INCD is promoting, through the auspices of UNESCO, the Convention on the Protection and Promotion of the Diversity of Cultural Expression. It is an international convention that defines and seeks to protect cultural and linguistic diversity, along with support for open artistic expression.

A good example of what INCD is about is a 2007 study of television programming on Sweden's network channels, both public and commercial. Basically Swedish language shows are being marginalized by imported American shows. From 1998 to 2006 Swedish films, comedy, and drama series dropped 35 percent. They were replaced by imported English language, mostly American, shows. This is an international phenomenon where indigenous shows across all genres are being displaced by English language imports, including movies. Native languages are being pushed off screens and speakers across the globe at an increasing rate.

One of INCD's goals is to facilitate a global consensus that cultural diversity is central to one's concept of self, the cultural and social milieu, and economic development in an environment of increasing globalization. The smaller and weaker members of the international community are at greatest risk.

INCD thinks that there should be policies put in place to represent diverse cultures and put cultural protection on an equal footing within the WTO. To do this the INCD proposes that:

1   Governments must not enter into any agreements that constrain local cultures and the policies that support them.
2   A new international agreement, which can provide a permanent legal foundation for cultural diversity, should be created.

Globalization raised concerns that popular culture and other forms of mass communication may harm, displace, or destroy local cultures. Voices of local artists are being drowned out by imported mass production from other countries. From MTV to Disney, American media capture the hearts, minds, and money of vast segments of the global population. Entertainment giants, which are becoming larger and more concentrated, spread a homogenized global culture using their manifold channels of synergies across different media platforms. International trade bodies can worsen the situation by limiting the ability of nations to support or subsidize their own artists and cultural institutions. Likewise international financial institutions, such as the International Monetary Fund (IMF), may limit or even eliminate funding for cultural and other programs. Artists and audiences around the world envision a different kind of globalization: one which encourages cultural production within nations, and authentic exchange among them; one which encourages the dynamic coexistence of a diversity of cultures. The issue of the diversity of languages is also being heard more frequently.

In an open letter, many artists around the world, including Columbian Literature Nobel prize winner Gabriel Garcia Marquez, and American actor Danny Glover, criticize that the right of artists are at risk because of international trade courts or organizations, such as the WTO, ruling on artistic matters:

> It is time to secure the rights of artists globally. These rights are at risk because international trade courts are ruling on artistic matters . . . Some believe artistic creations are no different from conventional goods and services and they deny or ignore the powerful cultural importance of works of the human imagination. For some of the world's largest corporations, artistic works are commodities to be bought and sold like any other. They seek to dominate the world's markets with homogenized forms of popular culture and thus marginalize artists in many of our communities . . . help those countries that don't yet have the capacity to bring their stories, music and other artistic expressions to audiences everywhere. (INCD 2003)

There is actually a deceptively simple question: whether language and culture are commodities like bananas, computers, cars or whether they are a special and unique class with a non-economic value. Language acts as a central agent of socialization that shapes our selves and culture. If culture is just another commodity, it would be subjected only to the laws of free trade and free markets among countries. This is how the WTO frames it.

Yet the logic of a free market concludes that there ought to be no restrictions placed on goods and services which cross borders as part of global trade. If American movies, television shows, and music are found to be products that a family in Europe want to watch or listen to, than they should be allowed to do so without any import tariffs or other restrictions, such as content quotas. In addition, the UN Universal Declaration of Human Rights Article 19 proclaims, it is a basic right of all people to "seek, receive, and impart information and ideas through any media and regardless of frontiers." As a result any restriction of an individual's right by a government trying to preserve their native culture would be infringements of these basic rights. On the other hand, if culture is seen as art that manifests and shapes people and cultures, as well as nationhood, then diverse nations and communities have an interest in limiting the access and influence of a foreign culture, including language, to their own. So if the products in fact change attitudes and values, then local communities have reason to fear and restrict these imported popular movies, music, and television programs (Crothers 2006, 110).

The diverse issues, concerns, and rules governing international trade in popular culture have continued to drive international talks and law in the years since NAFTA was formed. In 2001, for example, UNESCO passed a Universal Declaration on Cultural Diversity. In that document the UN and the declaration's signatories insisted that cultural diversity is a "common heritage of humanity." It then called for the development of a treaty to promote and protect cultural diversity on a global scale.

The delegates to the 2001 conference then followed with a draft treaty in 2005. Sponsored by France and Canada, two countries that have long used subsidies and quotas to help their movie, television and radio industries to hold back American popular culture, the convention was inspired by a desire to shield culture from international agreements to liberalize trade.

The Convention on the Protection and Promotion of the Diversity of Cultural Expressions was adopted in 2005 and entered into force in 2007. The UNESCO vote on October 20, 2005 is illuminating. The vote was essentially cultural diversity versus cultural conformity or homogeneity. The outcome was 148 nations for and 2 nations – the USA and Israel – against. Even Canada and Great Britain, who almost always vote with the USA, recognized the implications of the hemogenic power of the USA in this sector. The treaty was intended to empower states to protect their interests in their cultural industries. The Convention on Global Diversity seeks to make the exemption of trade in cultural artifacts permanent, thereby protecting and promoting world culture from the apparently corrupting, imperial, and homogenizing effects of American popular culture. The Convention seeks to strengthen the five inseparable links of the same chain: creation, production, distribution/dissemination, access and enjoyment of cultural expressions, as conveyed by cultural activities, goods and services. It also seeks to preserve the sovereignty of governments and societies to implement measures to support diversity of cultural expression as well as encourage them to provide the appropriate support or aid for their own cultures. In addition, the Convention serves as a safeguard from trade agreements (fearing WTO actions) and provides a solid legal foundation for measures that promote cultural diversity. Furthermore, for those who adopt the new instrument and sign the declaration, they must agree that there can be no trade retaliation against measures enacted in conformity with the treaty.

As the specific language states, the objectives of the Convention on the Protection and Promotion of the Diversity of Cultural Expressions are:

- to protect and promote the diversity of cultural expressions;
- to create the conditions for cultures to flourish and freely interact in a mutually beneficial manner;
- to encourage dialogue among cultures with a view to ensuring wider and balanced cultural exchanges in the world in favor of intercultural respect and a culture of peace; and
- to foster interculturality in order to develop cultural interaction in the spirit of building bridges among peoples. (UNESCO 2005)

Adopting the convention was an important step in protecting threatened cultures, particularly in developing countries and it serves as a counterbalance to the WTO in future conflicts between trade and culture. However, many experts say they believe that its principal importance is symbolic: while it has reached no unambiguous definition of cultural diversity and how it should be promoted and protected, it has given voice to widespread concern about the perils of excessive domination by American popular culture.

The convention's supporters argue that the treaty will protect and promote cultural diversity in the face of cultural globalization, but the US believes it is intended to restrict exports of American audio-visual products, particularly Hollywood movies and television programs. Under the convention, governments will be permitted to use subsidies and quotas to promote their culture and, implicitly, to limit the access of Hollywood movies to their markets. It is seen by the US as an instrument of disguised protectionism and the US claims, not with an unbiased agenda, that it violates freedom of expression and information. A UNESCO meeting in Paris in June, 2008 outlined various strategies for the implementation of the Convention. The US delegation worked to undermine the meeting by various means.[2]

A sample of the implications of the American goals in the media sector is evident in a 2006 letter from INCD to the Office of the US Trade Representative concerning a free trade agreement involving South Korea.[3] The US position not only prevailed but the Korean film industry was all but decimated under the free trade agreement. When it comes to cultural matters, the deal ends up being for a one way flow, always favoring the US. Hollywood and the US television industry now focuses more and more on export markets, thus restrictive trade rules are a curse to them.

Global Alliance for Cultural Diversity

UNESCO's Global Alliance for Cultural Diversity is a project that aims to turn creativity in developing countries into sustainable cultural industries. One of its goals is to promote cultural diversity, support economic development and encourage job creation in a range of fields including music, publishing, cinema, crafts, and the performing arts. The different fields are recognized as a driving force in the world economy and hold great potential for developing economies. The Global Alliance for Cultural Diversity was launched as a pilot project in January 2002 by UNESCO's Arts and Cultural Enterprise Division and uses its experience in developing public–private partnerships to support programs and activities implemented under the Convention on the Protection and Promotion of the Diversity of Cultural Expressions.

Its mission is stated as promoting "cultural diversity by strengthening the capacity of cultural industries to produce and distribute goods and services and help them gain access to national and international markets." The Global Alliance achieves these aims in three main ways which are: creating public–private partnerships between its members to help get cultural initiatives off the ground and share know-how and experiences: working to promote the international respect and enforcement of intellectual property rights without which artists and creators cannot protect their work or turn their creativity into viable businesses: and supporting consultations between national authorities and private stakeholders to develop suitable sector policies and legislative frameworks to promote cultural industries.

The project is about collaborative action and some examples in the cinema and audio-visual sector include fostering Niger's film industry and developing quality pan-Arab television programming for children. Niger is one of the leading countries in African documentary filmmaking. Global Alliance has set up the first ever African Documentary Film Forum in the capital Niamey and sponsored a documentary filmmaking workshop for local young people. Now, the forum will be held every two years and focuses on helping raise public interest in film, and tries to inspire a new generation of filmmakers by at the same time promoting the development of the industry's infrastructure.

Developing quality pan-Arab television programming for children, which is essential to the education of children, is an ongoing project. One of the aims is to adapt "Sesame Street" to local realities but also to provide co-production opportunities for local producers. Moreover, part of the program includes training local technicians and developing various skills of employees of media organizations in broadcasting, production and post-production, publishing, advertising, music, media and marketing services.

In publishing, the Global Alliance promotes a project which provides African books for the neediest African libraries. The revenue generated after a special sale throughout the French-Belgian network of Maxi-Livres bookshops helped fund the donation of books produced by African publishers to libraries in several African countries.

Another project is aimed at capacity-building for cultural enterprises in developing countries. The Artists in Development (AiD) program is designed to hone skills among artists and creators in developing countries. Organized workshops foster individual professional growth and income-generating capacities and the program later aimed at strengthening existing cultural enterprises in developing countries. Eight initiatives have been carried out within the framework of the program, all supported by the Norwegian Ministry of Foreign Affairs. Some examples of the initiatives include the building of a film distribution and exhibition network for Cultural Diversity in Colombia, strengthening the link between Craft Link's business arm and its development (training) arm in Vietnam, and the innovation in the Crafts Sector in Latin America.

World Trade Organization (WTO)

The World Trade Organization (WTO) is an international organization dealing with the rules of trade between nations. It counts 152 member countries and the organization is designed to supervise and liberalize international trade and to help producers of goods and services, exporters, and importers conduct their business. Therefore, it also handles trade disputes and organizes forums for trade negotiations. The WTO has its headquarters in Geneva. The WTO came into being in 1995 as the successor to the General Agreement on Tariffs and Trade (GATT), created in 1947.

What is driving a greater sense of urgency for the INCD members is twofold. First, the WTO's new agenda, as part of the Doha Round, attempts to expand future negotiations to include audio-visual industries. To open the media sector to the prevailing rules of freer trade could have a significant impact for many nations. For example, such practices as subsidies for films, quota regulations for national broadcast media, or tax support for national broadcasters, such as the BBC, could be deemed improper under future WTO agreements as they apply to the audio-visual sector. Second, the US is aggressively promoting free trade across more and more sectors, including cultural industries. Historically, the US has defined media productions of all types as being commodities like all others, whether that be cars, planes, food, or furniture. For them the revenues from foreign dollar purchases are all alike. They count revenues from off-shore sales, whether for a hamburger, coffee, Disney video, television series, or Hollywood feature film, as all alike. The US believes in free flow of information, free trade, free markets, deregulation, liberalization, and privatization. Such philosophies underpin their domination of the global economy. No where is it more evident than in the cultural industries sector.

In contrast, the members of the INCD group have a vastly different view of cultural industries or audio-visual productions. They do not equate the audio-visual sector with other commercial products; rather they view them as part of their cultural legacy, encouraging cultural plurality, or as being central to their national identities, much like their languages. The US position on the other hand promotes a commercial model that over time could lead to cultural homogeneity rather than the rich and varied cultural diversity being sought by the INCD.

An insightful example of the above is the impact of the 1994 regional free trade agreement between Canada, the US, and Mexico called the North America Free Trade Agreement (NAFTA). During preliminary talks the Canadians exercised the cultural exemption option or card and kept their cultural industries off the negotiating table. But Mexico allowed its cultural industries to be included just like agriculture, wood, electronic components, oil and several other commodities. By 1998 the Mexican film production sector had produced only 20 films as compared with a decade earlier when the sector was much more vibrant with an output of over 100 feature films. Australia also negotiated a similar bilateral free trade agreement with the US and aspects of culture are included. Jane Kelsey (2005) makes the valid point that the US is adding telecommunications to regional agreements and with digitalization of many media formats the result will be to include critical media components.

History: GATT

The major Western powers agreed after the end of World War II to stabilize their currencies in relation to the US dollar. To accomplish this, institutions were established. These include the General Agreement of Tariffs and Trade (GATT) and the International Monetary Fund (IMF) to oversee currency exchanges and trade rules for international member states. These organizations also established free trade zones among themselves. After that, free trade became popular and zones like the North American Free Trade Agreement (NAFTA) and the European Union (EU) were set up.

The provisions of the General Agreement on Trade in Services (GATS) apply to trade in cultural services but any obligations regarding market access and national treatment are subject to a country making commitments. The GATS sector most closely related to culture is audio-visual services, where less than 20 countries including the US have made partial or complete commitments.

Examples like the creation of the North American Free Trade Agreement (NAFTA) proved that the tremendous dominance of US investments induces a rapid depletion of cultural diversity (in such a way that led to the actual collapse of the Mexican film industry after 1994). For the US, the art and culture market (inclusive music industry, film industry, television companies etc.) became the second most important industry. US producers already inundate the world market with their products. In view of these developments the INCD and their delegates from 39 states met in October 2002 in Cape Town at the edge of a world culture meeting, to adopt a convention for cultural diversity, which should exclude specific goods and services from the GATS context, especially those, which can be assigned to the section of art and culture. Ratios for native art, exclusion of foreigners at culture enterprises, even the mere subsidy are according to GATS logics handicaps to trade or distortion of the free market, and it is self-explanatory that a country like the USA, for which film for example is a main export good, wants to have for its culture-industrial products an unregulated global market access. The WTO exercises more and more pressure on numerous states to liberalize their markets for audio-visual media and culture services. The WTO is significantly influenced by the USA.

Conclusion

Cultural variety and diversity are artistic and social goals; at the same time they have become sophisticated theoretical concepts which have both economic and political ramifications. In connection with this the INCD attempts to raise its voice for programs that support diverse artistic, linguistic, and cultural activities and to protect these from unwanted interventions from external political or economic forces. The INCD takes a stand against the homogenization of culture. To date its major success has been to promote under the global auspices of UNESCO a Convention on the Protection and Promotion of the Diversity of Cultural Expressions. Collectively the INCD and UNESCO are trying to protect a significant sector, namely culture, from the free markets and liberalized trade movements. The major push from the latter is from the WTO and the powerful American media conglomerates. The future will show if the Convention has an impact on what is already a globalized market for cultural products. In this global market there are a few LDCs' media successes outside of the Hollywood world. These include India's Bollywood, Asian animation movies, or Brazilian and Mexican telenovelas. The US, on the other hand, is certainly trying to promote further their philosophies, such as privatization, liberalization, free enterprise, and market forces, as well as see their products go global – ranging from Disney, to the Simpsons and MTV, to Google and Microsoft.

The WTO is serving as the international ambassador of the American political position in opposing both the INCD and UNESCO. The WTO considers all forms of artistic or cultural expression as services and that they should be part of and be included in any future free trade agreements. This is the next frontier for the WTO after it concludes the current Doha Round which has become stuck on the issue of agriculture subsidies.[4] But once that issue is solved culture will take center stage at the WTO and weaker members, both culturally and economically, of the world community will feel the impact of liberalized trade agendas.

Notes

1　Canada's initial strong support of the INCD disappeared with the federal election of the Conservative Party which became more like the Republican Party in the US. Prime Minister Harper failed to grasp the importance and uniqueness of culture and promoted free trade policies similar to those of his friend President Bush. Harper cut funding for most of Canada's cultural agencies, including the INCD. At the same time he significantly increased the military budget.

2　The overall role of the US within UNESCO is almost unique. Since its return, the US delegation has been at odds with a number of UNESCO's programs. But that is not the real problem. Most of the deals about votes and dollars are made informally in the corridors or cafeterias of UNESCO. Formal votes just confirm what was agreed to previously. But the US staff is now off-site. Since 9/11, the US delegation has, for security reasons, moved out of its UNESCO offices to a fortress-like structure a few miles away. But the compound has left them even more isolated than before. The behind-the-scene deals are made without a US voice and that accounts, in part, for why they are so isolated on cultural and media matters in Paris. But the US's bunker mentality, where fear has trumped diplomacy, across the UN system has weakened the US's foreign policy impact and is diminishing its role in an unanticipated manner.

3　The following letter from the INCD captures the central matters of the debate very well.

The letter dated 24 March 2006 to the Office of the United States Trade Representative states, in part, the following:

> We are writing to express our concern about recent developments connected with the launch of free trade negotiations between the United States of America and the Republic of Korea. In January 2006, Korea announced it is reducing its movie theatre screen quota system by 50 percent, effective July 2006. Within days, the office of the United States Trade Representative announced the launch of free trade talks with Korea. We believe the agreement to reduce the screen quota arrived at between the United States and Korea interferes with the democratic will of the Korean people to have their political representatives protect and promote Korean culture.
>
> These developments highlight the wide gulf that exists between U.S. policy and the international community. Last October, over the opposition of the United States, UNESCO adopted a new convention on cultural diversity. The convention is designed to confirm in international law that cultural goods and services are vehicles of identity, values and meaning,

as well as having economic value; to recognize the link between culture and development; and to affirm the sovereign right of states to maintain, adopt and implement policies relating to arts, culture and the media.

We urge the United States government:

- To propose an unrestricted and unlimited exemption for cultural goods and services from the terms of the free trade agreement with the Republic of Korea. The language of such an exemption is outlined below; and

- To exercise leadership to promote cultural diversity internationally, and within the United States itself, by ratifying the *UNESCO Convention on the protection and promotion of the diversity of cultural expressions.*

We have no doubt that the Korean film industry will be severely damaged by the decision to slash the screen quota. Any decline in production will result in fewer choices for movie goers everywhere. We anticipate there will be continuing pressure on the government of the Republic of Korea to further reduce or to eliminate the screen quota, and to eliminate television content quotas that reserve a share of screen time for Korean television programs.

4   The WTO has been tied up for nearly a decade over agricultural subsidies and tariffs. Known as the Doha Round, it is another example of how the industrial, wealthy countries have made life more difficult for those in the southern hemisphere. The high food tariffs across most wealthy nations make it very difficult to sell agricultural products in the richer Western nations. Also, many rich nations, particularly the US, provide enormous subsidies for their agricultural sector. And this sector has significant lobbying and political clout and they are adamant that the heavy subsidies continue. Thus because of the stalemate with the Doha Round, the attempts to capture the audio-visual or cultural industries has been delayed. But once the 152 member WTO sets its sights on this new frontier, it will only be a matter of time before the subsidies, the content rules for indigenous electronic media, protection of domestic cinema industries, and taxation policy will all be in play.

6

A Framework for Conceptualizing Technology in Development

Renée Houston and Michele H. Jackson

Introduction

Research perspectives in the field of development communication carry mandates that not only shape scholarly investigations, but that also guide social and educational interventions. These differences are represented in marked divisions in the field. Kumar (1986), for example, suggests that the "language of the field" recognizes three paradigms: modernization; dependency theory; and culturalist or alternative approaches. The modernization paradigm is often optimistic with regard to ICT and development (e.g., Sein and Harindrath 2004), and culturalists pessimistic, holding that ICTs will not lead to development unless social context is accounted for (e.g., Avgerou 1998; Morales-Gómez and Melesse 1998). Further, although the three paradigms signal an evolution that can be traced through the history of the field, all three may be present in contemporary development efforts. Indeed, Kumar (1986, 2) argues, carry-through effects from previous efforts results in multiple paradigms operating concurrently:

> Each of these paradigms has emerged as a critique of the inadequacies of earlier dominant paradigms, but both the practical implementations and the theoretical premises underlying previous paradigms tend to remain operative in the culture of developing countries. Thus, in a given country, we would find different paradigms operating side by side.

Perspectives, then do not supplant one another in practice regardless of whether they do so in the literature. In fact, they may be cyclical or co-present. Thus, a discussion of perspectives along purely historical lines is insufficient for guiding critical discussions and comparisons.[1]

In a review of the field, Servaes and Malikhao (1991) suggest that perspectives develop in opposition to previous traditions. However, these oppositions vary depending on the level of discussion. For example, on a planning and policy level, this opposition is between the *diffusion* perspective, which adopts a one-way, hierarchical, pre-planned view of communication and development efforts, and the *participatory* perspective, which adopts a two-way, self-management view. On an assumptive level, the opposition is between, on the one side, "one world, multiple cultures" or "multiplicity" theories on the other.

Developing a thorough explanation of this shifting relationship between perspectives is beyond the scope of this chapter. What we wish to draw attention to is this: Each succeeding perspective has been formed as an opposition to an existing perspective. In other words, the impetus for a new perspective has been to oppose some assumption or implication of the then-dominant perspective. Thus, in Kumar's (1986) presentation, modernization begets dependency, which in turn begets culturalism.

We propose that the oppositional nature of the perspectives or paradigms in development communication has made it difficult to engage in constructive dialogue among these perspectives. In other words, the development of new perspectives has proceeded according to the particular nature of the historical or political context rather than according to a set of *a priori* principles. Evaluations of these perspectives have been equally tied to context. Yet, situating perspectives in terms of their relation to a previous perspective shapes and limits the nature of the debate that can take place, naturally tending toward clarifying oppositional qualities. One alternative is to begin from a set of criteria or characteristics derived independent of any particular perspective. Such criteria might be used to compare and critically evaluate the perspectives in relation to one another, and might also serve to generate new perspectives that emerge from principle rather than opposition. The aim of this chapter is to suggest such a starting place. Whereas we recognize the importance of the historical contexts in which the major research perspectives developed, we propose a discussion that begins with assumptions about the relationship between technology and context. The nature of this relationship is principled rather than historical, which we hope can both contribute to an understanding of each perspective and also foster a dialogue across the perspectives. As Wilkins and Mody (2001, 387) note, we need to "be self-reflexive and interrogate ourselves." Further, we highlight the relative contributions and critiques of emphasizing the technological artifact over the social context and vice-versa, and we propose that the integration of technology and context can provide an agenda for planning and implementing an alternative development perspective.

We begin by laying out a framework for conceptualizing technology in terms of the assumed relationship between a technology and its context. We then use the framework to analyze and critique development research on information and communication technologies (ICTs) in order to illustrate dominant assumptions in the literature from the 1940s to the present. Finally, we suggest some implications of the framework for further planning and evaluation. However, before turning to the main argument of the chapter, we wish to address the issue of terminology. As Servaes and Malikhao (1991) suggest, the use of a particular phrase signals an association with a particular perspective. So, for example, they argue that "development communication" is associated with top-down, hierarchical perspectives. We wish to avoid the bias of terminology. We are primarily concerned in this chapter with development efforts that use ICTs for educational purposes. The focus on education provides a narrower scope to this chapter, but the choice is not unreasonable. Schramm noted in 1977 that over a quarter of a billion students were living in developing regions. Efforts to meet those needs, through the use of ICTs, have been extensive. Further, the evolution of perspectives guiding educational efforts shows the oppositional pattern found in development communication in general (Carnoy and Levin 1975; Cuban 1986). Consequently, we use ICTs as a way to describe educational development efforts while attempting to avoid bias toward any particular perspective.

The Technology-Context Scheme

Our analysis adopts Jackson's (1996) technology-context scheme. Advanced as a heuristic for the comparison of communication technology studies, the scheme focuses on the nature of the technological artifact itself. How one conceptualizes the artifact is one of the most fundamental issues for any study of technology. Jackson argued that dominant perspectives may be organized in terms of how each views the relationship between technology and context. Jackson's scheme concerns only one particular characteristic of the artifact: whether the constitution – the very make-up – of the artifact is dependent on the context in which the technology is situated. "Technology" is the material, or what Winner (1977, 11) calls "apparatus":

> [T]he class of objects we normally refer to as technological – tools, instruments, machines, appliances, weapons, gadgets – which are used in accomplishing a wide variety of tasks . . . For many persons, "technology" actually means apparatus, that is, the physical devices of technical performance.

Can we know technology apart from its context? A consequence of this separation, Jackson argues, is to make possible a second question: can we know context apart from the technology that comes to be located within it? Context is what the technology (i.e., the material artifact) is introduced into; it is what is left behind when the technology leaves. Here context is important in its role as the necessary backdrop for technology. The boundary is necessarily conceptual and fluid. The purpose of the distinction is *not* to delineate two sets of elements. Rather, it is to call attention to the assumptions a perspective makes about artifacts, particularly in the way that it conceives of their constitution. The temptation to identify context as a set of elements must be avoided. So should the urge to delineate that set of elements. In a belief contrary to that which is typical in development research, *the constitution of context is unimportant*. Given the history of communication research in technology, delineation of context is tempting. Both technology-centered perspectives, such as modernization, and social-centered perspectives, such as multiplicity, have attempted to identify the elements that play a role in effecting change, with the difference being mainly the elements emphasized. In the technology-context distinction, the importance of "context" is not in its use as an empirical tool, but instead as a conceptual tool.

Thus we arrive at the first question forming this scheme: *Can we know technology apart from its context?* This is a familiar question within sociological and philosophical studies of technology (e.g., Latour 1987, 2005; Law 2002; Winner 1977, 1986). To determine further how one would answer this question from a given perspective, one can ask this set of related questions:

- Is technology essentially acontextual?
- Can technology be removed from context, with no residue of context left over in the artifact?
- Or, stated in reverse, is the definition of technology dependent on the context in which the material artifact is located?
- Is it meaningful to talk of technology apart from context? (Jackson 1996, p. 240)

The second question forming the scheme is the corollary to the first: *Can we know context apart from the technology that comes to be located within it?* Related questions include:

- Is context essentially atechnological?
- Can technology be removed from context, with no residue of the technology left over in the context?
- Or, stated in reverse, is the definition of context dependent on the material artifact located within it?
- Does a technological artifact become an inherent part of context? (Jackson 1996, p. 240)

Again, we are not concerned here with answering these questions empirically, but instead with the work that can be done by the resulting separation of the concepts of technology and context. Logically, the answers to these questions produce four distinct perspectives, each bearing different assumptions regarding the relationship between technology and context (see figure 6.1). The function of the technology-context (T-C) scheme is to enable the location of existing communication technology theories in relation to each other and therefore to promote a principled dialogue among them.

The separation of context and technology provides a distinct method for comparing existing theories and for furthering theory building. For example, to say that context and technology are

		Q1: Is the constitution of technology separable from context?	
		Yes	No
Q2: Is the constitution of context separable from technology	Yes	1: Determinism	3: Context as filter
	No	2: Technology as change agent	4: Integration

Figure 6.1   Technology-context classification scheme

separable from each other is to say that technology is an acontextual "black box" introduced to a context. In this view, what *counts as* technology does not depend upon context – rather, technology is acontextual. What *counts as* context does not depend upon the technology – context is atechnological. An alternative is to regard the separation as conceptual, a reflection of a *perspective* of reality. Other perspectives are generated easily by varying the combinations of the technology-context separation.

The advantage of this scheme over the traditional oppositional or evolutionary organizational schemes is that theories are located according to their fundamental assumptions of how technology and context relate to one another. In other words, the T-C scheme does not catalog existing theories; rather, the scheme is based in principle and is prior to any particular theory. The scheme does not imply that perspectives from any one of the cells are necessarily preferable to those in another. In other words, it does not merely replace a binary opposition with a four-fold one. Rather, it provides a mechanism to overcome the oppositional stance that has made comparing theories difficult.

In this scheme, the first perspective, in cell 1, is *determinism*, which holds that technology and context are constituted as separate from one another. Conceptually, what this separation implies is that technologies and contexts remain independent and discrete. This is the ordinary, common-sense view of the relationship between technology and contexts. Technological artifacts consistently and predictably cause change to contexts because the features of each, though variable, are themselves independent. Artifacts have physical, tangible features – e.g., wireless networking connectivity, small size, or a graphical user interface – that can act upon or act within a context, affecting communication in such ways as altering communication patterns and information flows. Effects are anticipated, indeed planned, while deeper institutional or cultural factors remain unchanged. Further, when technology is not being diffused, researchers want to understand barriers to the process (Orlikowski and Iacono 2001). Thus, technological determinism is the central characteristic of the cell 1 perspective.

Determinism maintains a clear and definite boundary between the constitution of an ICT and the constitution of the context in which it exists. Effects traverse this boundary without altering it. In the second perspective, *technology as change agent*, this boundary is softened in that the constitution of contexts may indeed change. For example, theories and approaches classified as cell 2 typically may provide descriptions of "single" technologies that are implemented across a number of contexts, and then observe the extent to which the introduction of the technology changes the character of the context. For example, do the contexts become more creative, more participatory, or more controlling? Importantly, this is a one-way effect. Artifacts do not change, they remain constant regardless of any contextual changes. Technology, as an autonomous agent, changes the intrinsic nature of its surroundings. Thus, technology as change agent is the central characteristic of the cell 2 perspective. This introduces somewhat more complexity on the assumptive level, as theories must adapt to the possibility of a more active and unstable context.

The third perspective holds that context is separable from technology, but that technology is not separable from context. We depart somewhat from Jackson's (1996) conceptualization of the third perspective, *context as filter*. Jackson emphasized the psychological processes that would cause context to intervene, to "filter," the user's experience with the artifact. Hence, context would be always prior to technology in terms of an individual's cognitive processes, and therefore a context-independent artifact would be inconceivable. Key to this perspective is that contextual elements alter perceptions of technologies: technology is never acontextual. However, this perception could be socio-political and strategic rather than cognitive or psychological. In other words, theories operating from this perspective would see cultural elements as enduring and technologies needing to adapt and fit these deeper currents. Reframing the perspective in this way is well suited to work in development communication.

The final perspective, *integration*, recognizes technology and context as mutually and recursively constitutive. Neither is independent of nor prior to the other. In this perspective, there is no boundary between technology and context, the two, in fact, are integrated as one entity. The implication is that there is no separate, objective ground or standpoint from which to perceive technology; rather, it is constructed continually anew as the material and social elements are integrated.

We use the technology-context scheme in several ways. First, we use the scheme to interrogate theoretical perspectives within development communication according to their assumptions concerning technology and context. Second, considering each cell separately, we analyze the ways in which research has evolved over time. Of particular interest to us is understanding how research from each perspective identifies particular problems and concerns, and whether addressing those concerns has been possible while still remaining true to the assumptions of that perspective. Third, we attempt to use the scheme to encourage dialogue among these perspectives. For example, the scheme provides a means to argue for the advantages of research consistent with a certain cell because the differing assumptions will cause research in each cell to perceive different aspects of a development program. We offer such an argument for the integrationist perspective.

Comparison and Analysis of Existing Research Perspectives

Determinism

Cell 1 illustrates determinism: The constitution of technology is separable from context, and the constitution of context is separable from technology. The initial research that cultivated the use of media technology in education for development stemmed from work done by Paul Lazarsfeld, a communication research scholar at Columbia's Bureau of Applied Science Research (BASR). During the 1930s and 1940s, a great deal of development was based on the "hypodermic needle" model of effects, which touted immediate media effects on human behavior. Formulating a change from traditional attitudes and psychological characteristics to a modern one would include a greater ability to empathize with a wide range of people, greater secularization, a detachment from traditional indigenous culture, identification with Western culture and a belief in human efficacy.

Modernization theory   Now that communication researchers had the key to "unlock" media effects, scientists thought they could transfer this technology with the same value-free neutrality as the physical sciences, although the agendas for research on development were viewed as largely determined by political forces (Kumar 1986). The first conceptualization of technology transfer was the modernization perspective, prevalent from 1945 to 1965. Researchers and decision makers operating from this perspective focus on the mass media as an important causal element for development (Stover 1984). This model of change is based on the notion that there is a direct causal link between five sets of variables, namely, modernizing institutions, modern values, modern behavior, modern society and economic development (Inkeles and Smith 1974). Thus, modernization tends to support the agenda to transfer not only technology to "traditional" societies, but also the sociopolitical culture of modernity. The acceptance of this perspective gave rise to the argument that ICTs, then labeled as "mass media" contribute to literacy, urbanization, and industrialization. Development, within modernization, is defined largely in terms of economic growth.

Perhaps the one of the most quantitatively successful examples of the use of an ICT under the modernization approach was the experimental Radio Mathematics Project (RMP), developed by Stanford University's Institute for Mathematical Studies in the Social Sciences for Nicaragua (Suppes, Searle, and Friend 1978). This program created and introduced an ICT known as interactive radio. The RMP produced radio lessons to act as surrogate teachers, "completely self-contained and understandable to the children without intervention" (Friend, Searle, and Suppes 1980). The summative program evaluations on student learning concluded that at all grade levels students learned topics taught by radio lessons better than students in traditional schools, the radio lessons helped rural students overcome the performance deficit they showed compared to urban students, and students of all abilities showed significant learning gains after radio mathematics lessons (Friend, Searle, and Suppes 1980).

Through sustained attention to all facets of development education: quality education; human and economic considerations; and long-term sustenance, RMP was able to provide primary schoolchildren in Nicaragua a high quality educational system within the economic means of an underdeveloped nation (Suppes, Searle, and Friend 1978). Due to a political revolution that could not be forecasted, the program was disrupted after four and a half years of continued success.

A more recent example illustrates an important evolution in the deterministic perspective toward an appreciation of the complexities involved in successful ICT implementation. The Acacia program, supported by the International Development Research Centre (IDRC) and initiated in 1997, seeks to establish the potential of ICTs to empower Sub-Saharan African communities, "helping Africans harness the transformative potential of ICTs" (http://www.idrc.ca/acacia/ev-5895-201-1-DO_TOPIC.html). The program proposes that access to ICTs alone is meaningless unless accompanied by measures to ensure affordability and ease of use in four areas: policy; infrastructure (including human resources); tools to facilitate use and local content creation; and applications that would be shaped by or respond to needs articulated at the community level. Program assessment centers on contribution to the promotion of access to and effective use of ICTs at the community level. Originally, development sponsors supporting Acacia hypothesized that access to ICTs would empower communities to take control of their own development and thereby leapfrog traditional stages of the process. In actuality, programs met with mixed success. For example, the "lessons learned" from Acacia's SchoolNet projects in nine countries illustrate the work that can be done from a deterministic perspective: steady and cumulative assessment or program elements; precise identification of model strengths and weaknesses; and clear and concrete assessment for improvement (http://www.idrc.ca/acacia/ev-32015-201-1-DO_TOPIC.html).

Critique of approach   A number of the criticisms of this approach are more properly criticisms of modernization. For example, research using the modernization approach to development communication emphasizes observable and quantifiable criteria that may be assessed in a short timeframe to the exclusion of social and cultural factors more deeply embedded and emerging only as these currents alter their course. The manner in which the technology transferred to less developed countries interacts within a cultural context is typically explored. Further, the role of communication is treated as a traditional, one-way transmission. As Wilkins and Waters (2000) note, "this approach promotes communication as a hierarchical channel for the transmission of information, avoiding reference to the content or context of communication processes." The limitations of this perspective reflect what critic Banuri (1990) sees as the artifacts of the culture which produced modernization theory. The modernization perspective believes that the modern life style is superior, therefore development is perceived as an effort to "catch up" the Third World. Further, the concept of context is altogether ignored, therefore the "successful" planning and implementation of the RMP was unable to predict the discontinuance of the project in light of the country's political unrest.

Recasting these critiques using the technology-context scheme illustrates the work that determinism is performing as compared to other assumptions. Criticisms of method and western-centricity, for example, could be overcome with a broader perspective and richer methods of data collection, and do not require abandoning deterministic assumptions. Another example is the criticism of the over-reliance in deterministic research on measurable effects as the indication of success. Research may appear simplistic and mechanical. Yet, a different and more productive way to frame this criticism would be to hold deterministic research to its own tenets: to insist on a thorough identification of the factors that must be taken into account in planning, implementing, and assessing development efforts. It may be that deterministic research should be held to a standard requiring highly sophisticated statistical analysis, such as network analysis or modeling techniques. At the very least, we should expect deterministic research to be nuanced and responsive to complexities of rapid change, in both artifact and context, that is the hallmark of contemporary ICTs (cf. Anderson and Schrum 2007).

One point for dialogue between this perspective and others is this conceptualization of effects and the underlying perception of the social system in which technology operates. Although recent examples recognize that the system is highly complex, the assumptions of determinism require the system to be closed. Banuri (1990), for example, recognizes this in acknowledging that modernization may apply to a limited number of situations. Critics and advocates of this perspective might center their exchange on what is at stake in assuming a closed system. For example, advantages include simplicity, measurability, and efficiency of determining effects. Disadvantages may include inability to perceive important contributors to success or failure. In terms of values, the worth of aspiring to the construction of a "complete picture" might be debated. Indeed, a deterministic viewpoint might provide an interesting entry point for critical scholars who advocate for a more engaged and informed understanding of the details context and against a detached, top-down view (cf. Mamidipudi and Gajjala 2008).

Technology as change agent

The technology as change agent relationship is represented by cell 2: The constitution of technology is separable from context, but the constitution of context is not separable from technology.

Human capital The human capital perspective advances the idea that the specific investment in the number of years spent in education would have an economic corollary. Thus, the improvement of the human workforce is seen as a form of capital investment, thereby justifying the economic expenditure on education. One example of the human capital perspective comes from an effort involving American Samoa (1964–75) in which television was used to modernize primary and secondary schools to improve students' performance. This program was sustained for 15 years and comprised 35 percent of classroom time. Eight minutes of television lessons were used to instruct primary students, whereas the secondary students viewed 25-minute units. An evaluation of the program produced mixed results of effectiveness. After 7 years, 59 percent of the students achieved US norms, whereas in 1935, they had already achieved 60 percent. The program's failure was attributed to three causes: a) the high cost per year for each student ($166 per student); b) the failure to involve teachers in curriculum planning and development; and c) power shortages during the 1974–5 school year. Finally, in 1975, the political government perceived the project as a failure and terminated the program (Anzalone 1987).

One strength of the "technology as change agent" approach is that it highlights the resistive nature of the social and political environment. Thus, constraints are seen as an expected and inevitable by-product of this integration. Such explanations seem to be important, given the variety of internal structural arrangements and external environmental constraints on the adaptation possibilities. The failure of a development effort can be cast as a failure on the part of the technology to change the environment sufficiently. Reported failures of innovations introduced in less developed countries provide good case studies exemplifying these internal and external constraints. External pressures that constrain the organization's ability to adapt are legal constraints, legitimate ability to change, and the collective ability for certain organizational types to change. Even when government officials agree to support a program, a problem common to many educational programs is that they are the agendas of external agencies. As Bock and Arthur (1991, 319) note:

> To force the acceptance, no matter how gently or well intentioned, of an inappropriate reform program, and of implementation strategies that are contrary to the prevailing political culture, may weaken and endanger the very elements within the host government which are to our best interest, and the long-term interest of the evolution of a more democratic institution, to encourage.

The focus on changing context is an important strength of this perspective, for it mandates that programs carry through to provide for the needs of each context. One more recent illustration of this is an educational effort led by the United Nations Research Institute for Social Development (UNRSD) in Senegal. As a part of the World Links for Development (WorLD), in 1996 the World Bank financed instructor training and equipment as well as software, while the State paid for the Internet service provider (ISP), consumables and wages for project coordination. By 2000, 20 schools were connected, however a number of problems highlight a lack of attention to the needs of the context. The schools, for example, must pay additional costs and, because their budgets were not sufficient for "normal" functioning, several months after the computers were received, three schools were unable to pay the ISP. Further, no specific provision was made for retrofitting or replacing obsolete equipment. Beyond these technical problems, Sagna (2000) noted that the failure of this program stems from the context – that introducing ICT in an educational system makes profound changes to which teachers are often hostile, or are at least unenthusiastic.

Critique of the approach   From the above discussion, it appears that one weakness of this perspective is that it has been utilized more in a post hoc fashion to explain failure rather than in a proactive manner to plan for development. This analysis draws attention to the need for further anticipation of contextual contingencies that will be created by technologies. A substantive problem highlighted by this perspective is the relative strength of social structure vis-à-vis technological change. Research in this perspective tends to assume that the social structure of any given society will favor or discriminate against certain classes among the society. As a result, the direct causal link between human investment and improvement in occupation or income is unclear. Furthermore, the investment in ICTs can produce unintended effects (Sproull and Kiesler 1991), some of which are counter to the reasons for which development was initially invested. For example, one concern raised is that educational developments may draw able students away from rural areas to the cities, where they lose touch with the needs and problems in the rural areas (Watson 1984). The difficulty for the technology is that the measurement techniques of determinism do not fit here. Instead, metrics must take into account the more complex dynamics occurring as a result of constitutive changes in context. In terms of the critique of this perspective from the other perspectives in the technology-context scheme, the conceptualization of the technology as separate from the context can be seen as failing to recognize the importance of how the local context shapes and uses the technology. A one-way causality remains at the center of this perspective; an impersonal worldview that assumes all human actions are reducible to the impersonal act of human behavior (Banuri 1990). Finally, though the perspective holds technology as separate from the environment, having no social context or social implications, it would be difficult to imagine an example of technology use in which the context did not imprint some unique use of the technology as a product of the community's values.

Context as filter

The third cell of figure 6.1 illustrates the relationship we call context as filter, in which the constitution of technology is not separable from context, but the constitution of context is separable from technology.

Classical dependency A substantial amount of the design in ICT research reflected the thought cultivated in the modernization and human capital perspectives. However, another line of thought, the dependency perspective, emerged in the 1960s and continued into the early 1980s (Frank 1972; Wallerstein 1983). This perspective aims to represent the goals of emerging nations for political, economic and cultural self-determination within the international community of nations. Much of the development promoted in this perspective is concerned primarily with political decisions focused on relationships between and within societies in regard to social, cultural, political and economic structures. Continuous controversy about the relative merits and effects of development through education and the argument that the less developed regions were created by the activities of rich countries characterizes the years during which this theory was dominant. These debates have undergone a steady process of adjustments which have been described as moving from "the age of innocence to the age of skepticism" (Weiler 1978). Overall, dependency theory is criticized as focusing too heavily on externalities and for being exaggerated in its claims that dependent development is always caused by outside investment. However, the dependency perspective added to our understanding of the political processes and the possible negative effects of technology transfer.

Liberation/participative movement In relation to the concerns of the assumptions associated with modernization, a cry of paternalism surfaced, bringing with it a new perspective for development, the liberation/participative movement. This movement responds in part to the biases found in diffusion research, some of which included: a) a pro-innovation bias that assumes that all innovation is desirable; and b) a lack of sociometric analysis (Holmes 1972). The liberation/participative perspective also challenges the oligarchic view that communication is one-way, moving from a higher to a lower level, from the communication rich to the communication poor (Servaes and Malikhao 1991). Therefore, this perspective favors grassroots movements for greater democratization and social change within less developed countries (Freire 1970; Servaes, Jacobson, and White 1996). Overall, emphasis in this perspective is placed on the process of communication, that is, the exchange of meaning, and its significance – the social relationships created by communication and the social institutions and context that result from such relationships (Servaes and Malikhao 1991).

Importance of context In participation theory, issues of cultural identity and context take precedence. In 1985 Mody noted that, "communication hardware, communication programs, and communication institutions take distinct forms in distinct economic, legal, political, and ideological conditions" (p.136). Further, Hancock (1984) proposed four criteria to gauge the extent to which ICTs have been absorbed into cultural contexts and to promote sustainable and successful ICTs. These criteria are: a) the use of a given technology for purposes other than those for which it was originally intended; b) adaptation of local materials to meet the recurrent resource requirements of imported ICTs; c) modification of the technologies themselves to meet local needs; and d) modifications in personnel requirements, operational processes, and the like to suit local conditions. This survival ethic for ICTs is one that does not depend on state of the art technology, but rather on the willingness of the people at various levels to remain flexible and open in order to enhance the health of ICTs in the new context. Corea (2007) notes that the understanding of context helps shape the effectiveness of ICT-based projects. It is hoped that modifications of the acquired ICT indicate that the technology is being recreated locally (Mayo 1989) and in "intelligent, culturally appropriate ways that are organic to the developing society in which they occur" (Corea 2007, 50). Constraints of this perspective include a limited ability for evaluation and an overly optimistic attitude toward development.

One illustration of the "context as filter" perspective comes from an evaluation of a development effort (Houston and Heald 1995) that attempted to provide a better understanding of Honduran schoolteachers' decisions to discontinue use of the interactive, radio instruction program "La Familia de Los Numeros." Because teachers play a vital role in the use of educational innovations, Houston (1993) argues that factors influencing their decisions to continue or discontinue using an innovation need to be understood. Houston found two conditional factors contributing to discontinuance: first, the relationship between teachers' assessments of existing conditions (i.e. quality of materials, supplies, availability of technical support, etc.) and their decisions to discontinue using the educational innovation, and second, the degree to which teachers need to coordinate instruction with other teachers. Results suggest teachers' negative assessments of existing conditions influenced their decisions to discontinue using the educational innovation. Further, results suggested that, when the degree of coordination required increases, teachers consider the beliefs of their peers when deciding to discontinue using an educational innovation. This research provides support for Bell's (1989) and Kimberly's (1981) arguments that different processes may govern the adoption of various types of innovations depending on the organizational location of both the innovation and potential advocates.

Critique of the approach   In theory, this perspective on development is quite useful, given that development is realized and enacted by local participants. It emphasizes the ability of local communities for self-determination. The strength of the theory is that it begins with context and examines what is needed from the bottom-up to build an effective implementation. Still, a main weakness comes from research that does not hold true to this perspective; many of these projects are initiated in the developed world. For example a development effort might be proposed and supported by a northern NGO, yet implemented locally. As Van Tuijl (2000, 619) noted:

> NGOS intend to be innovative, flexible and participatory, but a closer look at the reality of their work shows that many of their supposedly "unique selling points" are often overstated and feeble. NGOS do not hesitate to question the legitimacy or conduct of everyone else in the world, but have no adequate answer if their own accountability is questioned.

However, some might argue it is difficult for a grassroots movement to emerge in the absence of knowledge of "other-wise" (Bakhtin 1990). The weaknesses of this perspective, then, simply are the challenges that face any participatory type of initiative, rather than problems inherent to the perspective itself. How can a researcher hold to the primacy of context over the technology, without inaccurately idealizing the social situation? For example, research within this perspective often glorifies and idealizes local relations, yet they may be laden with exploitation. It assumes that the local community will act equitably and efficiently, yet this is not always the case (see, e.g., Mody 1985). Local relations may include hierarchies or castes which will serve to reify relationships with the local culture rather than elevate the group as a whole. Indeed, idealism is a central danger of this perspective, which often assumes that development is an end point – higher standards of education or living will tie up all the loose ends in the social structure and create a global player – yet most would argue that development, "is a slow and uneven process" (Edwards 1989, 116).

Integration

In the integration relationship, cell 4, the constitution of technology is not separable from context, nor is the constitution of context separable from technology.

Alternative development In Latour's (1987, 2005) social constructionist approach to technology, the meanings and use identified with technology are constructed as a social artifact reflecting the values of our society. In concert with this idea, Escobar (1992), Laclau and Mouffe (1987), and Schuurman (1993) indicate the rise of new social movements in developing nations signals the end of a unified and single subject. In place of previous development paradigms, alternative development proposed that multiple subjectivities comprise the basis of a multipronged attack on various axes of oppression. Local resistances, as Foucault (1978) calls them, serve to counter the multiple sites of oppression at work simultaneously in developing nations. Alternative development recognizes the end of the privileged and one-dimensional subject, thus highlighting the awareness of human diversity while serving to illuminate the need for a diverse set of strategies to improve the human condition. As Wilkins and Waters (2000) note, "This perspective draws attention to interactive technologies that promote community, participation, and resistance, and contributes to this framework by situating the process of social change within contexts differentiating levels of power. The practices of social movements can be interpreted as strategic acts of resistance." Alternative development attempts to deconstruct the discourse of development, thereby offering a new way of thinking about a complex problem.

Up to this point, perspectives have focused on the purposes and planning of development. Initially, development was defined only in terms of economic growth. The shift to a participatory, grass-roots movement replaced the deterministic one-way, top-down orientation, yet, all things considered, one general observation of these perspectives is that typically they are *evaluated* by their ability to plan, predict, and document change. The problem with such an evaluation criteria is that, from the integration perspective, this would require the separation of technology and context. Integration holds, however, that such a separation is impossible. The two are integrated on a *constitutive* level making traditional, evaluative procedures involving the identification of variable relationships, measurement, and causal analysis lose their meaning. Technology cannot be an independent variable, for it is *redefined* as a consequence of adoption in a particular situation. Similarly, the substance of the context is changed after the introduction of a technology so that it is no longer the same construct as existed prior to the study.

For research from the integrationist perspective, development is not so much a question of outcomes as it is a question of processes. The relationship between technology and context does different "work" here, it becomes a site for exploring and teasing out other dynamics of the socio-technical milieu. Development efforts become an "occasion for structuring" (Orlikowski 1992), which can highlight underlying tensions and problematics for the purpose of understanding broader concepts and problems. New social movements research, for example, illustrates how the assumptions of integrationism can focus research on questions of power and social change.

Integrationism is better suited to offering explanations for complex phenomena than it is to predicting or measuring development processes. This may be a weakness, for although the perspective may more easily speak of positive social change, it is more difficult to use as a tool in negotiating with policy makers and institutions in the cause of that change. In other words, while research may seem to have stuck to a control perspective, a need for a deterministic understanding of the effect of development technologies, there may be important practical reasons for such control. Yet, in light of our inability to make any linear combination of possibilities "work," perhaps it is time to reconsider how we view development problems and how we go about planning for change. One way to do this is to conceive of the tension as one between managing development and understanding the process of development, and to ask if this tension can be resolved while remaining within the integrationist perspective. Certainly, it is possible to assign the management function to determinism, or perhaps to the remaining perspectives to a somewhat lesser extent. Integrationism can then be left to the function of providing understanding. Such division, however, may be premature, based on practical considerations rather than principled ones. Resolution of the tension may not depend on shifting our assumptions of technology and context so much as on finding a method that is better suited to integrationist assumptions.

Emergence of a nonlinear process as an integrationist perspective on development   A theoretical frame for understanding an alternative development perspective grounded in new developments in science illustrates an integrationist perspective. Often referred to as the emergent systems approach, this frame underscores the importance of examining how pattern, structure, and process emerges relationships (Capra 1997). As previously noted, our current level of inquiry limits us to examining simple relationships. Although traditional, deterministic reasoning does generate insight, local human interaction, coupled with environment, creates global, emergent patterns. For example, individual actors in societies create local activity patterns which emerge and overlap into different individuals, groups, regions, and then to the nation as a whole. Problems ensue when we assume local conditions are related in a linear relation to the larger system. Under linear systems, cause and effect are related proportionately. As Davies (1987, 23) notes, "Small changes are expected to produce proportionately small effects and large changes result in large effects." Additionally, "aggregationists" expect large changes as a result of numerous small changes. In contrast, nonlinear systems expect that the environment is itself constantly changing, which means that change is disproportionate (Briggs and Peat 1989).

Local relationships provide one way to examine development efforts. Within a small set of interactions, guided by simple local structures or rules, predicting outcomes is relatively easy. For example, if a local group creates an agricultural process that sustains the region's food supply, it works perfectly well. On the other hand, as those processes are picked up and interpreted by larger entities, the meaning ascribed to them changes, which introduces change. These changes become magnified during the reproduction of action, which transforms the initial process. This explains why predicting local behavior can be easy when it represents an equilibrium-like state, whereas on a global level, although patterns may be self-similar, they are not predictable because the meaning ascribed to any process has changed in the process (Anderson and Houston 2005).

These patterns are accounted for by the process of *emergence*, which Stacey (1996) explains is the production of global patterns of behavior by humans in a complex system interacting according to their own local rules of behavior. Although the outcome is patterned by individual behaviors, and that behavior may be expected, the global pattern is recognizable but not linearly related in any simple cause–effect manner. The local behavior that emerges from human interactions does not represent calculated practices that intend to create the global *patterns* of behavior that emerge. So, although local rules may predict local behavior, they may not be used to predict global behavior, or, as Stacey puts it, "global patterns cannot be reduced to individual behavior" (1996, 287). Global practices then reflect the unintended outcome of local activity where small changes in local adaptation cast other changes throughout the system. This means that reductionist approaches searching for simple causal relationships will never create a complete understanding of the role that ICTs play in national development.

These propositions, structure, pattern, and process, associated with emergent systems, highlight the contribution of the integrationist perspective. An integrationist perspective accentuates the relationship between perspectives that we would traditionally hold in opposition; that is, no single perspective is necessarily inconsistent with the other or is the "correct" perspective. Rather, the decision as to what perspective is appropriate has more to do with what questions we want to ask and/or what assumptions we are willing to live with.

Metatheoretical and theoretical responses to the development crisis have been important to the creation of approaches that seek to articulate better the relationship between ICTs and development. However, all the theorizing and innovation in the world amount to nothing if empirical strategies and attitudes continue to perpetuate theoretical weaknesses. It is precisely at the empirical level that true changes in development thinking manifest themselves, both in the approaches of researchers and the practical interventions that affect people's lives. Development scholars need to rethink the concepts of change and change agents in their theorizing about the relationship between ICTs and national structures and processes.

Conclusion and a Coda

When the first version of this argument appeared in *Communication Theory* the notion of reconceptualizing the artifact to consider the role context plays in the constitution of technology was novel

(Orlikowski and Iacono 2001). Since that time, a number of scholars have pressed on this issue (Dourish 2001; Jackson, Poole, and Kuhn 2002; Leonardi 2008). Research across disciplines generally acknowledges the biases, assumptions, and values that lie behind any development technology. Despite their physical materiality, technologies are not ahistorical, acontextual, and value neutral. We remain surprised, however, by the dominance of the top-down, "managerial" perspective in development research. As the conceptualizations of technologies and their relation to context have become more sophisticated, so have the ideas of how to be more strategic in using technologies for change. In other words, it is even more clear today that researchers and developers can choose how they conceive the relationship between technologies and contexts, and that this choice continues to carry implications for the questions that come to be asked and the positions that come to be defended.

Early views held that ICTs should be employed to bring about specific desired goals as formulated by a mechanistic worldview (McGinn 1996). As a result, questions ranging from who decides on a community's or country's need or how we develop or define education needs were often left unaddressed. Although the leading Western development elite argue that the application of the development model represents the rational, linear step towards the apex of national development (i.e. industrialization and all its social implications), they fail to acknowledge this is an inherently political act which suppresses global diversity. This is but one example demonstrating the most common means for differentiating among perspectives in the field of development communication technology: opposition and evolution. Each new perspective has held promise for overcoming previous limitations or has sought to make better predictions.

Yet it stands that no perspective has been successful in resolving all of the problems posed by its predecessor. No perspective has been so self-evident as to supplant what has gone before. Each enjoys limited success in explaining development successes and even less success in explaining failures. The argument we have posed here is that by changing the basis for comparing and evaluating these perspectives, we might be able to gain insight into why perspectives persist, into whether the dominance of certain perspectives cycles over time, or the situations in which perspectives may be co-present. Funk (1999) reports on several projects in pursuit of sustainable development. Of the many examples she cites, most fit within a cell 1 perspective. Her study, coupled with a complete review of recent cases, reveals that cell 1 is attractive to development researchers. Because the nature of development research is social action, or the ability to create a change in current conditions, it is easy to see why cell 1 research is pursued. The ability to report that life outcomes are changed is a great motivation for pursuing development with an immediately measurable outcome.

Further, it stands that the attractiveness of the cell 1 approach demonstrates why an integrationist approach is not appealing. Since an integrationist approach proposes that implementation of programs may or may not be predictable, it would be difficult to support a program that has no immediately arguable outcome. However, even an integration perspective based on self-organization theory grants that local conditions can produce measurable outcomes. For example, investment in education for women often results in fewer children within those women's families. Yet, the global, emergent pattern materializes over the *longue durée* (Giddens 1984) that creates other complex effects. For example, overpopulation is often treated as an independent variable, but it is much more complicated. Yapa (1991) argues that for poor families with little land, children play an important role in contributing to the household. Fertility then becomes a coping mechanism by which couples with few economic assets meet their needs. In the long run, overpopulation reflects an economic system in which people are forced to create coping strategies (Yapa 1991). We propose that the pursuit of perspectives that meet the integrated criteria proposed by the technology-context scheme might allow us to examine the more dynamic relations in developing societies. The relative failure of the way complex issues have been diagnosed in development efforts points to the need to reexamine the way we conceptually define development and to change our approach to the problem.

Notes

1 Kumar goes on to argue that the field is circling back to a modernization paradigm due, primarily, to advances in technology. Thus, the idea of "evolution" may be inappropriate altogether.

7

The Global Digital Divide

Mitchell F. Rice

Introduction

A United Nations' report has noted that "the world is undergoing a revolution in information and communication technologies (ICTs) that has momentous implications for the current and future social and economic situation of all countries of the world" (United Nations 2000b, 3). The report identifies several important benefits to countries and their populations from the wide application and use of ICTs. The benefits include:

1 direct contribution of the ICT sector's output to the economy;
2 improvement to public sector administration, in particular that transparency in the procurement process for public service contracts had reduced corruptive practices;
3 tremendous potential for improving education, including distance learning and training;
4 important improvements in the delivery of services such as health care, including . . . the application of tele-medicine; and
5 enabling countries to monitor ecological situations and maintain environmental stability (United Nations 2000b: 4–5).

These benefits suggest that ICTs can be an important weapon in the fight against world wide poverty (Peters 2003). Supporting this point, the Secretary General of the United Nations has observed that "Narrowing the digital divide is a crucial part of achieving global anti-poverty goals" (Secretary General 2008). Further, Navas-Sabater, Dymond, and Junutumen (2002, 1) of the World Bank note that ICTs impact poverty reduction in the following ways:

- ICTs promote integration of isolated communities into the global economy.
- ICTs promote productivity gains, efficiency and growth.
- ICTs improve the delivery of public services.

ICTs and technology transfer can benefit and move a country ahead in economic development, human capital development, and social development (see Sahay and Avgerou 2002; United Nations Development Program 2001). Technology transfer is the communication, use, and application of the latest knowledge, skills, and practices for mitigating and adapting to change and it covers the processes of transfer in and between developed countries, developing countries and transition economies (United Nations Industrial Development Organization 2002; Wangwacharakul nd).

Yet, ICT transfer and adaptation has been slow in finding its way into many less developed countries (LDCs). At the same time, some LDCs that are transforming to transition economies are surging ahead in ICT application and use while other non-transition or slower-transition LDCs are not. Examples of transition economies include: Armenia, Azerbaijan, Belarus, Georgia, Kazakhstan, Kyrgyz Republic, Moldova, Russia, Uzbekistan (Commonwealth of Independent States); Czech Republic, Estonia, Hungary, Poland, Slovenia (recent applicants to the European Union); Lithuania, the Slovak Republic (Central Europe and the Baltics); and Albania, Bulgaria, Croatia, and Romania (Southeastern Europe) (see Clarke 2001). A large number of non- or slower-transition economies are located in Sub-Saharan Africa and parts of Asia (particularly South Asia). Africa and Asia have the smallest number of PCs per 100 inhabitants (Peters 2003). Recent estimates of Internet usage show that Africa, Asia, the Middle East, and Latin America/Caribbean have the lowest population penetration (population usage) of the Internet with 5.3 percent, 15.3 percent, 21.3 percent, and 24.1 percent, respectively (Internet World Stats 2008).

The marked gap between the number of countries that are high level ICT participants and the number that are low level ICT participants has been referred to as the "global digital divide" (World Economic Forum 2000). Put another way, there is a stark gap of ICT diffusion between industrialized countries and LDCs as measured by the number of phone lines per inhabitants (teledensity), the number of Internet hosts, the number of Internet users, the number of households that own computers, and/or the number of cell and mobile phone users (Campbell 2001; Peters 2003). The global digital divide, as well as the digital divide within countries, is also referred to as: "technological divide," "racial Digital Divide," and lack of "digital inclusion" (Rice 2001). The digital divide represents the latest addition to the already existing chasms between developed countries and the southern hemisphere.

Why does the digital divide continue to persist in LDCs? The lack of opportunities for business and the low level of economic progress that characterizes most of the developing countries is certainly the primary reason for the digital divide. Another reason is that the governments of poor countries challenge themselves with more pressing concerns, such as food, health care and security, rather than technological improvements. As a result, the population of these countries does not reach higher levels of education and is not provided with the knowledge that is necessary to utilize them. As a result, on March 15, 2005 the United Nations launched the Digital Solidarity Fund to finance projects that deal with "the distribution and use of new information and communication technologies" and "enable excluded people and countries to enter the new era of the information society" (United Nations Secretary General 2005). Other global initiatives launched to close the global digital divide have included: the Business Council for the United Nations 2003 (June 18–19) "The Net World Order: Bridging the Global Digital Divide" conference held in New York City (see UNAUSA 2003) and The World Summit on the Information Society held in Geneva, Switzerland in 2003 and in Tunis, Tunisia in 2005 (International Telecommunications Union 2005).

The lack of the application and diffusion of ICTs in LDCs is exacerbated by the fact that more than 80 percent of all websites are in English, a language understood by only about 10 percent of the world's population (BBC News Online 1999a; OECD 2001) including a very, very small percentage of the world's poor. Further, minority languages are dramatically under-represented on the World Wide Web (Kenny 2002). Bolt and Crawford (2000) have described this condition as the "World White Web." McNair (2000) notes that the use of ICTs has resulted in a global occurrence whereby "the educated (information rich) become richer and the non- or less-educated (information poor) become poorer." Graham (2002, 36) argues that ICTs:

> Extend the power of the powerful; underpin intensified unevenness through tying together international divisions of labour; allow socio-economically affluent groups selectively to bypass the local scale; and be culturally and economically biased, especially in terms of the wider development of what we might term the emerging "international information marketplace."

Graham (2002, 37) continues: "thus, the uneven growth of the Internet and other ICT-mediated systems, represents a subtle, often invisible, but immensely powerful process of *dualization* within and between settlements" (emphasis added).

This chapter explores the global digital divide and discusses some of the conditions and circumstances that have contributed to its creation. An important issue this chapter examines is whether there is a convergence or absolute convergence or divergence or relative divergence in the application and diffusion of ICTs between developed countries and LDCs and, if so, which of these conditions will continue. Another issue addressed by this chapter is what are the basic conditions required in a country to facilitate technology transfer, application and diffusion of ICTs. This chapter draws on several highly respectable data sources and an extensive body of literature to provide a fairly clear picture of how the ICT revolution is shaping up globally. However, the chapter does not pretend to be a full assessment of the ICT global situation between countries.

ICTs and a Country's Development

ICTs are "general- purpose technologies and permeate production and consumption activities" (Sciadis 2003, 11) and ICTs cover a broad range of services, applications, and technologies using various types of contemporary equipment and software. Modern ICT services include cellular and mobile telephones, fax, email, transfer of files from one computer to another computer, and the use of the Internet. These services are called "readiness" indicators (OECD

2001). ICT applications include videoconferencing, teleworking, distance learning, management information systems, and stock taking. Simply put, ICTs are "the set of activities [and services] which facilitate by electronic means the processing, transmission and display of information" (Rodriguez and Wilson 2000, 10). In a broader sense, ICTs include the use of television and the radio (Kenny 2002; Rodriguez and Wilson 2000). Both developed (industrialized) countries and some LDCs are benefiting from the rapid growth, development, and application of ICTs. According to the Commission of the European Communities (2001, 7):

> ICTs are already important to the function of developing countries and emerging economies ... Large businesses and governments depend on their communications networks and computer applications to function effectively in terms of administration, analysis, and information dissemination, and to reduce transaction costs.

This observation suggests that ICTs are reshaping the flow of investments, goods and services in the global economy. International businesses, local companies and even governments see strong and highly developed ICT networks as requirements for investment, growth, and economic development (see Clarke 2001). Succinctly stated, ICTs have "rocked the way we deliver and receive information and the way we do business" (BBC News Online 1999b).

By September 2001, Norway and Sweden had the highest percentage of households with a fixed telephone lines (one hundred percent telephone penetration rate) (see National Office for the Information Economy 2002). Sweden had the highest percentage of persons 16 years and older with Internet access at home and work (107 percent) followed by the United States (101 percent), Norway (100 percent), Australia (92 percent) and Ireland (78 percent). Sweden also had the highest percentage of persons 16 years and older with Internet access using the Internet (78 percent) (National Office for the Information Economy 2002). Further, by September 2001, the United States was ranked number one in the adoption and use of ICTs. Sweden, Australia and Norway were ranked second, third and fourth, respectively, of the top 14 ICT countries listed (National Office for the Information Economy 2002). Interestingly, countries that have high levels of adoption and diffusion of ICTs see significant levels of economic and social developments and interactions in their societies. As a result, ICTs have (and can) become indispensable tools for a country's immediate and long-term development and ICTs contribute to a country's improvements in social policy areas such as poverty, health care, and education (United Nations Development Program 2000).

Considering the ways in which countries are different, Rodriguez and Wilson (2000, 23), through empirical analysis, conclude that there are two fundamental factors that separate highly technological countries from those that are not: "an economic environment conducive to investment, and a climate of civil liberties conducive to research and expansion of communications." Investment is difficult to have unless there is a focus on human capital development, a low level of unproductive government expenditures, security of property rights, a low level of expropriation risk, and basic political freedoms (see Barro 1997). Human capital development is important especially in the areas of education and health because these areas have a synergistic relationship to higher levels of technological investment (see Rodriguez and Wilson 2000).

Political freedoms and other civil liberties, government transparency, and protection of property rights are central to technological transfer, diffusion and innovation in a country. A minimum level of government interference facilitates a market mechanism that allows the flow and exchange of goods, services, and information. It is the absence of these conditions within LDCs that contribute to a "market efficiency" gap – "the difference between the level of service penetration that can be reached under current plans and conditions, and the level one would expect under optimal market conditions" – which in turn facilitates the "access gap" or the lack of affordability of ICTs (Navas-Sabater, Dymond, and Juntumen 2002). LDCs, more often than not, tend to have governments that are politically volatile and unstable with uncompetitive industries and dysfunctional public bureaucracies (Sahay and Avgerou 2002). From this perspective, the legal, political, and economic settings under which a country operates gives some indication of a country's "e-ready" condition (InfoDev 2002).

Therefore, under the right circumstances, ICTs can greatly expand a country's economic growth, create or enhance a country's participation in global markets, dramatically improve human welfare and human capital, and promote political accountability (United Nations Development Program 2000). Kenny (2002, 1) points out ICTs are "powerful tools for empowerment and income generation in LDCs." ICTs then have tremendous enabling potential for the individual, community, or country (especially a LDC). ICTs can be mobilized and shaped in ways that can help to make the effects on a country's human capital development more progressive and positive (Graham 2002); particularly through e-Government, e-Health, e-Education, etc. (Global Envision 2007). However, because of ICTs potential in promoting democratization and human capital development, a country can be ambivalent toward ICTs' widespread general application and use. Countries under authoritarian regimes recognize the power of ICTs, especially the Internet, to create political instability and political change. As a result, authoritarian regimes shape the growth and diffusion of ICTs to their political advantage by exerting control and censorship over ICTs use (see Kalathil 2001; Kalathil and Boas 2001).

ICT Comparisons Between Developed and LDCs

The level of access to ICTs for LDCs is quite low according to the Organization for Economic Cooperation and Development (OECD). The OECD came into force on September 30, 1961 and comprises 30 member countries: Australia; Austria; Belgium; Canada; Czech Republic; Denmark, France; Finland; Germany; Greece; Hungary; Iceland; Ireland; Italy; Japan; Korea; Luxembourg; Mexico; Netherlands; New Zealand; Norway; Poland; Portugal; Spain; Sweden; Switzerland; Slovak Republic; Turkey; United Kingdom; and United States. The OECD defines the ICT sector "as a combination of manufacturing and services industries that capture, transmit and display data and information technology . . ." (OECD 2002, 19, 81–2).

The OECD notes that at the international level the most basic and important indicator of the digital divide is the number of Internet hosts per 100 (or 1,000) inhabitants (OECD 2001). A host is defined as "a domain name that has an IP (Internet Protocol) address record with it" (OECD 2001, 40). An Internet host includes any computer

Table 7.1 Number of Internet hosts per 1,000 inhabitants between OECD
countries and non-OECD countries (October 1997 to October 2000)

	October 1997	October 1998	October 1999	October 2000
OECD countries	23.00	34.00	55.00	82.00
Non-OECD countries	0.21	0.38	0.59	0.85

Source: Based on OECD (2001)

connected to the Internet via full-time, part-time and by direct or
dial-up access (OECD 2001). Table 7.1 compares the number of
Internet hosts between OECD countries and non-OECD countries
over the four year period from October 1997 to October 2000. In
1997 there were 23 Internet hosts per 1,000 inhabitants in OECD
countries as compared to 0.21 inhabitants in countries outside of
OECD. By October 2000 there were 82 Internet hosts per 1,000
inhabitants in OECD countries in contrast to 0.85 hosts in non
OECD countries (OECD 2001). By July 2001 the number of Internet
hosts in OECD countries reached 112 million persons. Other OECD
data show that the US had the highest number of Internet hosts with
more than 272 hosts per 1,000 inhabitants (OECD 2002, 40).
Canada, Finland, Iceland, and Sweden had around 180 Internet hosts
per 1,000 inhabitants. In contrast Mexico and Turkey had no more
than 5 Internet hosts per 1,000 (OECD 2002, 40).

Further, comparing the number of Internet hosts in OECD countries to the number of Internet hosts in countries in Africa may
provide an even starker contrast. In Africa, where all countries are
finally connected to the Internet (Eritrea was the last country connected in November 2000), most of these connections have only one
Internet service provider (Miller 2001). Some 90 percent of the
Internet market in Sub-Saharan Africa is in South Africa, where 90
percent of all users are in the main urban areas (Navas-Sabater,
Dymond, and Junutumen 2002). Moreover, while the number of
Internet hosts provide an indication of the size of the Internet in a
country, the number of active websites gives information on countries' relative development of Internet content. The US, Germany
and the UK, respectively, have the most active number of websites
(OECD 2001).

Table 7.2 Number of Internet hosts per 1,000 inhabitants by global geographic region (October 1997 to October 2000)

Global region	October 1997	October 1998	October 1999	October 2000
North America	46.28	69.74	116.41	168.68
Oceania	26.81	34.76	43.84	59.76
Europe	6.13	9.45	13.41	20.22
Central/South America	0.48	0.91	1.67	2.53
Asia	0.53	0.87	1.28	1.96
Africa	0.17	0.21	0.28	0.31

Source: Based on OECD (2001)

Table 7.2 shows the number of Internet hosts per 1,000 inhabitants by global geographic regions from October 1997 to October 2000. Central and South America, Asia, and Africa have the lowest number of Internet hosts per 1,000 inhabitants. As was noted earlier, Africa is the least connected to the Internet of all the geographic regions. North America, Oceania, and Europe have the highest number of Internet hosts per 1,000 inhabitants. Given the higher Internet host penetration rates in industrialized global geographic regions, Graham (2002, 34) observes that "the Internet remains the preserve of a small global elite of between 2 percent and 5 percent of the global population." This condition has been called a "global ghetto" by the United Nations (United Nations Development Program 1999). Put another way, what has resulted is the concentration of "electronic economic power" in the hands of a small number of countries (or global firms) (Graham 2002).

The US, Canada, and Western Europe combined represent some two-thirds of all the world's Internet users and more than two-thirds of all the Internet users in Asia are in the countries of Japan, Korea, Singapore, Hong Kong, and Taiwan (Navas-Sabater, Dymond, and Junutumen 2002). These countries and Western Europe have achieved very high "infostates" – accumulated "stocks of ICT capital and labour, including networks and ICT skills" (referred to as infodensity) and "the uptake and consumption flows of ICTs" and their intensity of use (referred to as info-use) (see Sciadis 2003, ix, 6). Put another way, a high Infostate equals high infodensity networks plus high literacy and education plus high info-use and intensity of

Table 7.3 Infostate[a] characteristics

Infodensity[b] (telecommunication networks)	Skills (literacy and education)	Info-use[c]

• Main telephone lines per 100 inhabitants
• Waiting lines/mainlines
• Digital lines/mainlines
• Cell phones per 100 inhabitants
• Cable TV subscriptions per 100 households
• Internet hosts per 1,000 inhabitants
• Secure servers/Internet hosts
• International bandwidth (Kbs per inhabitant)
	• Adult literacy rates
	• Educational enrollment rates
	  – Primary education
	  – Secondary education
	  – Tertiary education
		Uptake
		• TV equipped households per 100 households
		• Residential phone lines per 100 households
		• PCs per 100 inhabitants
		• Internet users per 100 inhabitants
		Intensity
		• Broadband users/ Internet users
		• International outgoing Telephone traffic minutes per capita
		• International incoming telephone traffic minutes per capita

[a] aggregation of infodensity and info-use
[b] sum of all ICT stocks (capital and labor)
[c] consumption and flows of ICTs (uptake and intensity)
Source: Based on Sciadis (2003)

use through broadband and international outbound and inbound rates (Sciadas 2003, 15). Table 7.3 shows in more detail the characteristics of Infostate.

ICTs and Poor Global Populations

The World Economic Forum observes (2000, 9) that:

On every relevant measure – from size and penetration of telecommunications market or the extent of internet diffusion to level of global electronic commerce and so on – the vast majority of economic activity related to information and communications technologies is concentrated in the industrialized world. Conversely, developing countries, and especially, the least developed countries – account for a small fraction of the global digital economy.

Stated another way, ICTs are "irrelevant to the three billion people in the world who live on two US dollars per day. A large majority of these individuals are in Sub-Saharan Africa and South Asia (Pigato 2001). For an estimated two billion people, "access to fresh water or electricity is a daily challenge of more fundamental concern than access to the information society" (Campbell 2001).

A similar point is made by Sachs (2000, 99) who says:

> [T]oday's world is divided not by ideology but by technology . . . A small part of the globe, accounting for some 15 percent of the earth's population, provides nearly all of the world's technology innovations. A second part, involving perhaps half of the world's population, is able to adapt these technologies in production and consumption. The remaining part, covering around a third of the world's population is technologically disconnected, neither innovating at home nor adopting foreign technologies.

Poor populations in LDCs have several common characteristics. First, as previously noted, they live on less than two or three dollars per day and in many instances less than one dollar a day. Second, they live in rural areas. Third, they are unemployed or subsist on farming or as unskilled wage laborers. Fourth, they are uneducated. Fifth, they are a part of minority "ethnolinguistic groups." That is, they do not speak the official language or the most popular language of the country in which they live (Kenny 2002). Each of these characteristics reduces the likelihood of poor individuals' use of the Internet and other advanced ICTs. In particular, the lack of education may significantly reduce Internet use in poor countries (Duncombe 2000). Much of the world's poor live in the countries of Bangladesh, Brazil, China, India, Indonesia, Mexico, Pakistan, Russia and on the continent of Africa. Table 7.4 shows the use of ICTs in Sub-Saharan Africa. The radio, followed by the TV, mobile phone,

Table 7.4   ICTs use in Africa (2001)

Ratio	Number (millions)
1 in 4 have radio	205.0
1 in 13 have a TV	62.0
1 in 35 have a mobile phone	24.0
1 in 40 have a fixed line	20.0
1 in 130 have a PC	5.9
1 in 160 use the Internet	5.0
1 in 400 have pay-TV	2.0

Source: Based on Global Envision (2007)

Table 7.5   Global poor characteristics

Characteristic	
ICT poor usage	
Poor population (%)	36.4
Personal computers (per 1,000 capita)	7.4
Fixed telephone lines (per 1,000 capita)	36.5
Mobile phones (per 1,000 capita)	7.9
Radios (per 1,000 capita)	196.0
Education, Literacy, and Language	
Female adult literacy (%)	46.0
Male adult literacy (%)	27.0
Population not speaking widely-used language (%)	48.0
Population not speaking official language (%)	53.0
Rural	
Rural population total (%)	67.0

Source: Derived from Kenny (2002)

fixed line, PC, Internet, and pay TV, respectively, are the most commonly used ICTs.

Table 7.5 shows the characteristics of global populations in the categories of income, education, literacy, and language, and rural conditions. There are only 7.4 personal computers and 7.9 mobile phones per 1,000 capita among the global poor populations. Only 46 percent of the global poor females and 27 percent of the global poor males are literate. Some 53 percent of the world's poor do not speak the official language in the country where they live. About two-thirds of global poor populations live in rural areas and the largest city in a rural area has only about 171 telephone lines per 1,000 inhabitants. Table 7.5 also points out that the radio is the most common electronic communication technology used by global poor populations. The radio has several advantages as an ICT. According to Noronha (2003, 168–9):

> it [the radio] is cost-efficient . . . It is ideal for the huge illiterate population that still remains marginalized, especially in the rural areas . . . Its language and content can be made most suited to local needs. It is also relevant to local practices, traditions, and culture.

For more costly ICTs, global poor populations are unable to afford telephones (even if telephone line connections are available) and personal computers.

The telephone is the most basic and necessary tool for access to ICTs and it "is the leading indicator for the level of universal service in telecommunications" (OECD 2001). The telephone is also "a fundamental measure of the international digital divide" (OECD 2001). One condition for accession to the OECD is a country's commitment to provide universal telecommunications service and/or universal access including the Internet (Global Internet Liberty Campaign (GILC) 2000). Universal service is commonly viewed as a telephone in every household, while universal access is seen as everyone should be within a "reasonable distance" of a telephone (GILC 2000). Access to telecommunications is critical to a country's commerce, public safety, governance, and overall human development (United Nations Development Program 2000). Yet, "one-third of the world's population has never made a telephone call. More than 3 billion people have no money to spend on communications services, or live in rural or remote areas" (Commission of the European Communities 2001, 2). In 1999, both New York and Tokyo and the country of Thailand had more telephones and cell phones than the entire continent of Africa (Rice 2001; United Nations Development Program 1999). However, access to mobile and digital wireless telephone networks may be changing the telephone access dynamic for the better. The attractive features of wireless telephone networks, such as shorter waiting time to gain access, competitive

Table 7.6 ICT connectivity in Central and Eastern Europe in the 1990s

	GDP per capita ($)	FCIC[a]	Phone lines	Teledensity[b]
Albania	1,290	early 1990s	63,900	1.74
Belarus	5,000	1993	2,128,000	21.0
Bosnia-Herzegovina	600	1998–9	326,000	8.9
Bulgaria	4,630	1989	2,647,500	32.0
Croatia	4,300	mid-1990s	1,389,000	31.0
Czech Republic	11,100	1996	2,817,200	27.0
Georgia	1,350	1995	567,400	10.5
Hungary	7,500	1995	2,661,600	28.0
Macedonia	960	1995	367,300	17.0
Moldova	2,400	1995	593,300	14.0
Poland	6,400	early 1990s	6,532,400	17.0
Romania	5,200	early 1990s	3,161,200	14.0
Russia	5,200	?	25,914,500	17.5

[a] First commercial Internet connection
[b] Number of telephone lines per 100 people
Source: Derived from GILC (2000)

prices, and value added services, can improve a country's basic telephone access capabilities in a much shorter period of time (Kauffman and Techatassanasoontorn 2005; Waverman, Meschi, and Fuss 2005).

Table 7.6 shows the GDP per capita, the year of the first commercial Internet connection, the number of telephone lines and teledensity for poor and relatively poor countries in Central and Eastern Europe including the OECD countries of the Czech Republic, Hungary, and Poland. Two countries, Albania and Bosnia-Herzegovina, have fewer than ten telephone lines per 100 inhabitants. The countries of Belarus, Bulgaria, Croatia, and OECD countries Czech Republic, and Hungary have 21, 32, 31, 27, and 28 telephone lines per 100 inhabitants, respectively. The first commercial Internet connections occurred in most of the countries in the early to mid-1990s.

Telephone mainlines as well as the number of scientists and technicians are "technological inputs" (Campbell 2001) that are required for the transference, application, and use of technological outputs

(ICTs) (Rodriguez and Wilson 2000). Instead, LDCs' poor populations have used traditional ICT, the radio, as their "community telephone" (Kenny 2002). Unlike other ICTs, the radio is the least expensive to operate, requiring no literacy – only batteries. Kenny (2002) estimates the cost of operating a radio for 2,000 hours per year (about 6 hours a day) is about one US cent per hour. Yet, even this amount exceeds poor individuals' expenditures of approximately US$10.00 on annual communications (Kenny 2002). Most countries' (except LDCs') households and individuals spend approximately 2 percent of their income on telecommunications (Navas-Sabater, Dymond, and Junutumen 2002).

Conclusion and Final Observations

OECD countries have substantially higher investments than LDCs in technological inputs or "soft infrastructures." OECD countries invest nine times more in Research and Development, have about 17 times more technicians, and eight times as many scientists per capita than sub-Saharan countries (Rodriguez and Wilson 2000). In 1998, in OECD countries, 72.1 per 100 inhabitants had telecom access (fixed and mobile) as compared to 7.8 for non-OECD countries. Some 30 percent of individuals in developing countries had Internet access as compared to 2 percent in LDCs (Commission of the European Communities 2001, 2). High-income countries have 22 times as many telephone lines per 100 inhabitants as low-income countries (International Labour Organization 2001). ICTs not only allow access to information and knowledge, they are also enabling and facilitating technologies and can be used to save time and money and improve the quality of both work life and home life, whether in developed countries or LDCs. ICTs are increasingly playing an important role in a country's economic development, education, health, and well-being.

Even if LDCs significantly increase the application and diffusion of ICTs a very important question remains. Will the poor in these countries benefit? This question is important because of what the literature argues about income inequality in developed countries. For example, in the US personal computer ownership and access to the Internet is highly associated with family income. The family income threshold is $75,000 (see Chinn and Fairlie 2004; Rice 2001). Further, ICTs benefit workers who possess greater levels of education. Educated workers are better able to use ICTs than low-educated or uneducated workers. This situation widens the ICT gap between low-income and high-income individuals. Under this circumstance, in developed countries ICTs reinforce existing patterns where individuals' skills, capabilities, and income are markedly different (Rodriguez and Wilson 2000) and the "haves" benefit disproportionately from the application and diffusion of ICTs. Unlike the poor and low-income individuals, in developed countries higher income individuals take advantage of ICTs to gain more resources for further growth and development. Therefore, without concentrated efforts in human capital development in LDCs, it would appear that ICTs may be contributing to a widening technological gap between developed countries and LDCs.

The points above lead to a final set of observations. It is important that LDCs eliminate or reduce several significant barriers that impede technological transfer and technology development within their borders. These barriers can be placed into at least four categories: economic and financial, organizational, institutional, and human resources related. First, LDCs have a poor economic base and lower overall incomes which provide little stimulus for savings and investment. Second, there are little or no incentives to encourage business, entrepreneurship, and market development for technologies. Third, business and market structures in LDCs must advance from a monopoly or oligarchy to one of competition and fair pricing. This point leads to a quite interesting question: to what extent do LDCs' government policies inhibit a competitive private sector or reserve significant economic activities for government controlled organizations (see Dasgupta, Hall, and Wheeler 2002)? This question is important because as Eggleston, Jensen, and Zeckhauser (2002) note, in a proper market structure arrangement, ICTs can enhance market functions for both producers and consumers. In this situation a more positive impact can occur on the living standards of the poor. Fourth, LDCs need to enact explicit national policies that support technology acquisition and development and upgrading of indigenous skills and knowledge. These developments may lead LDCs to possess overall stronger capacities to assess their technology needs and, perhaps at some point, to influence global thinking on future technology development and technology research. Fifth, LDCs need to engage in human resource training and skill development in project development, management, and operations for application in technological organizations. Sixth, LDCs must find ways to enhance the personal incomes of their populations; thereby making ICTs more affordable. Finally, LDCs must improve their telecommunications infrastructure for more radio use and both land-based (fixed) and wireless (digital) communication networks.

8

Feminism in a Post-Development Age

Luz Estella Porras and H. Leslie Steeves

In seeking to connect development communication and feminism and to identify opportunities for inquiry, we suggest the need to explore streams of thought beyond the positivistic and Marxian traditions. We draw a map that includes recent theoretical trends and paths that redefine the meaning of development. These trends include: spirituality as liberation; post-development thought (including postcolonial studies); and the embodiment of female experience (see table 8.1). These diverse yet overlapping views open up a range of questions for the development communication field by integrating gendered experience, knowledge and voice.

Thus far the dominant emphasis in scholarship and practice has been on the material aspects of development, resulting in the predominance of the modernization and political economy approaches. The modernization approach is evident in the women in development or WID framework of the 1970s and 1980s, which argued for integrating women into mainstream economic development. Many studies showed, however, that these changes were cosmetic and did not alter the capitalist-patriarchal basis of modernization. The latter approach, political economy of communication, primarily considers the dynamics of media ownership and denounces concentration, employment inequities, the manipulation of audience markets and access to media use. Feminist political economy scholars have sought to extend critiques, by considering the gendered and class relations of power in analyses and calls for reform.

Non-material dimensions and practices of development most notably include spirituality for liberation, which has been insufficiently studied in relation to development communication (Freire 1970; Melkote and Steeves 2001; Steeves 2001).

Table 8.1 Frameworks on feminism, communication and development

Frameworks	Issues / ideas	Communication mainly seen as . . .	Tools	. . . what about gender?
Modernization	Transcending tradition Engagement with global capitalism Western societies as developed models of social organization Technology, urbanization, secularization. Individual rights	Mass media / information systems Communication campaigns for behavior change Free press Digital world	Diffusion of innovations Social marketing Free information flow Transference of Western technology and knowledge to developing regions	Women in Development (WID) Gender included in the agenda but disconnected from historical roots of oppression Liberal feminism focuses on expansion of women's rights
Political economy of communication	Control over media Concentration of ownership Commodification of audiences/news/ cultural products Labor, presence of women in decision-making Access to media and telecommunications Digital divide Impact of global free markets	Multinational media corporations Private vs. public Local independent media Telecommunications and information technologies	Media reform International regulation Change of ownership Challenge capitalism (social protest) Alternative/independent/ public/community/ citizen's media	Access to media is gendered Communication as women's right Access to media is insufficient for gender equality Segregation and underrepresentation of women workers in media Global feminization of poverty

Spirituality for liberation	Spiritual resources from diverse traditions (Buddhism, Christianity, Islam, Hinduism) Community empowerment Social justice	Interpretation of sacred texts Connection to local realities Intrapersonal and interpersonal communication	Concientizacion Liberatory education / Freire's dialogue Collective action and social mobilization Personal growth	Collective empowering practices do not necessary include feminist interests Gender issues relevant to women's roles in spiritual and religious practices
Post-development thought and postcolonial studies	Criticism of oppressive systems / discourses Rejects causal theories and grand narratives Rejects essentializing social groups Deconstruction of nation and "otherness"	Meaning-making Narratives construct a symbolic order Social movements and local production of knowledge Visual and textual representation in art, popular culture, film, advertising, etc.	Questioning development and communication interventions and the power within Unmasking the discourse of modernization and its mythologies Listening to divergent voices, local ways to define change and gendered production of knowledge Unpacking language and ideology of representation. Self-representation and circulation of other discourses Emphasis on community media, citizen's media, and counter-colonial representations	Explore the paradoxes and complexity of experiences of women engaging in globalization Woman is not an individual subject as in liberal feminism but immersed in social location and multiple forms of oppression Intersectionality of identities: race, class, religion, culture, urban experience, sexuality, age, environment. etc. Account for systems of power: colonial systems and current Western liberal neo-colonization practices Decentering the historically dominant male voice in projects and programs

Continued

Table 8.1 *Continued*

Frameworks	Issues / ideas	Communication mainly seen as . . .	Tools	. . . what about gender?
Embodiment	Body politics Body is not private territory but connected to social and cultural environments Attentiveness to the subjective embodied experience Body as site of convergence of multiple oppressions Body and place as contingent non-essentialized experiences Expression and enunciation of one's voice is an embodied experience.	Communication is sensorial experience. Communication requires attention to place, body, emotional well-being and quality of the encounter Individuals use their bodies to engage and produce technology	Communication encounters and listening practices as embodied acts of caring Use of the inviting gesture to break down the embodiment of fear and silence "Midwifery of communication"	Bodily experience is gendered, is socially located and political Recognition of embodied experiences such as health, work, aging, sexuality, motherhood, violence and the gendered experience of the place in the everyday life Recognition of diverse non-rational dimensions of the sensorial body: Emotion, sensuality, sexuality, sisterhood, motherhood. Women's bodies learn the gendered habits of care and subsistence, alongside gendered habits of fear and silence

In this chapter we include two additional approaches. These new layers incorporate non-material dimensions of language and meaning; the discourse and symbolic order that constitute both modernization practices and patriarchy. They also include the layer of embodiment, which links material and non-material experience by highlighting the corporeal life of women as a unique place to raise questions on how development processes affect women at the most basic level, which arguably grounds other dimensions of experience. Each of these five approaches to development communication will be considered through a feminist lens. We argue for a holistic approach that includes the consideration of non-material elements of development including discourse and spirituality, as well as political and economic questions, with a foundational awareness of women's embodied experience.

Modernization

Development understood as a process of modernization is rooted in Western ideas of progress as a product of economic growth, free trade, urbanization, secularization, individualism, and technological progress. It represents the effort to transcend traditional ways of organizing social life that are perceived as obstacles of progress and industrialization. Consistent with modernization, communication and information are seen as the tools to extend values, diffuse innovations, and push for reforms. At the macro level, this means reshaping the institutions and infrastructure of non-Western regions in order to integrate them to the free-market global economy. At the micro level communication and information take the form of social marketing campaigns and other persuasion-oriented programs to affect individual behaviors of target audience members and to achieve certain development goals.

Many modernization-as-development programs designed by governments and aid organizations are directed to women and depend upon women's participation. However, many of them have failed to consider gender relations. Boserup (1970) was among the first to document this phenomenon. She showed how sub-Saharan African women's historically productive roles in agriculture were harmed by colonial and postcolonial aid policies favoring men in the new cash economies. There, women had been traditionally responsible for food planting, cultivating and processing, and men assisted with land clearing and cultivation. Development increased women's workload, as men's work was shifted to non-food cash crops or employment in cities. Women became almost solely responsible for food production and childcare, plus were forced to earn cash by selling in the informal market. Other subsequent critiques have supported Boserup's observations, showing how development aid often neglects gender roles and privileges men (e.g., Staudt 1985; Wilkins 1999).

Many social marketing projects in the modernization tradition, which apply commercial marketing principles to development goals such as family planning, have been similarly critiqued. For instance, Luthra (1991) examined USAID's multi-million dollar social marketing contraceptive campaign in Bangladesh and found considerable evidence that the project privileged commercial marketing considerations over the project's social mission and women's needs, even harming women in the process.

A central criticism of social marketing addresses its design, which defines people as consumers of products or services, not as citizens. Social marketing asks for obedience not empowerment, as noted by Gumucio-Dagrón (1999). Individual behavior-change campaigns may include women's issues, but seldom analyze the engendered systems that reproduce gender oppression. Thus, communication campaigns are designed towards goals of integration, assimilation or adaptation to the dominant model of development, keeping intact historical structural orders and gender asymmetries. However this limitation does not necessarily mean that all modernization projects fail to help women. For instance, the Meena communication campaign is a popular UNICEF-funded project using comic books, animated films, television, and radio series to educate Southeast Asian audiences about girls' rights (UNICEF 2008). This case shows how message-oriented strategies can include women's interests. While praiseworthy in many respects, such projects remain consistent with a liberal perspective on individual rights that is at the core of modernization.

Another feature of modernization is its faith in technology to deliver information. New information technologies like the Internet and mobile telephony generate optimism because of their potential to challenge modernization's top-down direction of development projects. There is room in the network systems for women interconnecting, exchanging information, participating in public debates, self-expressing, promoting mobilization locally and globally, organizing protests, and generating low-cost publications, as long as women have access to the necessary resources: money; time; training; access to technology and software; and language and literacy skills (Huws 2008, 48, 50). The phenomenon of the Cuban blogger Yoani Sanchez, a struggling digital journalist who became a storyteller of everyday life while challenging censorship and engaging thousands of online readers in daily political conversations illustrates the opportunity posed by online communication.[1] Huws (2008) suggests that minority women, women with disabilities, and other marginalized social actors find the anonymous experience of the Internet empowering. However, she and Gallagher (2008) acknowledge that, while the dream of "globalization from below" seems possible, there is a history of gender inequality engrained in the conception and use of this technology. Internet and cell phones, despite their potential, are just tools that reflect the priorities of the designers and the social conditions of their production from which women are usually absent (Gallagher 2008, 23).

These questions of access, production, labor, and material gender inequalities in communication lead us to political economy frameworks.

Political Economy of Communication

Gallagher (2005) notes a critical difference between seeing media existing "out there" separated from gender relations, and media "inside" the space of reproduction of gender inequality. Global events like the World Summit on the Information Society (WSIS), held in Tunisia in 2005, include calls for women's participation in media systems; however, their rhetoric inadequately addresses material constraints that hinder the possibility for women to control, use, own, produce, and work for media (under just conditions), and decide about telecommunications, media content, and policies. Political economy scholars consider these and other questions about the material conditions of communication in the context of the free market orientation of global media systems.

Political economy focuses primarily on the issue of economic class as a site of oppression. It studies the commodification of media content, cultural products and even audiences that are bought and sold in the markets of global advertising (Meehan 2008). Neo-liberal policies push for deregulated markets. The rule of the market then manifests itself in concentration of media ownership, monopolistic conglomeration processes, and pressures on local media and independent outlets. These processes in turn shrink democratic debate and make gender oppression irrelevant and invisible. In this context, audiences are seen as commodities/consumers, not as citizens, as previously noted; they miss the opportunity to shape values and cultural products they consume, as well as ideas of development, gender equality, or social justice.

Political economists interrogate the course of transnational capital that dictates the flow of news, information, and circulation of cultural products, affecting the range of genres, aesthetics, and formats that are produced and consumed globally (Schiller 2001). Analyses by feminist political economists may include issues of labor in media and information environments showing pervasive gender underrepresentation, segregation in news rooms, the high cost for women of doing "flexible" work at home, the poor work conditions in electronic manufacturing or outsourcing telecommunication jobs (Joseph 2004; McLaughlin 2008; Mosco, McKercher, and Stevens 2008; Sreberny 2005; Steeves and Wasko 2002).

Shade and Porter (2008) connect the trends of feminization of poverty and the myth of women's "nimble fingers" in the case of global corporate media which produce both media content/hardware and other retail products in international sweatshops. The authors analyze the Dualstar Entertainment Group that on the one hand makes astronomical revenues in media, hiring celebrities like the Olson Twins, and on the other hand exploits girls' labor in the garment factories of Bangladesh and other export processing zones.

To address these issues women have organized to gain power in media and technology. SEWA, the Self-Employed Women Association in India, is a well-known example of producing media to strengthen a women's organization (Joseph 2004). The Association for Progressive Communications (APC) works to redefine sustainable development and gender justice by promoting open communication sources, communication rights, and other issues among activists around the world (Sreberny 2005). There are many other examples of activist campaigns to boycott corporations and to educate consumers such as the Clean Clothes Campaign and the work of the National Labor Committee that have helped raise awareness on gender and global inequalities (Shade and Porter 2008). However, despite these efforts, the deep-rooted structures of global capitalism and its dynamics of oppression remain essentially intact.

Spirituality as Liberation

Nussbaum (2000, 78–80), while discussing human development, argues that beyond survival needs there is another set of non-material dimensions crucial to social change, including the ability to "imagine, think, and reason . . . to sustain emotional bonds . . . to affiliate with and show compassion for others . . . to laugh and play." She includes spirituality among the capabilities of the senses, imagination and thought. Nussbaum recognizes that "while religious traditions have been a source of oppression for women, they have also been powerful sources of protection for human rights, of commitment to justice and of energy for social change" (p. 178).[2]

Development scholars have largely underestimated the importance of religion and spirituality. Within the modernization mindset, religion is equated to tradition and irrationality; seen more as a barrier to change than an asset. Among critical scholars influenced by Marxian thought, the pattern is to see religion as the opium of the masses, an ideological reflection of social institutions or "apparatuses" that propagate ideology, as evident in institutions such as the media, the family, and the school (Steeves 2001). In turn, some Western feminists tend to see religion as one of causes of "Third World" women's victimization. In response, southern feminists have rejected the label of passive victims as inaccurate and ethnocentric (Mohanty 1991).

For many women and men religious affiliations are central to their lives, bringing personal fulfillment as well as an opportunity for collective engagement with social issues. There are many examples of liberation through spiritual and religious activism. Particularly notable is the Base Ecclesial Community (CEB) movement in Brazil that played an important role in the political resistance and social mobilization that pushed for the end of the dictatorship in the 1970s. Members of this movement engaged in religious education practices and readings of sacred texts that generated questions about the living conditions of the poor. In contrast to conservative churches, the CEB movement was committed to addressing injustice in *this present life*, without waiting passively for providential solutions or a better chance in the next life.

This movement was framed in the "theology of liberation" tradition, which was importantly influenced by Brazilian educator Paulo Freire and his philosophy of adult education, which blends notions of religion, spirituality, communication, and education.

For Freire (e.g., 1970), development is neither capitalist economic growth nor a Marxian alternative. Rather it is a process of emancipatory dialogue with the goal of expanded individual and communal consciousness and empowerment. According to Freire, once people were able to name their sources of oppression as well as their sources of power, they would be capable of identifying appropriate solutions. Development communication practice therefore should be primarily characterized by face-to-face egalitarian dialogue, involving reflection and action, and with no hierarchal distinctions between participants, recognizing that both oppressors and oppressed are equally in need of liberation.[3]

Freire, however, fails to consider whether liberation and collective reflection on oppression benefit women and men equally. Steeves (2001) and Melkote and Steeves (2001) attempt to address this gap via case studies, including the above noted CEB movement in Brazil, and the Sarvodaya Shramadana movement in Sri Lanka that incorporated teachings of Buddhism in community work. In both cases women gained a heightened awareness of social injustice by participating in collective political actions; however, they were often frustrated in their efforts to gain positions of leadership or to challenge prescribed gender roles.

These two cases illustrate the difficulty of including gender equality in the practice of spiritual liberation, but also the opportunity and need to learn the ways in which dialogical communication and spiritual awakening represents an important resource for women's empowerment and social change.

Post-Development and Post-Development Feminism

As discussed above, modernization perspectives ask questions about how to make development more efficient but do not question the problematic aspects of pressing communities to become modern. Political economy of media focuses its attention on global inequalities in terms of capital distribution, labor, and access to media and ownership. Spiritual perspectives, grounded in interpretations of sacred texts from liberation perspectives, view development communication ideally as emancipatory dialogue that leads to expanded individual and communal consciousness and power.

There is yet another non-material perspective, post-development, that attends to the fundamental enterprise of development: its sets of knowledge, assumptions, narratives, and the symbolic order it reproduces that perpetuate dynamics of inequality. Post-development includes postcolonial feminist frameworks and perspectives.

Since the 1990s post-development thought has aimed to unpack the myths, language, and practices of international development interventions. Post-development scholars question the very idea of development as a powerful discourse. In his groundbreaking book, *Encountering Development*, Escobar (1995) discusses the issue of development from a post-structuralist perspective: as a *discourse* that constructs reality. Development as *discourse* consists of a set of assumptions that shape the social imaginary. According to this view, discourse creates the machinery of agencies and programs and also defines the populations and regions in need of development. In this way development under modernization is made to seem "neutral" and "logical." The dominant development discourse acts as an overarching regime that informs policies, programs, and methods and produces knowledge that legitimizes the practice of development. It also contains resources that validate its premises, i.e., technical knowledge, value-free science, efficiency, and the invention of The

Other (women, the poor, native people, people of color, the entire "Third World") as categories for intervention.

Many issues remain unseen or non-existent under the logic of development discourse: power inequalities; politics of intervention; complexity of local needs; failure and discontent of particular social actors; gendered experience; and cultural and environmentally negative consequences. Therefore post-development, as Saunders (2002, 17) writes, implies a "full recognition [that] development cannot be universalized, is environmentally destructive and grounded in exploitative social relations." She and other feminists such as Mies and Shiva (1993) discuss not only the degradation and unsustainability of modern industrial life but also the [modern] mentality that devalues subsistence-based communities. From observations of farmers in India, Mies and Shiva assert that many peasant women in the South in their everyday practice of subsistence have learned to respect the sacredness of life and to preserve life on earth (p. 19), which is a knowledge dismissed by patriarchal societies and projects grounded in modernization.

There has been much discussion of how social science researchers, humanitarian agencies, development programs, feminists and even journalists who intervene in or study the so called Third World regions tend to understand the experience of diverse women from a Western viewpoint. Mohanty (1991) pointed out that Western feminists tend to see women's lives and struggles through their lenses and imagination. Their lenses often universalize the experience of women seeing them as perpetual victims or as natural and traditional, while assuming that notions of progress, freedom, and ideas of wellbeing and gender equality carry the same meanings and value for everyone in different contexts.

Post-development feminists specifically examine the contradictions of integrating women into development. They argue that development is gendered, that women and men engage and experience the impacts of modernization and globalization in different ways, and that women in their local contexts and social groups deal in diverse and complex ways with poverty and gender inequality. Thus, when modernizing agencies or non-governmental groups propose welfare projects, women's lives do not necessarily improve and the culture of gender oppression remains unchallenged. As an example, Rodriguez's (2001a) discourse analysis of a Colombian agricultural program sponsored by the World Bank finds that women are symbolized as passive and ahistorical subjects, while men are depicted as agents. In other cases, even though the rhetoric of agencies emphasizes women's agency, the actual gains and costs of their participation in development stays unnoticed, as in the case of the community food programs carried out for poor women in the slums of Lima during the 1980s. Lind (2003) suggests that these programs are regarded by many international agencies as a success, but women, after few years of participating in them, reported feeling exhausted, still in deep poverty and marginalized.

Post-development scholars look at how local groups engage with globalization, and the ways that people interact, negotiate, and deal with transnational power dynamics at the micro levels. As an example, Babb (2001) describes the socialist (Marxian) and neoliberal (modernization) strategies for women in Nicaragua following the Sandinista revolution. She shows how both failed the poor and how women and other marginalized groups responded by mobilizing informally at the micro level of their barrios looking for alternatives to survive those very models of development designed to support them.

Movements emerging at the local level gain political power forming collective identities and connecting with places and actions charged with cultural meanings. Escobar and Alvarez (1992) discuss how "new" social movements have emerged in Latin America not only around economic issues, but also around cultural and identity dimensions of their lives and a meaningful connection to *place* and environment. Therefore post-development feminists recognize that feminism is plural, and the many ways in which ethnicity, sexual orientation, class, race, political militancy, and more define the mobilization of women and ground conceptions of social justice.

Post-developmentalists have denounced the dominant Western narrative that assumes one way of understanding the complexities of people in economically poor regions of the world. For post-development feminists, the main challenge of communication and the media is to de-center the monopoly of truth and knowledge of development by circulating diverse counter-narratives, women's stories about social change, other referents of knowledge, and other imaginaries of development. The citizen's media projects documented by Clemencia Rodriguez (2001b) moves toward that direction by giving visibility to emerging voices and knowledge, plural movements, and local conversations.

Under a post-development feminism, communication is not only about mass media arrangements, social marketing or information campaigns, but about a broad range of communication opportunities in which the voices of women are expressed and the nuanced paradoxical, complicated threads of life are shared. Communication is about telling and listening to what is hard to enunciate, the contingent experiences and meanings, the tales that do not talk about one "normal" way to be women and to develop, but the multiple fluid ways of existing and of representing the experience of women and other marginalized groups who decide collectively what they want to be. Communication efforts may include exploration of the variety of *modes* local communities use to communicate within themselves and to make meanings of their experience, place, history, identities, resources, and engagements to the global world.

Post-development perspectives have certainly been criticized. Some critics assert that this perspective does not offer clear alternatives for social change. Others point out the romantization of local movements and women's political leadership, placing too much weight on women's expression. However, post-development feminism, as Lind (2003) says, asks that we imagine a post-development era, a place in which progress is not measured just by WalMart and McDonald's, but by social justice and other grassroots indicators of social change.

As development under modernization followed the independence of dozens of previously colonized states following World War II, postcolonial studies and critiques emerged alongside post-development thought. Postcolonial studies address the ways in which dominant cultures play a role in reproducing and normalizing oppression among subaltern groups in postcolonial societies, often due to powerful cultural images and assumptions about The Other or subaltern (Said 1978; Shome and Hedge 2002). Postcolonial feminists examine racial, class, and ethnic oppression and the ways these forms of oppression are enmeshed with the colonial experience of women. One central theme in postcolonial thought is the critique of representations that essentialize subaltern groups. Scholars ask how culture and tradition are inventions linked to notions of nation and authenticity that excludes and devalues the experience of the subaltern.

Postcolonial studies often examine varied visual and textual representations, showing how these representations reinforce power inequalities. These studies frequently reveal ways in which postcolonial images, stories and texts depict local people as "primitive," "savage" and "exotic." At the same time the colonizer sees and represents himself as the "center," or "norm," and the experience of colonization as an idyllic adventure. Studies by postcolonial feminists look more specifically at how colonialism and patriarchy merge to cast women in particular ways, for example, as "passive victims" in contrast to Western women who are "modern" and "free."

In sum, post-development and postcolonial scholars aim to challenge dominant representations and their ideological work by unmasking and critiquing them, as well as by supporting the production, circulation and consumption of the anti-colonial work of various "Third world" and minority artists, scholars, and filmmakers.

Embodiment

While ideology and representations constitute an important realm of critique, we also recognize that women (and men) construct their sense of self in connection to their experiences and perceptions of their bodies. Women laboring the fields, pregnant women, aging women, women expressing their sexuality, women walking the streets at night, women migrating, women using a camera – or watching television experience particular sensorial connections to their bodies and their environments. The embodied experience of women is located and it is political. Harcourt and Mumtaz (2002, 37–8), for instance, discuss "the fleshy political being," meaning the body is a political site that mediates women's lived experience linked to material expressions of the family, community, or public space. The body is not only a private realm, but a site where multiple social oppressions and liberating experiences converge. While rejecting an essentialist argument that seals women to their biology, these authors recognize that the diverse lives of women are still constrained by biological and material realities such as race, age, illness, and being a rape survivor. These experiences are not isolated but affect and are affected by a range of social and cultural exclusions or inclusions, and connected to powerful or disempowered states that together constitute one's political identity.

Such a focus is related to development communication in that women's participation requires their whole sensorial experience and their active bodies engaging in communication. However on the ground, the tired body is overlooked. Porras (2008) reports that women participating in a community project in Colombia feel exhausted during meetings. They usually leave home before 6:00 a.m., work in the informal sectors as street vendors or maids, then in their own barrios at the community daycare, and later in the afternoon or in the evening they attend community meetings. They often walk or take the bus home when it's already dark, and when they are back they have to face the "second shift,"[4] i.e., the dual labor of women in the economy outside home and in the household doing domestic chores and taking care of elders and children. A woman talks about feeling *taxed* in her rear end after sitting for hours in low-engaging meetings. This comment offers clues about the disconnection between community development interventions planned only at the content/mind level, versus the need for other approaches that recognize the participant's motivations, needs, everyday practices and their embodied experiences. This split between the communication content/message and the holistic presence of women and their bodies reveals consistency with the modernization tradition that separates mind and body (as well as mind and spirit, material and non-material), and privileges mind, leaving the experience of the body unnoticed.

Embodied experience and development communication are further linked by *the gesture* that invites expression and participation. Technological gadgets such as media equipment may intimidate users, and many women report feeling fearful in front of a camera or microphone. Fear, as Martín Barbero (2002) asserts, is the feeling of being disempowered by discourses that exclude people as subjects, and reinforces gestures that dismiss history, voices and experiences. Fear in front of the microphone, or the ancestral shyness that feeds the culture of silence[5] needs to be broken by communication opportunities that recognize power dynamics by making gestures that undress the power of media or public speech. The concept "midwifery of communication" may be used to describe the nurturing gestures that smooth the path to expression and the birth of one's own voice. Porras (2008) reports how a group of Colombian communicators for development use humor, games, sensorial experiments, and olfactory and tactile activities with community leaders in communication workshops. These playful experiments are designed to build women's confidence in expressing concrete sensations, emotions, ideas, and powerful stories and thus fight fear and detachment from embodied dialogue.

Conclusion

We examined five trends in the scholarship of development communication and feminism: modernization, political economy, spirituality as liberation, post-development, and embodied experience. The latter four represent critiques of the dominant modernization perspective, which foregrounds economic development via private enterprise and globalization, and they suggest different ways of thinking about and gauging the success of development and social change. These latter perspectives need not be mutually exclusive, as all highlight important issues and questions for women: of labor and access, ownership and control; dialogue, community, and collective action; unmasking development narratives for a new symbolic order; and recognizing the role and constraints of the gendered body in development.

Post-development and postcolonial thought incorporate elements from political economy and liberation perspectives, recognizing the power and biases of the institutions, agents, and machinery of development, and extending an invitation to imagine a world in which local organizations and social movements redefine in their own terms the very ideas of progress and well-being (Lind 2003). Post-development feminists are quick to point out that the roots of oppression and gender exclusion remain unexamined within the modernization discourse. They challenge us to consider the contradictions and paradoxes in the experiences of the women within the global development economy and the need for grassroots expression and voice to share alternative views of social change.

We close with the embodiment perspective, as a reminder that abstract theories too often forget that men and women are living, breathing, human beings, whose capacities to act individually or collectively may often be affected by their gendered sensory experiences and constraints. In fact communication itself is a sensorial experience, limited by the body's capacity to initiate and respond. In developing countries, gender socialization may be inseparable from and importantly shape one's sensory capacity and experience. Clearly economic resources, ownership and control, spirituality, and ideological meaning all point to important gendered questions in development. Yet interviews with women remind us of the sensory basis of communication, and that women's bodies constitute an equally important consideration.

Notes

1   Yoani Sanchez is a philologist who lives and works as a journalist in La Havana. Her popular blog "Generacion Y" (http://desdecuba.com/generaciony/) is translated by volunteers around the world to nine different languages. She obtained the 2008 Ortega y Gasseet Award for Digital Journalism, but the Cuban government would not issue her a permit to leave the island and receive the award in Spain.
2   Nussbaum draws on the "capabilities approach," which states that people should have real choices in order to engage in concrete practices that make them fully human. Amyarta Sen, who won a Nobel Prize in Economics and helped to create the Human Development Index (HDI), is also the proponent of an alternative approach in which development expands the capabilities of people to be able to do and be what they value (Sen 1994).
3   See also Steeves (2001, 400).
4   Arlie Hochschild coined the concept in her book by the same name.
5   Martín Barbero (2002, 25) follows Freire's reasoning on the culture of silence instituted in Latin America since colonial times explaining that "the essence of the alienation (from speaking *la palabra*) is not only imposition of the values and ideas but the radical devaluation of one's own existence. The colonized people, dispossessed of their land and traditions . . . learn to devalue their own language and culture."

9

Sonagachi Project: A Case-Study Set in India

Satarupa Dasgupta

Introduction

"People's capability and opportunities to shape their own destiny is an ideal supported by virtually everybody, including the decision-makers at the highest level. Still, most people around the world do not have this option" (Mefalopulos 2002, 836). One of the objectives of development-based communication is to generate such an option for disempowered groups to gain control over their own destinies. As Mitchell and Chaman-Ruiz (2007) observe, communication forms an integral part of such development initiatives. Figueroa, Kincaid, Rani and Lewis (2002) note that communication itself can serve as a tool for facilitating empowerment among the marginalized and voiceless.

The realm of development communication has evolved considerably, the current emphasis being on participatory approach in place of the diffusion strategy (Jacobson and Storey 2004). Participation is defined in terms of local involvement in development initiatives, "sometimes as involvement in program implementation, sometimes as involvement in program design, sometimes in both" (Jacobson and Storey 2004, 100). Participation is noted to generate agency among disempowered groups by rendering them active facilitators in the process of development.

The objective of this chapter is to explore participation communication by utilizing its theoretical attributes to analyze a particular health intervention project. The project in consideration is a HIV/AIDS intervention program undertaken in what is referred to as the red light district of Calcutta, India. The initiative is referred to as the *Sonagachi Project*, owing to its origin and location in the district by the same name. The project in question started in 1991 to ascertain and arrest the incidence of sexually transmitted diseases (STDs) and HIV/AIDS among sex workers in and around the Sonagachi district in Calcutta (Jana, Basu, Rotheram-Borus, and Newman 2004). The project was funded by a national healthcare research institute and later by the state-based West Bengal AIDS prevention council (Jana, Basu, Rotheram-Borus, and Newman 2004). The said project was initiated by a group that comprised a local physician, an Ethiopian public health worker, and healthcare and social service professionals from Calcutta. But later, the project was spearheaded by the sex workers themselves who acted as peer outreach workers (Jana, Basu, Rotheram-Borus, and Newman 2004). The Sonagachi Project is still going on in Calcutta as a peer outreach and participation-based program, under the guidance of the sex workers. Statistics from UNAIDS and NACO show a significant drop in the incidence of HIV infection and a significant increase in condom usage in Sonagachi since the project's implementaion. The original aim of the project was to disseminate awareness information about STDs and HIV/AIDS among sex workers, and arrest the infection incidence among the latter population. However the project ended up achieving outcomes that were not foreseen by the program coordinators (Jana, Banerjee, Saha and Dutta 1999).

This chapter endeavors to elaborate the theoretical presumptions of participation-based development communication, and to explore the extent to which the Sonagachi Project reflects the theory. An elaboration of the theoretical frameworks inherent in development communication is also included. Dominant paradigms of development such as modernization theory and Freirean principles are analyzed to understand their relevance in the Sonagachi Project. The chapter also tries to assess whether the Sonagachi Project conforms to the notions of empowerment communication – a specialized form of a development communication approach that offers analytical means of addressing structural inequalities among marginalized groups.

The chief objective of participatory process in communication is to "extend the fruits of development in a sustainable way to all the citizens of the developing world" (Stiglitz 2002, 179). The chapter endeavors to analyze whether the Sonagachi Project subscribes to the said aim of participation-based development communication by facilitating an environment of sustainable empowerment among the sex workers.

The Sonagachi Project as a Model of Participation Communication

"Development communication is a client-oriented strategy, contributing a powerful set of tools for the success of development initiatives. (Mitchell and Chaman-Ruiz 2007, 1). Often incorporating a participatory process, development communication emphasizes community, interpersonal interaction, and understanding based on mutual regard. The concept of participation is noted to generate a discourse that "evolves from people serving as a mirror of their aspirations and needs rather than being imposed upon by others. It allows people to become subjects of their own development and not simply objects of technology or processes" (Thomas 1994, 475).

A successful development communication program based on participation has to possess a comprehensive understanding of the needs and perspectives of the client/target population (Mitchell and Chaman-Ruiz, 2007). While participation-based communication programs can be aimed at the individual for social or behavior change, the collective involvement of a community for facilitating health and welfare is also quite common. As Figueroa, Kincaid, Rani and Lewis (2002) observe, "there is a wide-spread belief in the field of development communication, that community participation is a valuable end in itself as well as means to a better life" (p. iii). Notwithstanding whether the communication technique is directed at individual or community level, the basic tenets of participation entail generating unhindered dialogue and active social engagement; also "it requires that individuals have a voice in the decisions that affect them" (Stiglitz 2002, 165).

The Sonagachi Project involved a participation-based communication intervention that was undertaken at three concurrent levels – community, group, and individual. At the community level, the STDs and HIV/AIDS incidence was defined as a problem for the entire local community and its mitigation was articulated as the responsibility of all members. At the group intervention level, the sex workers were mobilized as peer outreach workers. The latter were given requisite training to serve as sources of preventive health information and knowledge of safe sexual practices among their colleagues. At the individual level, the intervention entailed the empowerment of the individual sex worker in multiple ways. For instance, "outreach workers served as models for their sex worker peers that it was possible to gain literacy, respect, employment, and self-confidence" (Jana, Basu, Rotheram-Borus, and Newman 2004, 410).

The definition of a common problem at the community, group, and individual level helped in facilitating community dialogue and collective action, thus serving as an example of participatory process. As Jana, Banerjee, Saha and Dutta (1999) note, efforts were made to identify and appreciate a broad array of issues that determine the priorities of the sex workers and to localize these issues in their general environment. "Whatever the objective of the program may be, it has to take into account and build on what the targeted community perceives as their immediate and urgent needs" (Jana, Banerjee, Saha and Dutta 1999, 3).

In this regard, an example may be cited. In case of the Sonagachi Project, adoption of condom usage and safe sexual practices were not the initial priority of the sex workers. Rather obtaining healthcare facilities for themselves and for their children were noted to receive greater attention. The Sonagachi Project sought to prioritize meeting the personal needs of the sex workers instead of gearing the campaign towards an occupational health initiative. Such an approach conforms to the client-oriented strategies of participation-based communication techniques. As Stiglitz (2002) notes, "processes, not just outcomes, are key to this broader interpretation of participation . . . the stress on processes is a natural outgrowth not only of the increasing emphasis on equity, but also of a greater recognition of agency problems" (Stiglitz 2002, 165). The Sonagachi Project put its focus on the process of achieving greater community empowerment of the sex workers rather than emphasizing its immediate goals directed towards changing sexual health behavior.

One of the important aspects of the Sonagachi Project was its initiative of re-articulation of issues related to sex work – including the status of sex work itself – and stressing the right of sex workers to avail material resources and opportunities. Jana, Banerjee, Saha

and Dutta (1999) emphasize that there was no endeavor to reha-
bilitate the sex workers, rather the latter "were accepted for what
they were" (p. 2). Sex work was reconceived as a valid form of
employment. Sex workers sought to demand benefits, such as
healthcare for themselves, and educational opportunities for their
children. As Jana, Basu, Rotheram-Borus, and Newman (2004)
observe, "by engaging sex workers in roles of power and decision
making within the program a set of principles emerged that
assisted in reframing the problem of HIV from an issue of
individual motivation, will, or behavioral commitment to a problem
of community disenfranchisement" (p. 407). Such a mode of
operation emphasized a participation-oriented process based on
shared knowledge of common problems and also created understanding based on mutual respect. By refusing to generate alternative professions for the sex workers, the project succeeded in
creating a respectable status for the target population, besides mitigating the stigmatization of the latter's profession. The project thus
created a public space that facilitated community dialogue and
public action. This is concurrent with one of the facets of participation-based development communication which allows "members of
a community to take action as a group to solve a common problem
. . . this leads to reduction in the prevalence of problematic health
behavior but also creates social change that increases the collective
capacity to solve new problems" (Figueroa, Kincaid, Rani and
Lewis, 6).

An interesting aspect of the Sonagachi Project was the identification of stakeholders within the sex work industry. The latter included
individuals both within and outside the realm of sex work such as
landowners of sex workers, pimps, clients, law enforcement agencies, and members of political parties. One of the objectives of the
project was to emphasize the status of sex work as a labor industry
and to focus on the losses of the stakeholders in case of a high
incidence of HIV/AIDS infection among the work force. As Jana,
Banerjee, Saha and Dutta (1999) observe such an initiative also
helped in forming public opinion against harassment of sex workers
by agencies such as police and pimps. Such identification and mobilization of stake-holders appear to be in concurrence with the following observations of Michelle and Chaman-Ruiz on efficacious
participatory communication:

> A more effective approach frames communication as an integral "two-way" process that engages stakeholders, understands their socio-political context . . . throughout the development process . . . this integrated two-way process constitutes a new communication approach, providing a better understanding of the development context, tailoring development initiatives into design and implementation, and contributing to more sustainable results by allowing project managers to better recognize and mitigate risks. (Mitchell and Chaman-Ruiz 2007, 2).

The Sonagachi Project facilitated relationships between the sex workers and the stakeholders; the project framed sex work in a way that it was deemed useful in maintaining the financial interests of the latter. The program was useful to sex workers for a variety of reasons such as reduction of HIV and STD incidence, free healthcare, credit opportunities, vocational training facilities etc. It was useful for the stakeholders by maintaining a viable and healthy workforce (Jana, Basu, Rotheram-Borus, and Newman 2004). An integration of the interests of the stakeholders and the target population facilitated an understanding of issues relevant to the development initiative – this is identified by Mitchell and Chaman-Ruiz (2007), and Figueroa, Kincaid, Rani and Lewis (2002) as one of the characteristics of efficacious participation-based development communication geared towards social change.

Participation-based development communication programs often involve the employment of opinion leaders who mobilize public opinion. These opinion leaders can be public figures such as politicians, media celebrities, religious leaders or civil society representatives (Mitchell and Chaman-Ruiz, 2007). Opinion leaders are sought because "societies listen best to their opinion leaders" who "can become a third voice . . . this voice is particularly effective if the initiative's key champion has low credibility or if the initiative is not favored by public opinion" (Mitchell and Chaman-Ruiz 2007, 22). Importantly, the Sonagachi Project did not use public figures as opinion leaders. Rather the sex workers themselves sought to mobilize opinion by peer outreach projects. It is an interesting attribute of the Sonagachi Project that it subverted a common facet of development work by repudiating utilization of public figures as opinion leaders. Perhaps the Sonagachi Project serves as a relevant example of development work in which the target population serves as the primary means for facilitating behavior or social change. Finally, it may be noted, that notwithstanding its unique attributes, the Sonagachi Project displays characteristics of participation-based development communication and may be considered as a relevant model of the latter.

Paradigms in Development Communication: Relevance to the Sonagachi Project

The following section endeavors to assess the Sonagachi Project in light of theoretical paradigms that are inherent in development communication.

Modernization theory and the Sonagachi Project

The history of development communication in the southern hemisphere comprises dominant theoretical paradigms one of which is modernization theory. Since modernization theory was covered in Chapter 1, the basic tenets of modernization theory can be summarized briefly as follows:

> The model of modernization exhibits certain components and sequences whose relevance is global . . . everywhere, for example, increasing urbanization has tended to raise literacy; rising literacy has tended to raise media exposure; increasing media exposure has "gone with" wider economic participation (per capita income) and political participation (voting). (Lerner 1958, 46)

The modernization paradigm conceives the West as providing the most developed model of societal attribute – "From the West came the stimuli that undermined the traditional society . . . for reconstruction of a modern society the West is still a useful model" (Lerner 1958, 47). Development when contextualized by modernization theory tends to be a repudiation of all socio-cultural attributes that are traditional. In Third World nations like India, health-related development and intervention programs are often financed by

international donor agencies. The latter draw heavily on modernization theory and emphasize the rejection of traditional socio-cultural
norms in order to achieve development (Nath 2000).

The objective of the Sonagachi Project was to disseminate awareness information about STDs and HIV/AIDS among sex workers in
Calcutta. The project also aimed to arrest the infection incidence
among the latter population. But in the long run the project resulted
in generating literacy campaigns and vocational training to the sex
workers and their kin. The project facilitated forming loan and
micro-credit facilities for the sex workers. It also resulted in the
unionization of the sex workers of Sonagachi. In a way, such development appears to subscribe to the basic facets of modernization
theory that postulate the correlation between gaining literacy with
economic and political agency. Yet the outcomes of the Sonagachi
Project cannot be recounted as progressive and gradual urbanization, because the sex workers are already in an urban setting, Sonagachi being in the heart of Calcutta. Neither did the project make
any effort to dislodge traditional elements of culture and society.
Modernization encompasses "dismantling all things non-Western
including traditional culture . . . traditional culture includes religion . . . it also includes indigenous gender roles to be replaced by
Western norms" (Melkote and Steeves 2001, 94). The Sonagachi
Project focused on mitigating the marginalized status of sex workers
and repudiating cultural stereotypes that enforced such marginalization. For this purpose the project emphasized re-articulation of
issues related to sex work, including the status of sex work itself by
defining the latter as a valid form of labor. The project stressed the
right of sex workers to avail healthcare and education opportunities.
But this cannot be said to be a reconstruction of traditional gender
roles. No efforts were made to dismantle the hierarchical social
system of India, based on class, caste, and gender.

As Oza (2001) notes, among the Indian Hindu population there is
a general propensity to perceive life-threatening venereal diseases
among sex workers as *karmic* or as a form of religious retribution
for profligacy. The Sonagachi Project endeavored to integrate sex
workers and their kin within the mainstream population. But it did
not attempt to transform traditional religious beliefs of the sex
workers or the public that might corroborate or sanction ostracization of sex workers as fallen women. The Sonagachi Project also did

not effectuate one of the tenets of modernization theory. The latter postulates that "stress on self-orientation serves to energize the individual, leading to technological innovation and rising economic productivity" (So 1990, 22). No attempts were made to emphasize the individual identity of the sex workers, rather the community identity of the latter was stressed. Rather endeavors were also made to integrate the sex workers within the greater Bengali community of Calcutta.

Encapsulating a Freirean philosophy and the Sonagachi Project

The HIV/AIDS intervention program undertaken at Sonagachi is participation oriented and based on the tenets of development, but does not subscribe to the modernization paradigm. Perhaps the postulations of Freire can be utilized to analyze the nature of the intervention program of the Sonagachi Project. Freire offers a vision of bypassing oppressive structures and facilitating social and political engagement among disenfranchised groups. As Downing (2001, 834) notes:

> Freire's pedagogy can serve as the core philosophy within which to think through the nature of the activist producer–active audience relationship . . . it proposes a democracy of the communication process, once more acknowledging the audience as joint-architects with the media producers, radically unlike the "they watch it, so we must be giving them what they need" ideology of commercial media.

Freire's conceptualization of the communication process incorporates dialogue that dismantles oppressive structures and democratizes socio-political participation. Freire's theory finds a reflection in the observations of Bakhtin for both put an emphasis on dialogue as an alternative and potent form of communication. "Bakhtin's emphasis on the dialogue of voices . . . could equally be applied to radical media as a dialogic, demographic public sphere within popular culture . . . both Freire and Bakhtin provide support for a dialogic vision of radical alternative media . . . that at their best are engaged with 'audiences' at their most active, producing as well as receiving media content" (Downing 2001, 835).

One of the characteristics of the Sonagachi Project was that the target population – the sex workers – were not considered to be passive recipients of information lacking in choice or agency, but instead they were treated as change agents themselves. (Blankenship, Friedman, Dworkin, and Mantell 2006; Jana, Banerjee, Saha and Dutta 1999). As noted previously, the peer education program generated by the Sonagachi Project succeeded in achieving outcomes beyond its immediate objectives of controlling transmission of HIV/AIDS and STDs. The community outreach programs brought sex workers together and facilitated a sense of camaraderie among them. Training of the sex workers by the program management as outreach workers, and subsequent dialogue among the sex workers themselves, helped to decrease the perceived powerlessness of a heavily marginalized community (Bandopadhyay, Ray, Banerjee et al. 2002). Perhaps such action undertaken by the sex workers themselves can be said to be in concurrence with Friere's observation that "the oppressed must intervene critically in the situation which surrounds them and whose mark they bear . . . while conviction of the necessity of the struggle is indispensible to the leadership, it is also necessary for the oppressed" (Freire 1970, 54).

Importantly, Freire did not emphasize mass media for achieving effective communication but focused on interpersonal interaction. The Sonagachi Project also did not utilize the mass media tools but rather focused on "face-to face interactivity" that Freire considered at the center of a communication process (Downing 2001, 834). The dialogue initiated by the sex workers with their peers effectively helped in disseminating awareness information about sexually transmitted diseases and safe sex behavior. Also it increased social participation by resulting in the formation of a sex workers' self-governed organization that looked after the needs and rights of its members. Perhaps the guiding principles of the Sonagachi Project can find a resonance in Freire's idea of a humanizing pedagogy "in which the leadership establishes a permanent relationship of dialogue with the oppressed . . . the method ceases to be an instrument by which the teachers can manipulate the students, because it expresses the consciousness of the students themselves" (Freire 1970, 55–6). Such a case as the Sonagachi Project in which the mantle of leadership is assumed by the oppressed themselves can propose a unique case-study especially when analyzed in the context of Freirean ideology of emancipation and empowerment.

The Sonagachi Project as an Example of Empowerment Communication

Empowerment communication has its theoretical framework based in participatory and development communication but is specifically geared towards fostering research agendas that facilitate social transformation and justice. As Mefalopulos (2002) observes, communication for development is motivated towards generating participation, dialogue, and dissemination of vital knowledge – "Communication can assist development by advocating and adopting models that genuinely require dialogue as a form of collaboration among all stakeholders and that genuinely require sharing knowledge as the best form of mutual education" (Mefalopulos 2002, 836). Yet empowerment of the target population often remains a desired but not achieved result. Empowerment communication, with its emphasis on power differentials, potentially offers analytical means of addressing structural inequalities in groups that historically have been marginalized. As White (2004) observes, empowerment needs to be based within the universal principles of social justice: "one framework of public responsibility that has broad cultural and political acceptance is the language of human and collective rights" (White 2004, 830).

Perhaps the following observation of Mefalopulos offers a description of empowerment communication in the most succinct way:

Empowerment communication intends to be a step further towards its development that gives control over their own lives to the very people who have traditionally been made passive, or partially active, recipients of those efforts by those in charge of development policies. While still within the boundaries of the current paradigm, empowerment communication also advocates its demolition, basing it on the genuine application of democratic ideals, which should by now pay more attention to the universal human rights regardless of other factors, e.g. nationality, religion and socio-economic status. (Mefalopulos 2002, 836)

Sex workers in India are vulnerable to HIV/AIDS infection due to reasons not restricted to unprotected sex alone. Their marginalized position in the social hierarchy results from a combination of factors like gender, class and social stigmatization, and ostracization. Their social exclusion compounds their marginalized status and enhances material deprivation. More than often they are rendered powerless to take decisions about their own health and welfare, and hence often do not respond favorably to behavior change intervention techniques (Jana, Basu, Rotheram-Borus, and Newman 2004). Consequently, conventional communication, which is aimed towards generating behavior change, may prove to be inadequate towards achieving the desired goal of adoption and implementation of safer sexual practices among the sex workers. "Given these conditions sex workers as a group will have to be enabled to break through the structural barriers that keep them excluded from access to resources as well as participation in society" (Jana, Banerjee, Saha and Dutta 1999, 6). Perhaps the implementation of empowerment communication in such a situation might be prudent. As Mefalopulos appropriately notes on empowerment communication, "even when paved by the best intention, communication cannot be the road to people's empowerment, unless a new paradigm will provide a plausible option for refusing or negating an external imposition to any given community or group of people" (Mefalopulos 2002, 836).

   While it can be postulated that the application of empowerment communication may be appropriate among sex workers in India, can the Sonagachi Project fall in the ranks of the said variety of communication? Evidently, the Sonagachi Project incorporated activities that were not included in the agenda of the initiative originally. The project succeeded in achieving its targeted outcomes – significant increase in condom usage and significant decrease in HIV/AIDS infection incidence. But in addition the project also generated literacy programs directed towards the sex workers and their kin, loan services, micro-credit initiatives and provident funds for the sex workers, and finally caused the trade unionization of the sex workers. The Sonagachi Project undertook efforts to prevent harassment of sex workers by the police, local anti-social elements, and pimps. The project also managed to incorporate the sex workers' children in mainstream schools. Out-of-school education and vocational training were also imparted to these children. Hence, the Sonagachi Project endeavored to mitigate the stigmatization of the targeted women both within and outside the realm of sex work.

In order to effectuate the peer outreach program, the sex workers were also given "on-the-job training and special capacity-building sessions" (Jana, Banerjee, Saha, and Dutta 1999, 4). Jana, Banerjee, Saha, and Dutta (1999) note such interactive training sessions increased the sex workers' self-confidence and paved the path for future initiatives such as forming their own micro-credit society. The sessions also inspired the sex workers to combine and form an exclusive platform for themselves. Referred to as the *Durbar Mohila Samnwaya Committee* (DMSC) the sex workers' collective evolved out of the Sonagachi Project and offered them an opportunity to assert their collective voices. "The DMSC furthered in-group recognition among sex workers, and the articulation and demand for their rights as workers" (Jana, Basu, Rotheram-Borus, and Newman 2004, 411). Importantly DMSC now participates actively in AIDS and sex-workers' conferences across the world and involves itself in issues pertaining to sex workers internationally (Hogg, Cahn, Katabira et al. 2002; Nath 2000).

Evidently the Sonagachi Project obtained outcomes that were not anticipated by the project initially. As Jana, Basu, Rotheram-Borus, and Newman (2004, 411) note: "even as the Sonagachi Project began with a vision of occupational health, it was not foreseen that over the course of a decade the sex workers would become a quasi-trade union." Additionally the Sonagachi Project facilitated vocational training and financial programs for the sex workers and their kin. It is evident that initiatives like the Sonagachi Project can ultimately transcend their primary agenda and facilitate greater outcomes. Perhaps it will be right to refer to such a mode of participatory communication and intervention as evidenced by the Sonagachi Project as empowerment communication. As Mefalopulos (2002, 836) notes: "participatory communication, and even more, empowerment communication, is not just about decision making in the development context, but it affects every aspect of the social, economic and political sphere of life."

Thus the Sonagachi Project besides facilitating safe sex practices managed to provide social, economic, and political agency to the sex workers. By rearticulating prostitution the project endeavored to de-stigmatize sex work and mitigate social powerlessness of the sex workers. By forming credit unions the project aimed to provide financial self-sufficiency to the sex workers. And by offering the opportunity of forming a union the project facilitated political visibility of the sex workers. Notwithstanding its initial objective of being a health behavior change endeavor, the project started to operate within the framework of public responsibility and the universalist discourse of human rights, which White (2004) terms as the essential element of empowerment communication.

Conclusion

"Success in the long term occurs when the developmental nature of prevention programs is recognized" (Jana, Basu, Rotheram-Borus, and Newman 2004, 413). The Sonagachi Project appears to incorporate the guiding principles of the participation communication paradigm and may serve as a relevant case-study for planning sustainable interventions among disempowered or marginalized groups across the world. While the project does not conform to theoretical frameworks of development such as modernization, it appears to encapsulate the Freirean philosophy of emancipation and empowerment. The Sonagachi Project also appears to incorporate characteristics of empowerment communication. Perhaps it will be relevant to note here that a future study can explore further such participatory communication frameworks in the light of the Habermasian theory of communicative action. The creation of a space by the project for dialogue and collective action can be analyzed in the context of Habermas' conceptualization of "public sphere."

One of the drawbacks of the Sonagachi Project is the lack of data verifying the effectiveness of the project. The researchers cite statistics from UNAIDS and NACO which show a significant drop in the incidence of HIV infection and a significant increase in condom usage in Sonagachi after the project was implemented. But the researchers themselves admit that no studies were undertaken that specifically measured the efficacy of the Sonagachi Project. As the authors emphasize, "a randomized controlled trial has yet to demonstrate the efficacy of the intervention model" (Jana, Basu, Rotheram-Borus, and Newman 2004, 406). It is however not certain whether the effectiveness of the Sonagachi model was tested or not. For Basu, Jana, Rotheram-Borus et al. (2004) note that the Sonagachi Project was replicated among a group of sex workers in North-Eastern India. The latter study results show the efficacy of a community-based intervention process in increasing safe sex practices and decreasing HIV/AIDS incidence. However the said study does not mention whether the intervention in North-Eastern India managed to replicate the multiple outcomes of the Sonagachi Project that included empowerment of the sex workers within social, political, and economic realms. Bandopadhyay, Ray, Banerjee, et al. (2002) also conducted in-depth focus group interviews that demonstrated the efficacy of the participation-based community development approach adopted by the Sonagachi Project. Notwithstanding the lack of concrete data ascertaining the effectiveness of the Sonagachi Project, one may observe that the unique methodology adopted by the initiative and its multiple outcomes emphasize the importance of a sustainable participation-based community intervention program. On a concluding note, the Sonagachi Project may be termed as an example of "sophisticated epistemology" in the field of development communication that, as Huesca (2003, 566) emphasizes, creates "an understanding of social reality in between people, in material contexts and in communication." In sum, the Sonagachi Project may be a development communication model for both further academic research as well as aid agencies funding similar projects.

10

Roma Project: A Case Study Set in Europe

Eva Szalvai

Introduction

During the past few decades the conceptual framework for international development has changed. In particular, the understanding of development communication has undergone a major paradigm shift as outlined in the earlier chapters. The earlier view, based on hard economic indicators such as GDP growth and a Western-type of modernization approach, had been long criticized. Relying on Marxist ideology (Frank 1969; Portas 1974) and the basic need approach (Grant 1978; Streeten 1979), critical development communication scholars started to look into socio-economic change not only from a materialistic but also from a structural standpoint of view (Huesca 2003b). Incorporation of some postmodern theories to critical view, such as feminism, environmentalism, and subaltern research influenced a major shift in the long-held views about development in the southern hemisphere (Mody 2003). Thus the embracing, rather than rejecting of local culture, religion, and ethics, together with the accentuation of traditional communication methods resulted in a significant change in the theories and practices of development communication (Melkote and Steeves 2001).

George Soros, the social commentator and philanthropist, is the founder of the Open Society Institute (OSI), an international network of NGOs dedicated to initiating and supporting civic society activities (Open Society Institute 2006). Soros's philosophy and the roots of his praxis are based on the theory of the Open Society, a notion first developed by Karl Popper in the middle of the twentieth century (Popper 1945). This chapter examines the forms and practices of development communication in the OSI's longitudinal project with Roma people in Central and Eastern Europe (OSI Initiatives 2006). The case study identifies the corresponding development paradigms present in the OSI's practices and communication techniques. It provides examples of the manner in which the OSI deals with cultural and economic issues of Roma people, as well as identifying forms of communication the project uses to reach Roma ethnic communities in Bulgaria, the Czech Republic, Hungary, Romania, and Russia.

After referring to the three paradigms in development communication, this chapter details the core principles of the OSI. Referring to their historical roots, there is a summary of the Roma situation in Central-Eastern Europe and the reasons behind the OSI's Roma initiative. Analyzing the different development communication discourses in the Roma Initiative's online presentation, the OSI's path for social change and the type of development communication used in the different practices throughout the 15 years of its project are detailed. Finally, the chapter concludes with a report on the results of the Roma Initiative and about its successor, the "Decade of Roma Inclusion" sponsored by several international organizations and supported by the OSI and the World Bank.

Through this case study it is argued that although all three development communication paradigm (modernization, critical, and empowerment) may be present in development projects, the empowerment model should serve as relevant communication form in any sustainable development. The examples of the Roma initiative may serve as a starting point for further understanding a given model of sustainable development communication, both in theory and in practice.

Overview of Social Change Models

Since the late 1990s qualitative research and post-structuralism have enriched the scholarly works on development communication. Development communication endeavors to link the concepts of the southern hemisphere, development, and communication, together. At the beginning of the twenty-first century, the big questions are: What do you do for us, to us, against us? Several current researchers base their theories on three major development models: modernization, critical/alternative, and liberation or empowerment theories (Melkote and Steves 2001). In the earlier understanding, development referred to social change, and communication was cited mainly in terms, as "the maintenance, modification and creation of culture" (Melkote and Steves 2001, 31). Nowadays, the goal is to achieve sustainable development that includes environmental and gender concerns along with critical cultural concerns.

Sustainable development communication uses mostly non-linear models based on intrapersonal, interpersonal, and group communication (that often includes organizational communication) together with consideration of local culture specifics (Mody 2003). Since in the long run, social change cannot be stopped or prevented, development refers to a directed and active social change within a community. It should not deny participatory communication, as communities are encouraged to exercise their right to discuss and include their own view on development of the objectives, imperatives, and methods (Huesca 2003b).

Modernization model

Briefly the modernization model and ideas are rooted in the colonization period. Originally, change in the Third World was to occur through exogenous factors with new ideas introduced from the outside – from the former colonizers. This mainstream development paradigm, prominent from the 1940s through the 1970s, is oriented around "progress measurement" via material, economic, and technological indicators. It promotes a *dirigiste* approach in which social change should be directed by the government bureaucrats, technological experts or technocrats, and the business elite of corporations (Melkote and Steves 2001). The research in this development positivism heavily relies on statistical data. Regarding the communication aspect, the weight of mass media is overwhelmingly high. Top-down communication is based on secular mass media with the official oppression of local religion or culture. In addition, few local ethical considerations are present. Development projects are initiated and mostly executed by international organizations (UN, WTO, IMF, World Bank) and national governments. Therefore, the context is macro or micro settings and the unit of analysis tends to be a nation (Melkote and Steves 2001).

Critical/alternative model

By the 1960s, even economists realized that the old modernization paradigm was not successful. Economic indicators clearly showed that this top-down, linear, Western model neither reduced Third World poverty nor promoted sustainable development (Black 2002). Interdisciplinary scholars from various fields of sociology, political economy, and communication, introduced critical theories on development such as the decentralization models, tricontinentalistic Marxist theories, cultural imperialism, and subaltern theories.

This critical paradigm, that included some of the postmodern research on gender, race, and class issues, has already intended to embrace spatial and cultural considerations in their analysis. Nevertheless, it was the work of Paolo Freire (1983) that caused a direct shift in the understanding of development communication.

Empowerment model

The deconstruction of the dominant paradigm was grounded on the discourse (Escobar 2000; Sosale 2002) and also included economic, sociological, and psychological deconstruction. Culture and community with religion, gender (e.g., Wilkin 2005), and environmental issues became the focal point of examination. In communication studies, more researchers viewed culture and communications as one, as modes of representation or meaning (Arnst 1996; Belbase 1994; Melkote and Steeves 2001). Place gained over space, local over global, and community, as unit became the focus of analysis. Power started to be viewed dialectically. Protest and social movement became part of the idea of network societies. With this breach of global spaces, ordinary people started to gain voice and power for receiving and creating their own destiny. Such an approach aims to make local places alive, visible, and interconnected both with each other and the world. (Escobar 2000) A holistic view of culture is gaining place with the understanding of naturally interactive cultures and a-morph self-change. Therefore, the role of new development communicators is to build trust cautiously while acquiring local knowledge and spurring the involvement of local people (Melkote, in-class communication, July 2006).

Freire's empowerment paradigm is based on a different educational approach. Dehumanization stems from power and humanity is stolen not only from the oppressed, but also from the oppressor. According to Freire, "the great humanistic and historical task of the oppressed" is "to liberate themselves and their oppressors as well" (Freire 1983, 29) as freedom is the "indispensable condition for the quest for human completion" (p. 31). In essence: "If men produce social reality . . . then transforming that reality is an historical task, a task for men" (p. 37). Quite obviously he relates ethics to social change. Participatory communication becomes a necessity for such empowerment and change (Cadiz 2005; Huesca 2003b). The question then remains: how can power be shared following this new kind of social change? Since power is both created and exercised, institutions are needed that facilitate the paradigm of empowerment. Such an institution is The Open Society Institute.

Case Study Methodology

A large amount of detailed information is posted on the Internet regarding the activities of the Open Society Institute that includes submission guidelines for grants and scholarships, news on the various initiatives the OSI is engaged with, and reports on the progress of their projects. This case study is focused on the OSI's report and studies presented online on its Roma Initiative.

This analysis adopts an interpretive research method. It focuses on the discourse used by the OSI in these online communications such as studies, news, and reports, regarding its Roma project. Some of these studies are prepared by other organizations that are not directly affiliated to the OSI. Being a non-profit organization, the activities of the OSI are publicly monitored. Moreover, the OSI relies on extended network systems involving both vertical and horizontal relations with other large and small organizations across nations. *Overall, the professional reports of the OSI were highly valuable for the critical analysis on development communication discourse in the Roma projects.*

Open Society Institute (OSI)

With years of hard work, the well-known billionaire, George Soros created a network of non-profit organizations (including a university) that currently is present in 29 countries and active in more than 60 additional countries. For example, the Open Society Initiative for Southern Africa (OSISA) and the Open Society Initiative for West Africa (OSIWA), are governed by regional boards of directors and staffs and provide grants in 27 African countries. The OSIWA and the OSISA foundations seek to "locate visions of open societies in their respective regions which serve to combat negative perceptions about Africa. The initiatives' strength lies in their roots in communities and countries that stimulate and create African solutions to African challenges" (Open Society Institute 2006).

The OSI offers a great variety of grants, fellowships, and scholarship for development purposes such as: grants for "enhancing coalitions of women's rights and HIV/AIDS organizations in select African countries;" scholarship that aims at the "equitable deployment of knowledge and communications resources for civic empowerment and effective democratic governance;" or a fellowship that "enables innovative professionals – including journalists, activists, academics, and practitioners – to work on projects that inspire meaningful public debate, shape public policy, and generate intellectual ferment within the Open Society Institute" (Open Society Institute 2006). These foundations are independent, autonomous institutions in their pursuit of open society activities as the "priorities and specific activities of each Soros foundation are determined by a local board of directors and staff in consultation with George Soros and OSI boards and advisors" (Open Society Institute 2006).

Theoretical Background of the Open Society

Soros' life-long international work as a philanthropist is fundamentally based on Karl Popper's liberal democracy theory (1945) that defends the idea of a so-called Open Society. The idea of the open society is partly rooted in the works of the philosopher Berson, who wondered how the government's role could be enhanced within the capitalist system. Disenchanted from the Marxist view of economics, Popper (1945) expanded the notion of open society as the adversary of totalitarianism in defense of democratic liberalism. Just as Popper, Soros – the "critical-rationalist" as he self-professed – not only defends a type of globalization based on open societies, but equally stands for the scope of intellectual influence. Clearly a reformist activist, his theoretical approach to development and globalization rooted in his praxis (Soros 1994, 2000).

Apart from Popper, the theoretical thrust of Soros also relies on a modified version of Pierre Bourdieu's theory of practice (Bourdieu 1977). Endorsing Bourdieu's, reflexivity (Bourdieu and Wacquant 1992) – that social science researchers should be aware of their own interference with the research subject as the research objectivity of social sciences is always influenced by subjectivity of the researcher – Soros (1994) considers that events "are facts and observations that are true or false, depending on whether or not they correspond to the facts" (First section, para. 3). Thus, knowledge is incomplete, and this imperfect understanding of reality modifies reality itself, (Soros 1994). Rooted in years of experience in financial markets, Soros applies reflexivity in his philosophy and theories on economy. He believes that in an interconnected and interdependent world, societies should be open to the outside, allowing free flow of goods, ideas, and people; and open inside with free flow of thoughts and social mobility (Soros 2006). Overall, he recommends critical thinking through self-observation, reflection, and self-learning as responses to altered circumstances (Soros 2006).

In his global strategy, economic freedom is mingled with some governmental intervention through centralized economic planning in the field of environmentalism and social justice that may also include state ownership in the means of production. According to Soros (2003, 2006), well-established international laws could regulate private and government practices, while ensuring global justice and the civic society activities of cultures and nations. The Soros foundations clearly represent Soros' ideas on the open society while encouraging socially reflective and responsible actions.[1]

Through the past 17 years, the Soros foundations have grown considerably and gained international attention. His primary foundation has disbursed over $400 million annually in recent years (Open Society Institute 2006). In line with the philosophy and ideas of its founder, Soros, the mission statement of the OSI clearly states its interest in local initiatives. It also exhibits advocacy for some level of glocalization (Roberson 1992) while tying local and global interests together in a socio-cultural interdependency:

> The Open Society Institute seeks to shape public policies that assure greater fairness in political, legal, and economic systems and safeguard fundamental rights. On a local level, the OSI implements a range of initiatives to advance justice, education, public health, and independent media. At the same time, the OSI builds alliances across borders and continents on issues such as corruption and freedom of information. The OSI places a high priority on protecting and improving the lives of marginalized people and communities. (Open Society Institute 2006)

Working with marginalized communities is among the main goals of the OSI. They are active in five sectors of social life: freedom and democracy; human rights; education; public health and access to care; and transparency and access to information. By targeting discriminatory practices and developing local Roma communities, the OSI's Roma Initiative aimed to aid the inclusion of the Roma diasporic communities in eight countries (Open Society Institute 2006). The research reported in this chapter matches the five targeted sectors with the activities of the Roma Initiative, and attempts to determine the development communication paradigms used in the process of these practices.

The OSI'S Path for Social Change: The Romani Case

The OSI has worked for over 14 years with marginalization issues of the European Roma population. As such, the Roma Initiative was a social change project that targeted the situation of the Roma people (also called Romani or, commonly, "Gypsy"); it is one of the most controversial diasporic minorities in Europe. The Roma Initiative and it successor, the *Decade of Roma Inclusion*, is a cross-cultural longitudinal project that the OSI has worked for over 17 years.

Originally the Roma people originated from the Punjab and Rajasthan region of northern India. Their language, Romani, still maintains elements of Urdu that was commonly spoken in the region during the Persian Empire (Fraser 1992). They migrated away in retreat from the advance of Islam during the eleventh century. The Roma migrated across the Indian Ocean to the then Ottoman Empire and then on across the Mediterranean to the European Continent (Rishi 1976). They arrived in Central and Eastern Europe during the fourteenth and fifteenth centuries on the coat-tails of incursions by the Ottoman Empire (Romani.org 2008).

Although they are referred to as "Gypsies" in English or "Gitanos" in Spanish, they prefer to be called as Roma or Romani (Romani. org 2008). The Roma culture holds to traditions and has difficulties adopting changes in social structure (Fraser 1992). Their cultural cohesiveness has faced overwhelming pressures through centuries by continuous persecution from empires and neighbors alike. Although they lost almost 500,000 people, they survived the ethnic cleansing of the Holocaust during the Third Reich (Crowe and Kolsti 1991). In 2007, the number of Roma people in Europe was estimated at ten million, of which around 80 percent live in Central-Eastern Europe (OSI 2007).

The Roma people comprise Europe's largest trans-border ethnic minority (Rorke and Wilkens 2005). Their diasporic communities face strong discrimination – including racial and gender – practices that targets their way of life, belief system, social organization, and culture (Rorke and Wilkens 2005; ERRC 2008; Romani.org 2008). Unfortunately, the Roma people lost the social safety net offered by the socialist system. The fall of socialism in Central Europe in 1989 resulted in a worsening situation for the already marginal Roma people.

The Roma population's comparably limited prospects have barely improved over centuries of persistent stigma and discrimination on the part of the rest of the population, including governments at all levels in many parts of the country. Their overall economic situation arguably has gotten worse since the collapse of the Soviet era totalitarian regime, which tended at the very least to guarantee more jobs and a minimum level of support to all residents. (Hoover 2007, 36)

Another example is given by Will Guy, an OSI collaborator in Czechoslovakia, who observed that "the first tangible experience of this brave new world was not a sudden expansion of civic liberties but of harsh realities as any [Roma] were flung out of their predominantly manual jobs in the now virtually redundant heavy industries" (Rorke and Wilkens 2005, 8). It is mostly due to the aid of NGOs such as the OSI that the Roma situation gains public exposure and has the hope for social improvement and inclusion.

During the initiative, OSI employees cooperated directly with Roma individuals and community leaders in order "to help them mobilize their communities, to help themselves" (Rorke and Wilkens 2005, 4).Moreover, the OSI employs people with a Roma background in their projects in order to enhance culture proximity with targeted Roma communities (OSI Initiatives 2006). Employment affiliation with OSI projects also enhances the acceptance and credibility of Roma among people from the majority population (Rorke and Wilkens 2005).

The countries involved with the Roma Initiative are the so-called transitional societies. After the fall of the socialism in 1989, Central and Eastern Europe has been going through transition, consolidation, and expansion of democracy. Given the multi-country complexity, poisoned history and political sensitivity of the Roma situation, as well as their ingrained cultural stance as outsider-nomads, it is not surprising that only an NGO like the OSI would be well placed to tackle the trans-national nature of the issue.

The Roma Initiative is the OSI's umbrella program for all its Roma-related efforts. The Initiative tries to assess and aid the change in the Roma people's situation in these transitional societies. The Initiative aims to improve "the social, political, and economic situation of Romani populations while helping to build an indigenous Romani leadership" (*OSI News* 2005, 4). According to *OSI News*, more than $34 million has been spent in 12 years on different Roma community projects within the program. The Roma Initiative fills an organizational vacuum, seeks to redress discrimination and offers innovative solutions based on the latest development communication techniques.

Summary of "Current State" Roma Situation

An OSI report, *Equality for Roma in Europe: A Roadmap for Action*, (OSI 2006) identified a number of factors that makes the work with Roma diasporic group more difficult and limit the progress of community development. Among these factors they reported the following: lack of strategic focus of funded initiatives; low levels of Roma participation in public life; insufficiently robust legislative frameworks; the need for an integrated approach; high levels of anti-Gypsyism; challenges to the preservation of Roma identity and culture; and lack of political will.

These factors clearly indicate a high level of discrimination and the lack of willingness to change from the ruling majority (OSI Initiatives 2006). Unfortunately, there are many examples of discriminatory practices. Among them we found *stigmatization* of Roma, *discriminatory practices* in the labor and capital (e.g. bank loans) market, *segregated education system*, *insufficiency in health-care*, and strong *gender discrimination* against Roma women.

Development Communication in the Roma Initiative's Online Presentation

Development as discourse is "a set of interpretations that are structured through institutional statements about people, places, and problems" (Wilkin 2005, 199). Development communication discourse perpetuates the interest of agency, and is thus power-loaded. According to Wilkin (2005, 199), the "categories constructed through development discourse not only shape problems and those perceived to suffer from those problems, but also legitimize appropriate solutions." Studying the reports allowed me to interpret how the OSI assessed Roma people and their needs, and how these needs were addressed. The information obtained from the reports is also a good source for defining the OSI's view on development and determining which development model is prominent in their practices.

To begin with, the Roma Initiative counted on three major types of activities (*Open Society News* 2005, 4):

1 Part of the strategy of investing directly in Roma, the OSI offered support for Romani rights NGOs (e.g., European Roma Rights Centre, Roma Participation Program (RPP)) to combat discrimination and build alliances, particularly around the international Romani-led movement to desegregate schools.
2 The OSI's fellowships and its programs for women, children, and youth, in the fields of public health, media, justice, and education.
3 Pursuing fast and flexible grant making with a focus on the younger generation of activists and students; ensuring direct participation of Roma in project implementation, design, and evaluation; forging long-term partnerships based on coherent and sustainable strategies.

These activities accentuate participatory communication (PC), which is linked to the empowerment paradigm. Moreover, even development support communication (DSC) elements can be found in their educational approach and the Roma women's programs: the OSI supports Roma leadership in the abolition of local discriminatory practices in schooling and offers aid for the empowerment process of Roma women. "The categories constructed through development discourse not only shape problems and those perceived to suffer from those problems, but also legitimize appropriate solutions" (Wilkin 2005, 199).

Participation is a basic element in the empowerment model: "People who are the objects of policy need to be involved in the definition, design, and execution of the development process" (Melkote and Steeves 2001, 333). The results illustrate that the OSI often uses the empowerment paradigm in its work with Roma people. Nevertheless, sometimes elements of the modernization (e.g., top-down communication) and the critical/alternative models are also present in their approach – mostly when they must deal with the interconnected communities, both locally and internationally.

Years of Rappaport's research defines empowerment as a "mechanism by which individuals, organizations, and communities gain control and mastery over social and economic conditions . . . over democratic participation in their community . . . and over their stories" (Melkote and Steeves 2001, 355). The accentuation of this empowerment is used throughout the reports: "OSI's fellowships and its programs for women, children and youth, public health, media, justice, and education have also developed a wide range of initiatives to give Romani communities immediate assistance as well as empower them to secure their rights and end their marginalization" (Wilkens and Rostas 2005, 4), or "The Roma Cultural Participation Project supports the cultural inclusiveness and empowerment of Roma" (Rorke and Wilkens 2005, 12). Other reference shows that any funding "should be . . . guided by one simple criterion: whether in its intended or unintended consequences the initiative empowers Roma" (Rorke and Wilkens 2005, 6). These are good indicators that throughout the Roma development project the OSI intended to use the empowerment model.

Another important element of the empowerment model is participatory communication. According to Waters (2002, 91), participatory communication "stipulates that reflection and action should be guided by dialogue, that is communication that is democratic, collaborative, and open, geared toward the mutual engagement of social actors as equal subjects." Examining OSI online reports on the Romani cases (*Open Society News* 2005; OSI Initiatives 2006; Rorke and Wilkens 2005), the discourse clearly indicates elements of participatory communication. In the funding strategy approach the OSI included the need for "direct participation of Roma in program design, implementation, and evaluation" that clearly represents bottom-up communication during the project (Rorke and Wilkens 2005, 2). The same report points out the necessity of active involvement of Roma people in the projects: "substantive Romani involvement and partnership" (p. 5).

Participation in the Initiative was somewhat directed as the development projects had aimed to achieve certain goals such as improved education, liberation of women, or preservation of ethnic culture. Nevertheless, the Initiative relied mostly on the concept of Freire on conscientization. According to Freire's concept, it is necessary to facilitate the "conscientization of marginalized people globally of unequal social, political, and spatial structures in their societies" (Melkote and Steeves 2001, 339). We can observe such processes mostly in the educational and women-related projects. The OSI's trust in younger Romani activists who "possess the requisite skills to engage in grassroots campaigning as well as in international advocacy" (Rorke and Wilkens 2005, 5), also indicates the OSI's consideration for the active participation of local community members.

The OSI documentation also shows that the OSI stresses importance on constant dialogue with Roma communities. According to Freire "development communication should be practiced not as message communication but rather as emancipatory dialogue, a particular form of non-exploitative, egalitarian dialogue" (Melkote and Steeves 2001, 299). The OSI documentation claims that the success of the Roma development initiative "requires transcending conventional donor–recipient relationships and fostering dynamic partnerships with Romani civic organizations based upon trust, transparency, and reciprocity" (Rorke and Wilkens 2005, p. 5). One in particular, the major grant program, the Roma Participation Program (RPP) aims to "support Roma activism in Central and Eastern Europe to take charge of their lives, to participate in decisions that affect them, and to advocate for their rights as equal citizens of their own countries" (OSI Initiatives 2006).

OSI documentation also shows that the OSI stresses importance on constant dialogue with Roma communities. According to Melkote and Steeves (2001, 299) "development communication should be practiced not as message communication but rather as emancipatory dialogue, a particular form of non-exploitative, egalitarian dialogue." OSI reports claim that the success of the Roma development initiative "requires transcending conventional donor–recipient relationships and fostering dynamic partnerships with Romani civic organizations based upon trust, transparency, and reciprocity" (Rorke and Wilkens 2005, 5). Working with marginalized communities and achieving fluid information exchange is always a delicate process. Understanding the culture and the marginalization of the Roma is particularly delicate in extreme problems, such as drug abuse.

Participatory communication and community empowerment involves not only the members of the targeted community but also the development agents. Importantly, the OSI makes special efforts to prepare its staff properly and enhance their ability for conducting dialogue with Roma people: "Organizations working with Roma need to invest in staff training to ensure that their staff members are tolerant and unbiased" (Rorke and Wilkens 2005, 3). Participatory communication should be an educational process for the participants and for the researchers (Melkote and Steeves 2001, 338). As observed, educating the OSI employees is in accordance with participatory research. The role of the OSI employees involved with the Roma Initiative is collaborative as facilitators and activists. Creative solutions are necessary in order to ensure dialogue. Such a new initiative was the appointment of so-called "Roma health mediators" whose task is to improve the Roma community's access to comprehensive health care in Bulgaria.

> Launched in 2004, the initiative focuses on training Roma individuals to serve as links or "bridges" between their own communities and local healthcare systems, which are almost unanimously staffed by non-Roma. The goal is to identify and overcome the numerous impediments – primarily cultural, but also economic and educational – that limit the inclination or ability of community members to seek out and obtain health care, particularly preventive care.
>
> Mediators are trained to achieve these goals by focusing on both sides of the equation. On the one hand, they seek to raise awareness within Roma communities as to how, when, where, and why to place greater priority on health care. At the same time, they focus on improving providers' understanding of, sensitivity to, and response to cultural differences between themselves and Roma. (Hoover 2007, 75)

This example underlines the efforts that the OSI makes to achieve dialogue and social change. Learning more about Roma culture can help to reduce – and ultimately eliminate – discriminatory views of people from the majority culture. Freire's notions of empowerment only can be achieve with such culture mediation.

Development should offer a chance for betterment (Black 2002). Overall, the Roma Initiative aimed for the empowerment of Roma people, intended to achieve social justice for the Roma, and to help them to build capacity and equity. Unfortunately, the community development efforts were not as successful as expected. It is reported in the *Open Society News*: "Since the mid-1990s . . . mobilization for political activity has come not from the grassroots but from what I'd call the middle class – the few Roma who were educated under the former communist regime, who had some schooling, who finished high school and entered universities" (Bitu 2005, 11). Future programs such as the Decade of Roma Inclusion, should concentrate on the creation of a larger platform of community activists.

Roma Inclusion Projects and Development Communication Models

All five sectors of social life that the OSI defined in its Mission Statement were represented through the various projects of the Roma Initiative. Based on Melkote's comparative table on the theory of modernization and the empowerment paradigm (Melkote and Steeves 2001, 352), table 10.1 summarizes the different Roma projects indicating the type of development communication model used in these projects.

Participation is a basic element in the Empowerment model: "People who are the objects of policy need to be involved in the definition, design, and execution of the development process" (Melkote and Steeves 2001, 333). Thus, advocacy for community issues formed part of the Roma Initiative. The Roma Participation Program (RPP) aimed for the civic and political participation of Roma people while promoting equality of Romani ethnicities. To achieve this goal, the OSI helped Roma people to promote local community activists offering "direct investment in Roma and Romani-led NGOs through strategic coherence combined with fast and flexible grant-making" (Wilkens and Rostas 2005, 4). RPP not only offered institutional support for these grass-roots Romani NGOs, but also got involved with training programs. The OSI strongly supported self-development initiatives.

Critical scholars such as Escobar, Mody, or Wilkin noted that "participation, without concomitant changes in structural conditions, may not be efficient to foster substantive social change" (Wilkin 2005, 205). Therefore, the OSI's effort to work with conjunct communities and with larger – national and international – social structures is essential for the success of sustainable development in their Roma projects. The newly founded Romani NGOs aimed to achieve changes in the practices of ethnic communication

Table 10.1 OSI Roma Initiative projects and development communication models

Social sphere	Project	Goal	Focus	Development models[a]
Freedom and democracy	Roma Participation Program (RPP)	Civil and political participation Promote equality	Ethnic communication Roma internal policies Anti-discriminatory information and actions	Mostly EMP
Human rights	Roma Participation Program (RPP) and Equal Rights for Roma Communities (ERRC)	Right to equal protection under the law	Exposure to international affairs	EMP and somewhat MOD
	Network Women's Program	Empowering women	Addressing ingrained prejudices, leadership development, and women's rights training	Mostly EMP and CRIT
Education	Roma Education Initiative (REI), Roma Culture Initiative (RCI), and Roma Memorial University Scholarship Program (RMUSP)	Educational/legal reform Foster cultural diversity	Scholarships and educational initiatives Culture initiatives	EMP

Continued

Table 10.1 *Continued*

Social sphere	Project	Goal	Focus	Development model[a]
Public health and access to care	Public health program	Empowerment in the health care system	Information Data collection Increasing professional opportunities	EMP and MOD
Transparency and information access	Network media programs (NMP)	Media access and Romani media development	TV and radio news agencies Development of Roma reporters	EMP
	Roma translations	Language preservation	Language promotion and grants for reporters Books on Roma culture by Roma authors	

[a]Empowerment model (EMP); Critical paradigm (CRIT); Modernization model (MOD)

reinforcing anti-discriminatory actions (OSI Initiatives 2006). On the other hand, RPP also supports broad-based campaigns that target systematic national and international policy reforms.

The OSI advocates that the anti-discriminatory laws of the European Union (EU) need to be applied equally; thus "improve information about the laws and strengthen equality commissions and ombudsman's offices" is highly important (Rorke and Wilkens 2005, 17). In their approach, some elements of the modernization paradigm such as top-down communication and Westernization are also present as they must pass on the information and educate EU laws and practices. Nevertheless, being a cross-national ethnic group, exposure of Romani leaders, "both male and female," to international affairs is crucial to Roma communities (OSI Initiatives 2006). The *Equal Rights for Roma Communities* (ERRC) aimed to achieve right to equal protection under the law for Roma people (OSI 2006).

According to Wilkin (2005, 201): "in practice, gender appears to operate in a way that essentializes women according to their bio-logical conditions rather than account for their social, political, and economic relationships." Gender discrimination is a complex ques-tion when working in patriarchal minority groups. There is a con-tradiction between identity and gender equality particularly in Romani culture with its accentuated patriarchal system.

OSI projects and practices address women's issues from the root of gender discrimination. Gender and power relations have elements of critical and the empowerment development paradigm. In her paper on gender discrimination, Bogdanić, an activist of "Better Life," a Croatian Romani women NGO, reported to the Roma Decade:

> if one protects the rights of minority groups, then one also protects a minority culture that is patriarchal. The main point of this feminist argument is that multicultural liberalism argues for protection of the rights of minority groups, but ignores the unequal relations of power within minority groups and the gender discrimination that exists within them. (Bogdanić 2005, 2)

Thus, in order to advocate for gender equality of Roma women, development activists cannot rely on participatory communication exclusively. Information dissemination, thus top-down communication on women's right, teachings about motherhood based on equal roles in families, and so on, becomes a necessary communication practice. Unfortunately, such teaching can rightly be perceived as attempt to change cultural traditions. As Bogdanić also asserts: "There is a clear conceptual contradiction between the choice of framing the issue in these terms and any goal of Romani women's empowerment" (Bogdanić 2005, 2).

Despite the difficulties, it is essential to examine the empowerment of women and focus on their unique issues. With feminist criticism, their approach is based on the empowerment and also on the critical development paradigms. With the aid of Network Women's Program's initiative the OSI organized "leadership development and women's rights training to develop, link, and catalyze a core group of committed Romani women leaders" (Rorke and Wilkens 2005, 10). Giving voice to Roma women, sharing their stories in diverse forums such as conferences, in reports, on the Internet, may be considered one of the ways participatory communication will efficiently help to abolish gender discrimination and aid social change. As the OSI denotes, it is important to "figure out how all of us can develop a discourse about gender and equality within the Romani community without creating irreparable divisions and disruptions" (Bitu 2005, 11).

Yet Westernization or ethnic culture loss is a likely outcome from the immersion of ethnic children in the existing education systems. The modernization model often applied in any project such as ethnic minorities cannot determine the general school curriculum. Through the Roma Culture Initiative (RCI), community outreach is an important part of Romani minority culture and social acceptance. RCI is "focused on the promotion of greater cultural awareness among younger Roma and on supporting scholarly research covering new grounds" (Rorke and Wilkens 2005, 12). The initiative fosters diversity and includes ethical issues in the solution of discrimination. The OSI places special emphasis on the importance of a collaborative effort: "Success will require multinational strategies and cooperation. It will require sharing lessons learned and best practices" (Rorke and Wilkens 2005, 3). Therefore, the empowerment development discourse is clearly present in the culture preservation effort.

The Roma ethnic preservation effort is further strengthened by the OSI's Network Media Program (NMP) initiative. This initiative fosters the learning and use of the Roma language in the Mass Media. According to OSI, "current assistance covers close to 25 television and radio outlets and news agencies in 11 countries" (Rorke and Wilkens 2005, 13).Furthermore, there is a special program that promotes Romani written language. According to Rorke and Wilkens's report, the "Roma Translation Project supported the translation and publication of 28 titles on Romani history, culture, and society in the national languages of 10 different countries across Central and Eastern Europe" (p. 14). These programs offer efficient aid to Roma empowerment as adequate communication strategies emphasize Roma contributions to society, and promote the benefits of tolerance and diversity in a democracy. As Rourke and Wilkens wrote: "the outside world must learn more about Romani culture and people, and we must challenge the verdict that Roma are born guilty" (p. 17).

Applying Melkote's comparative table on the modernization and the empowerment paradigm (Melkote and Steeves 2001, 362), the OSI's Roma Initiative mostly corresponds to the empowerment communication model although also uses the other two types of development communication models. The Initiative is interested in the empowerment of Roma people on the basis of social justice. Using diversity as a standard, the OSI believes that underdevelopment stems from the lack of power and control of Roma people over economic, political, and cultural resources. The context of the majority of Roma programs is community based with OSI agency as facilitators, collaborators, and participants in the individual and community development of Roma people. OSI uses a non-linear participatory communication model while conveying information and helping Roma empowerment.

The Future of the Roma Initiative

After several years of grassroots efforts, the OSI's Roma projects resulted in a new Pan-European program, the Decade of Roma Inclusion (DRI) to run from 2005 to 2015. The DRI is an action framework, supported (although not administered) by the OSI and the World Bank. Designed to monitor the improvement of the socio-economic status of the Roma people across the region, the program is endorsed by the prime ministers of eight countries (Bulgaria, Croatia, the Czech Republic, Hungary, Macedonia, Romania, Serbia-Montenegro, and Slovakia), and supported by the European Commission, the Council of Europe, the Council of Europe Development Bank, and the United Nations Development Program (Decade of Roma Inclusion 2006). The participating states "made a political commitment to close the gap in welfare and living conditions between the Roma and the non-Roma and to break the cycle of poverty and exclusion" (OSI Initiatives 2006).

The establishment of this new 10-year program indicates that ethnic development projects involve long-term processes and the constant cooperation of all the related and connected institutions, communities, and their members. "The Decade represents the fullest recognition to date that ensuring Roma equal access to education, housing, employment, and health care is a European issue requiring a multilateral and long-term approach" (Wilkens and Rostas 2005, 4).

Development agents accumulate locally gained experience and knowledge through participatory communication (Melkote and Steeves 2001). This pool of information is created within the context of various cultures and based in the interaction of different majority and minority culture groups. It does not contain elements of power differences among participating cultures. Thus, this shared pool of information gained through participatory communication of OSI field workers and Roma people (Decade Watch 2007) creates a new realm of globalization. It can be applied in the context of community projects or in other locations and cultures. Through this exchange of information and experience, OSI is creating a global know-how using "interlocalization" as a tool (Szalvai 2008).

"Interlocalization" defines a domination-free interconnectedness of two or more cultures in an international context. As a result of interlocalization, participants of such processes "*navigate* the turbulence of cross-cultural dynamics in order to co-create a constructive future together with cultural others" (LeBaron and Pillay 2007, 58). Thus, the OSI's longitudinal project the Roma Initiative active in several European countries provides an example for new forms of globalization (Szalvai 2008).

Conclusions

The research presented in this chapter was based on three paradigms and introduced the major principles of the OSI. The analyses of the different development communication discourses in this OSI program provided an opportunity to identify the various development communication forms used in the different practices throughout the 15 years of the Roma Initiative. Its successor, the Decade of Roma Inclusion, makes way for further development of the original OSI initiative towards the betterment of the Romani situation in Europe as well as a greater understanding of the role of development communication.

Development projects can be performed across nations, even those that involve power relations among ethnicity/race, gender, and, class. Such efforts justify development communication activists and scholars in understanding and dealing with development in a community base and not in state settings. Longitudinal ethnic programs such as the Roma Initiative provide good opportunities to analyze the success and failure of NGO-supported development projects.

Development occurs with the participation of organizations and individuals. Staff as the agent of development communication should be properly selected, prepared, and trained for getting involved with community members. They are the individuals who conduct and foster participatory or development support communication. Through learning about the selection/hiring practices, training projects, and other human resource experiences of the OSI, HRM researchers could gain valuable insight into human resource management of development-related NGOs.

This case study of the OSI on Roma development indicated that different development communication paradigms, including the empowerment model, should be present in sustainable development projects. The complexity of development requires complex actions and adjunct projects in an increasingly interconnected global world.

Note

1   The Founder of the OSI is George Soros. Soros (originally: Schwartz György) was born in 1930 in a Hungarian Jewish family. He graduated from the London School of Economics in 1952, and moved to the US in 1954, with the intention of making enough money to become a self-supported writer-philosopher. In March 2008, his net worth was estimated by Forbes over $9.0 billion that made him ninety-seventh richest person in the world ("Forbes 400", 03.05.2008). Since 1979, he has given away a total of $5 billion from his wealth through his charitable organizations and group ("Forbes 400", 03.05.2008).

For his theoretical and practical contribution to human knowledge and social betterment he received honorary doctoral degrees from several universities in England, Hungary, and the US. As Paul Volcker, former Chairman of the US Federal Reserve Bank, wrote in the foreword of Soros' book, *The Alchemy of Finance*, in 2003:

> George Soros has made his mark as an enormously successful speculator, wise enough to largely withdraw when still way ahead of the game. The bulk of his enormous winnings is now devoted to encouraging transitional and emerging nations to become "open societies," open not only in the sense of freedom of commerce but – more important – tolerant of new ideas and different modes of thinking and behavior. (p. xiv)

11

Summary and Conclusions

Thomas L. McPhail

Introduction

This chapter pulls together the materials from the preceding chapters and attempts to integrate the materials from the first five chapters with the next five chapters, which were written by eminent scholars in the field of development communication. The contents reflect an interdisciplinary perspective. Following a review and highlights of the materials, a series of findings and insights from the interdisciplinary approaches will contribute to the reframing of the field.

Chapter 1 looked at the early phases of development communication. This was marked by US President Harry Truman's call in his inaugural address, following World War II. The address was a mixture of concern for the emerging threat of communism with a genuine concern about spreading the economic benefits of industrialization and capitalism to other regions of the world. Over the next two decades this concern manifested itself through a theory of modernization which led to several development communication projects across the southern hemisphere. The funding for these various projects came primarily from US Federal grants but some others came from university projects, or large US Foundations. Despite the concern and funding the great transition of the Third World into economic nations like the industrial countries based in the North failed to materialize. Some of the Third World nations became worse off as corrupt regimes siphoned off development aid to their military or family relatives.

Yet two fairly recent activities represent a positive movement in the development communication sector. The first is the launching in July, 2007 of the National Indigenous Television (NITV) in Australia. NITV is produced for and by aboriginals so that their culture and language may be portrayed in a positive light. The network supports locally produced shows on behalf of a number of varied aboriginal communities. The other is the creation of a global network of indigenous television broadcasters. Their goal is to create an international television network delivered via satellite. The first meeting was held in New Zealand in 2008 and the promotion and protection of the Maori language and culture was a central theme. Indigenous broadcasters and producers from Canada, Australia, Europe, Fiji, the Nordic countries, Hawaii, Taiwan, and South Africa were in attendance. Future meetings will be held in Wales in 2012, and Canada in 2014. Canada in 1999 started its own Aboriginal Television Network (APTN) to serve the widely dispersed aboriginal peoples across Canada, particularly in the North. There are other more modest media systems around the world but by and large they all receive some type of federal funding from their governments. This could be the exact type of subsidy that the WTO attempts to make illegal under future free trade agreements involving broadcasting.

During the same period a religious-based movement labeled Liberation Theology began to spread throughout poor regions, particularly in Latin America. It looked for means to spread social justice and soon focused on land reform as being central to long-term meaningful structural progress. This movement also failed since in the 1970s the top leadership of the Catholic Church crushed the actions of social activist priests and nuns. Currently a number of evangelical Protestant denominations are pursuing a number of development-related projects, including micro-banking.

Looking back, the Liberation movement failed due to its own success. It started to have an impact and this eventually would have altered the social order. Initially the movement sought economic and social justice for those who were at the bottom strata of society. But they eventually came to the conclusion that the needed structural change required political acumen and action. This is when they attracted attention from senior bureaucrats and politicians. Two cases outlined in the book reflect this. The first is the Canadian Broadcasting Corporation's (CBC) "Farm Radio Forum." It was a radio series promoting agricultural reform and after a few decades they calculated that meaningful reform would not come about without political action requiring members to run for Parliament in Ottawa. The federally funded CBC network soon found itself under political pressure to cancel the program or face disastrous funding cuts. The other case was the liberation movement across Latin America which gravitated to land reform as a root solution ultimately requiring political will. With the intervention and fear of losing property, a coalition of land owners, military, and US officials pressured the Vatican basically to outlaw the movement under threat of excommunication from the Catholic Church. The situation became so tense in Latin America that rogue military death squads, some of whom were trained in the US, murdered priests and nuns who were seeking social justice for the poor.

As a net result of the dual failures of modernization and liberation movements other theories related to development communication emerged. There were several theories over time as well as a number of well intentioned projects. The second chapter examined three major theories which sought to replace the economically driven modernization theory. They were cultural imperialism, participatory communication, and entertainment-education. In general they broadened the approaches in two key ways. First a more local, bottom-up strategy was called for and second, non- economic dimensions, such as cultural integrity, were added to the development agendas.

An excellent case-study utilizing the participatory communication theory and methods was the Sonagachi Project in Calcutta, India. According to journalist Satarupa Dasgupta, who participated in the project, it examined a HIV/AIDS intervention program undertaken in a red light district of Calcutta, India. The Sonagachi Project started in 1991 to ascertain and arrest the incidence of sexually transmitted diseases (STDs) and HIV/AIDS among sex workers in and around the Sonagachi district in Calcutta. The Sonagachi Project involves participation-based communication intervention that is undertaken at three concurrent levels – community, group, and individual. A vital aspect of the Sonagachi Project is its initiative of re-articulation of issues related to sex work – including the status of sex work itself – and stressing the right of sex workers to avail themselves of material resources and opportunities. The peer outreach model of the project involves the mobilization of sex workers as opinion leaders and purveyors of the project. One of the outcomes of the project is the attainment of healthcare facilities for the sex workers and their children, and also creation of literacy programs and vocational training centers for the latter. The project also resulted in the sex workers unionizing and forming their own provident fund and micro-credit societies. Dasgupta's chapter endeavors to elaborate the theoretical presumptions of participation-based development communication, and tries to explore the extent to which the Sonagachi Project subscribes to the said notions. Dominant paradigms of development such as modernization theory are analyzed to understand their relevance in the Sonagachi Project. The chapter also looked into Freirian notions of development to examine the dialogue initiated by the sex workers with their peers to disseminate awareness information about reproductive health. In addition the chapter tried to assess whether the Sonagachi Project conformed to the notions of empowerment communication – a new and specialized form of development communication approach. Empowerment communication has its theoretical framework based in participatory and development communication but is specifically geared towards fostering research agendas that facilitate social transformation and justice. Empowerment communication, with its emphasis on power differentials, potentially offers analytical means of addressing structural inequalities in groups that historically have been marginalized. Given the long running treatment of indigenous peoples around the globe additional participatory communication projects could be illuminating.

The third chapter looked at the various activities of the United Nations as well as a number of its specialized agencies. From a global perspective the UN has the mandate and the finances to impact development communication more than any other organization. In particular, in 1965 the UN created the UN Development Programme which has been the leading unit across the UN system for projects and planning for future positive development activities. Finally, a large and dispersed group under the umbrella of the World Social Forum (WSF) was detailed. Both the hegemonic power and control by the US and the activities of the UN in world affairs are frequent targets at WSF forums and conferences. A frequent complaint is that the UN provides aid funds to military and authoritarian regimes with little follow up as to where the funds actually go. Given the desperate situation in many Third World nations it is obvious

that the funds never made it the poorer classes of these impoverished nations.

There is a growing consensus that the various agencies of the UN
have a handle on the underlying structural issues involving development communication but they are handicapped in two fundamental
ways in terms of moving to the next level. The next level is actually
solving the basic structural issues. The two problems are the lack
of funds for the units or agencies looking into how to be more successful in implementing effective development communication projects, and the other is the inability to keep crooked regimes from
hijacking the aid funds and funneling them to their family, friends,
or military.

The fourth chapter examined the influential role of non-
governmental organizations (NGOs). The various types of NGOs
were outlined. Many were created to assist the parent UN system
achieve its goals across a broad range of tasks. Clearly the NGO
phenomena as it applies to development communication are reflected
by the large number of NGOs associated with the UN specialized
agencies, such as UNESCO and the ITU.

Recently the plethora of NGOs has resulted in greater competition
for both funds and media attention. Many competing NGOs have to
become more sophisticated at attracting attention to their causes.
They need "face time" in the media to make their case or raise funds.
To be interviewed by CNN or the BBC World Service is invaluable,
particularly if your group is in the midst of some national tragedy.
All NGOs are not created equal. Some are much more sophisticated
in terms of media savvy which often translates into enhanced fund-
raising and recruiting ability.

There was also a review of the role and function of major American
foundations. The big three, namely Carnegie, Ford, and Rockefeller
were described in terms of their support for development communication projects. Examples of their political agendas were also outlined. In particular their conservative boards tend to be dominated by
former senior US government officials or retired military or banking
executives. A good example is Henry Kissinger's relationship with
the Rockefeller Foundation as well as his personal relationship with
Nelson Rockefeller, the same person who attacked Liberation Theology. Currently some Third World nations also fear that CIA agents
are among those groups sent to monitor Foundation initiatives.

Finally, three different organizations with a connection to either NGOs or foundations were outlined. They were the World Social Forum which is worried about American hegemony, the Communication for Social Change Consortium, and the impressive International Development Research Centre of Canada. Canada, much like middle size powers such as Australia and the Nordic nations, has been able to launch projects in the southern hemisphere without the negative historical baggage which the US and other more powerful nations take with them.

The fifth chapter looked a three interrelated organizations. They were the new NGO, the International Network for Cultural Diversity (INCD), UNESCO as it pertains to a global cultural convention, and the WTO, particularly in terms of its future attempts to include cultural industries/audio-visual industries in its trade agreements. The first two organizations are pitted directly against what they perceive as the potential threat from the WTO.

Here is the basic issue. A growing number of nations fear that their culture, and in some cases language, are threatened by a homogenous global culture evolving from the media domination and hegemonic power of primarily American communication conglomerates. Given the fragile nature of several cultures and communities in the southern hemisphere, the economic determinism of future WTO treaties could undermine or indeed destroy small cultures and language communities.

The INCD recognized this threat early and managed to get UNESCO on board. As a result in 2005 UNESCO adopted a Convention on the Protection and Promotion of the Diversity of Cultural Expression. The goal of the Convention is to provide and empower nations to take steps or measures to protect and promote their indigenous cultures. It seeks to aid multiculturalism and sees diversity as a public good which should be expanded and not reduced or threatened. The WTO's take on the matter is entirely different. They want media outlets, production of artifacts, and generally anything that can be bought and sold to be subject to WTO trade agreements. The WTO does not see cultural industries as unique or requiring special protection as part of a countries' heritage. The WTO views the world through an economic lens. They see cars, steel, or lumber as being identical to music, movies, or video products and productions. Finally, it is not surprising that the US did not vote for the Convention and actively pushes the WTO to move toward including cultural industries in future trade agreements.[1]

The sixth chapter begins the series of commissioned chapters from experts reflecting an interdisciplinary approach. Renée Houston and Michele Jackson focus on development efforts that use information and communication technologies for educational purposes in developing nations. The oppositional nature of the approaches to development makes constructive dialogue among these perspectives difficult. Using Jackson's (1996) metatheoretical classification scheme, we sort development research based on four possible logical relationships among technology as an artifact and social context. Derivation of the scheme is principled rather than historical and independent of any particular theory. Focusing on assumptions about technology and context brings new understanding of each perspective and can foster much needed dialogue across the perspectives.

In Chapter 7, Mitchell Rice examines information and communication technologies and the global digital divide and discusses determinants and conditions that have contributed to its creation. An important discussion this chapter examines is whether there is a convergence or absolute convergence or divergence or relative divergence in the application and diffusion of ICTs between developed countries and LDCs and, if so, which of these conditions will continue. Another issue addressed in this chapter is what are the basic conditions required in a country to facilitate technology transfer, application and diffusion of ICTs. This chapter draws on several highly respectable data sources and an extensive body of literature to provide a fairly clear picture of how the ICT revolution is shaping up globally. However, the chapter does not pretend to be a full assessment of the ICT global situation between countries.

In Chapter 8 Luz Estella Porras and H. Leslie Steeves examine the significant and historically under-researched area of the role of women in development projects in general as well as communications in particular. They develop a typology that frames and integrates gendered experience, knowledge, and voice. From a feminist lens they focus on the non-material dimensions and practices of development communication. One of the dimensions is spirituality which was also touched on in Chapter 1 when the possible gains from Liberation theology were discussed. Finally, the authors discuss the material and historical constraints that hinder the possibility and potential for women to control, use, own, produce, and work for the media. Some of the constraints are contemporary policies perpetuated by religious and male-dominated hierarchies.

The ninth chapter on the Sonagachi Project was discussed previously under Chapter 2, when outlining participatory communication theory.

In the tenth chapter, Eva Szalvai attempts to seek and better understand the hegemonic process of globalization. Due to the power differences, globalization results in differential advantage and disadvantage for the involved nations and cultures. The dialectical criticism of globalization aims to monitor social injustice and advances concepts on media homogenization, uneven information flow, and cultural imperialism. This interdisciplinary study explores the practices of globalization that are less culturally biased. Particularly, it makes a first attempt to conceptualize a new globalization form, "interlocalization." Premised upon a competitive and free market system, the study explores the ways "interlocalization" might offer a more equitable relationship for the players of different cultures. Some "interlocalization" practices are also elaborated in a case study of the Roma project. Based on the Roma projects of the Open Society Institute in Europe, the case study presents research on the role of "interlocalization" in social change. Analyzing cross-cultural participatory communication, this study explores the use of "interlocalization" as a tool in the creation of global practices for sustainable development. The overarching goal for this research is the advancement of equity and justice in media and development communication practices globally.

Observations: Reframing

In terms of reframing the field of development communication there are pertinent observations in most chapters and the final external academic pieces are specifically designed to reframe how and what gets done in the development communication sector in the future.

There are a number of both general as well as specific observations that emerge from the review and materials in this book. Collectively they will assist in reframing the field. They are:

- The area of development communication, in terms of theory and practice, is in flux.
- There are no grand theories or quick fixes available.
- An interdisciplinary approach and teams need to tackle the problems besetting the field of development communication.
- Modernization theory has been challenged as naïve and overly optimistic; yet some researchers and foundations still cling to it.
- Top down approaches generally fail.
- Seeking only economic indicators or measures of so-called success fails to grasp the underlying nature of the task.
- Concern for culture, traditions, language, and other non-economic variables is now a necessary part of the mix.
- Local participation at the earliest possible stages is essential for success.
- The role and input from women is an under-researched area which will lead to more meaningful and fruitful results.
- The accounting of funds still plagues development communication projects; far too many authoritarian regimes have siphoned off vast amounts of project funds.
- In general, universities and government aid agencies do not support creative and path-breaking development schemes or radical experimentation.
- Creative attempts such as the Sonagachi Project and the Roma Project are experimental rays of hope in what for decades has been a wasteland of model projects.
- The needs, input, and hopes of those in the southern hemisphere need to trump the agendas of the granting agencies, foundations, or universities.
- The pure voices and oral and folk traditions of the southern hemisphere need to be heard and respected.
- Outsiders cannot be authentic insiders.
- In some situations there needs to be a recognition that not everyone wants to be saved; many do not want their life-style to be changed, they just want to make the best out of a bad situation.

For example, that their children get a chance at education or health care.

- Tied aid clearly hampers the ability of the local participants to truly succeed.
- Environmental and green concerns need to be taken into account at both the strategic planning phase as well as at the outcomes assessment phase.
- The United Nations and its specialized agencies need to rethink and likely rearrange their activities and funding priorities when it comes to development communication; given that the vast sums spent over several agencies have not produced either the leadership or positive change in the southern hemisphere.
- Some individual nations are doing well at implementing development communication related initiatives yet there needs to be a mechanism whereby there is some overall coordination which would leverage the funding in a more strategic manner within a multi-nation format.
- The expanding number of NGOS with an interest in this sector is resulting in a situation where there are now many more voices seeking fewer available funds; this reduces the likelihood that large interdisciplinary teams and projects will be forthcoming or sponsored by NGOs despite the need.
- The placement and spread of information technologies to those in most need across the Third World continues to be problematic and sporadic; this could be a natural area for the Bill and Melinda Gates Foundation to become engaged.
- The global concern about US hegemony, including both economic as well as military power, debases and undercuts the humanitarian motives of American aid, academic projects, or NGOs performing development communication initiatives.

Finally, the thrust of the chapters reflect the state of the field of development communication. No single theory or approach dominates the field. Rather, new projects or initiatives should draw from a range of approaches. The most fruitful approaches appear to be participatory, education-entertainment, avoiding cultural or religious imperialism, empowerment activities, interlocalization, and greater sensitivity to gender, social, linguistic, and cultural aspects of attempts to change behavior. It is by combining the most salient components of a range of approaches that positive social change will most likely come about. There is no "magic bullet" or sure fire way to approach development; but by learning from past mistakes and being open to new ideas and allowing those in the southern hemisphere to be included at the earliest stages could lead to more progress in development communication activities in the future.

Note

1 It is important to keep in mind that the US does not have a cabinet-level position for a Minister or Secretary of Culture. American culture is determined by the marketplace; writers, artists, actors, musicians, and others work in a commercial environment. In many instances the American model promotes a popular culture. By contrast, most other nations have a Department or Ministry of Culture with a high ranking and powerful cabinet-level Minister or Secretary in charge. Historically, from a public policy perspective, other nations view their culture as a vital part of nationhood and that it is not merely another commercial commodity to be bought and sold like soap or fish. Indeed, in some nations culture and religion are intertwined and that moves the sacredness or meaning of culture to another higher level of meaning and value.

Bibliography

AID Science and Technology in Development Series (1990). *Interactive Radio Instruction: Confronting Crisis in Basic Education*. Newton, MA: Education Development Center.

Anderson, I. (2000). Northern NGO Advocacy: Perceptions, Reality, and the Challenge. *Development in Practice*, 10, 445–50.

Anderson, J. and Houston, R. (2005). Complexity and Organizing: A Semiotic Analysis. In G. Barnett and R. Houston (eds.), *Progress in Communication Science: Self-Organizing Systems Theory and Communication Research* (Vol. 17). Greenwich, CT: Ablex.

Anderson, M. and Schrum, W. (2007). Circumvention and Social Change: ICTs and the Discourse of Empowerment. *Women's Studies in Communication*, 30(2), 229–53.

Anzalone, S. (1987). *Using Instructional Hardware for Primary Education in Developing Countries: A Review of the Literature*. Harvard University Basic Research and Implementation in Developing Education Systems Project (BRIDGES).

Arnst, R. (1996). Participatory Approaches to the Research Process. In J. Servaes, T. Jacobson, and S.A. White (eds), *Participatory Communication for Social Change*. Thousand Oaks, CA: Sage, pp. 109–26.

Attaran, A. (2005). An Immeasurable Crisis? A Criticism of the Millennium Development Goals and Why They Cannot Be Measured. *PLoS Med*, 2(10), 318.

Avgerou, C. (1998). How Can IT Enable Economic Growth in Developing Countries? *Information Technology for Development*, 8(1), 15–29.

Babb, F.E. (2001). *After Revolution: Mapping Gender and Cultural Politics in Neoliberal Nicaragua*. Austin: University of Texas Press.

Bagdikian, B.H. (2000). *The Media Monopoly*. Boston: Beacon Press.

Bakhtin, M.M. (1990). *The Dialogic Imagination*. Trans. M. Emerson. Austin: University of Texas Press.

Bandopadhyay, N., Ray, K., Banerjee, A., Jana, S., Saha, A., Kerrigan, D., and Mahendra, V.S. (2002). Operationalizing an Effective Community Development Intervention for Reducing HIV Vulnerability in Female Sex Work: Lessons Learned from the Sonagachi Project in Kolkata, India. *International Conference in AIDS*. 14.

Bandura, A., Ross, D., and Ross, S. (1963). Imitation of Film-Mediated Aggressive Models. *Journal of Abnormal and Social Psychology*, 66, 3–11.

Banuri, T. (1990). Modernization and its Discontents: A Cultural Perspective on the Theories of Development. In F. Apffel Marglin and S. Marglin (eds), *Dominating Knowledge: Development, Culture and Resistance*. Oxford: Clarendon Press.

Baran, P. (1957). *The Political Economy of Growth*. New York: Monthly Review Press.

Barker, C. (2005). Television and National Identities in the Era of Globalization. In M. Romero and E. Margolis (eds), *The Blackwell Companion to Social Inequalities*. Malden, Blackwell Publishing Ltd, pp. 503–22.

Barro, R. (1997). *Determinants of Economic Growth: A Cross Country Empirical Study*. Boston: MIT Press.

Basu, I., Jana, S., Rotherma-Borus, M.J., Swendeman, D., Sung-Jae, L., Newman, P., and Weiss, R. (2004). HIV Prevention among Sex Workers in India. *Journal of Acquired Immuno-Deficiency Syndromes*, 36(3), 845–52.

BBC News Online (1999a). Losing Ground Bit by Bit. <www.news.bbc.co.us/hi/english_report/1999/10/99>.

BBC News Online (1999b). Plugging into the Revolution. <www.news.bbc.co.us/hi/english_report/1999/10/99>.

Belbase, S. (1994). Participatory Communication in Development: How Can We Achieve It? In S.A. White, K.S. Nair, and J.A. Ascroft (eds), *Participatory Communication: Working for Change and Development* (3rd ed.). New Delhi: Sage, pp. 446–61.

Bell, S. (1989). Technology in Medicine: Development, Diffusion, and Health Policy. In H.E. Freeman and S. Levine (eds), *Handbook of Medicine Sociology*, 4th ed. Englewood Cliffs, NJ: Prentice Hall.

Berghahn, V.R. (1999). Philanthropy and Diplomacy in the "American Century." *Diplomatic History*, 23, 393–419.

Bhagwati, J. (2001). After Seattle: Free Trade and the WTO. *International Affairs*, 77(1), 15.

Bitu, N. (2005). No Longer Willing to Wait on Gender. *Open Society News*, (Summer-Fall), 10–11.

Black, M. (2002). *International Development*. London: Verso.

Blankenship, K.M., Friedman, S.R., Dworkin, S., and Mantell, J.E. (2006). Structural Interventions: Concepts, Challenges and Opportunities for Research. *Journal of Urban Health*, 83(1), 59–72.

Bob, C. (2005). *The Marketing of Rebellion: Insurgents, Media, and International Activism*. New York: Cambridge University Press.

Bock, J.C. and Arthur, G. (1991). Politics of Education Reform: The Experience of a Foreign Technical Assistance Project. *Educational Policy*, 5(3), 312–29.

Bogdanić, A. (2005). The Croatian National Programme for the Roma: An Example of Gender Inequality? In OSI (ed.), *Overcoming Exclusion: The Roma Decade, Part II. Reflecting on Social Impact: Employment and Gender*. <www.soros.org/initiatives/roma/articles_publications/publications/overcomingtwo_20050916/bogdanic_2005.pdf>, accessed May 2, 2008.

Bolt, D.B. and Crawford, R.A.K. (2000). *The Digital Divide: Computers and Our Children's Future*. New York: TV Books.

Boserup, E. (1970). *Women's Role in Economic Development*. New York: St. Martin's Press.

Bourdieu, P. (1977). *Outline of a Theory of Practice*. Cambridge and New York: Cambridge University Press.

Bourdieu, P. and Wacquant, L. (1992). *An Invitation to Reflexive Sociology*. Chicago: University of Chicago Press.

Boyd-Barrett, O. (1981–2). Western News Agencies and the "Media Imperialism" Debate: What Kind of Data-Base? *Journal of International Affairs*, 35(2), 247–60.

Braman, S., Shah, H., and Fair, J. E. (2000). We Are All "Natives" Now: An Overview of International and Development Communication Research. *Communication Research Yearbook*, 24, 159–88.

Briggs, J. and Peat, F.D. (1989). *Turbulent Mirror: An Illustrated Guide to Chaos and the Theory Wholeness*. New York: Harper and Row.

Cadiz, M.C.H. (2005). Communication for Empowerment: The Practice of Participatory Communication in Development. In D. Hemer and T. Tufle (eds), *Media and Glocal Change*. Sweden: Nordicom, pp. 145–58.

Campbell, D. (2001). Can the Digital Divide Be Contained? *International Labour Review*, 140(2), 119–41.

Capra, F. (1997). *The Web of Life: A New Understanding of Living Systems*. New York: Doubleday.

Carnoy, M. and Levin, H.M. (1975). Evaluation of Educational Media: Some Issues. *Instructional Science*, 4, 385–406.

Chan-Tibergien, J. (2006). Cultural Diversity as Resistance to Neoliberal Globalization: The Emergence of a Global Movement and Convention. *International Review of Education*, 52, 89–105.

Chinn, M.D. and Fairlie, R.W. (2004). The Determinants of the Global Digital Divide: A Cross-Country Analysis of Computer and Internet Penetration. Center for Global, International, and Regional Studies. Paper CGIRS-2004-3.

Clarke, G.R.G. (2001). *Bridging the Digital Divide: How Enterprise Ownership and Foreign Competition Affect Internet Access in Eastern Europe and Central Asia*. Washington, DC: Development Research Group, World Bank, July.

Commission of the European Communities (2001). *Information and Communication Technologies in Development: The Role of ICTs in EC Development Policy*. Brussels, December 14.

Comor, E.A. (ed.) (1994). *The Global Political Economy of Communication: Hegemony, Telecommunication and the Information Economy*. New York: St. Martin's Press.

Condon, C. (2005). Heading for a Showdown on Desegregation in Hungary. *Open Society News*, (Summer-Fall), 8–9.

Corea, S. (2007). Promoting Development Through Information Technology Innovation: The IT Artifact, Artfulness, and Articulation. *Information Technology for Development*, 13(1), 49–69.

Crothers, L. (2006). *Globalization and American Popular Culture*. Lanham, MD: Rowman and Littlefield.

Crowe, D. and Kolsti, L. (eds) (1991). *The Gypsies of Eastern Europe*. Armonk, NY: M.E. Sharpe.

Cuban, L. (1986). *Teachers and Machines*. New York: Teachers College Press.

Dalton, R.J. (2005). Social Modernization and the End of Ideology Debate: Patterns of Ideological Polarization. Prepared for the Conference on "Beliefs, Norms, and Values in Cross-National Surveys," University of Tokyo, Tokyo, Japan.

Danaher, K. (2001). *10 Reasons to Abolish the IMF and World Bank*. New York: Seven Stories Press.

Dasgupta, S. (2008). Sonagachi Project. A Paper Presented at the Annual Conference of the International Association for Mass Communication Research [IAMCR.] Stockholm, Sweden: July.

Dasgupta, S., Hall, S., and Wheeler, D. (2002). *Policy Reform, Economic Growth and the Digital Divide: An Econometric Analysis*. Washington, DC: World Bank, Development Research Group.

Davies, P. (1987). *The Cosmic Blueprint*. London: Unwin.

Decade of Roma Inclusion (2006). <www.romadecade.org/index.htm>, accessed May 10, 2006.

Decade Watch (2007). Roma Activists Assess the Progress of the Decade of Roma Inclusion. Internal document of the Open Society Institute.

De Moura Castro, C., Wolff, L., and Garcia, N. (1999). Mexico's Telese-cundaria – Bringing Education by Television to Rural Areas. *Tech-KnowLogia*, (September–October).

Dervin, B. and Huesca, R. (1997). Reaching for the Communicating in Participatory Communication: A Meta-Theoretical Analysis. *The Journal of International Communication*, 4(2), 46–74.

Deutschmann, P.J., Huber, E., and McNelly, J. (1968). *Communication and Social Change in Latin America: Introducing New Technology*. New York: Frederick A Praeger.

Dietrich, S., Heider, D., Matschinger, H., and Angermeyer, M.C. (2006). Influence of Newspaper Reporting on Adolescents' Attitudes toward People with Mental Illness. *Social Psychology and Psychiatric Epidemiology*, 41, 318–22.

Ditchev, I. (2007). Hegemony of the Global-Popular? (Or Cultural Studies as Accomplice?). *Inter-Asia Cultural Studies*, 8(3), 454–7.

Dourish, P. (2001). *Where the Action Is: The Foundations of Embodied Interaction*. Cambridge, MA: MIT Press.

Downing, J. (2001). Community Democracy, Dialogue and Radical Media. In A. Gumocio- Dagrón and T. Tufte (eds), *Anthology: Historical and Contemporary Readings*. South Orange, NJ: Communication for Social Change Consortium, pp. 828–40.

Draganova, V. (2005). The Challenge of Finding a Place in Two Worlds. *Open Society News*, Summer-Fall, 17.

Drissel, D. (2006). Internet Governance in a Multipolar World: Challenging American Hegemony. *Cambridge Review of International Affairs*, 19(1), 105–20.

Duncombe, R. (2000). *Information and Communication Technology, Poverty and Develoment in Sub-Saharan Africa*. Manchester, UK: Institute for Development Policy and Management, University of Manchester.

Edwards, M. (1989). The Irrelevance of Development Studies, *Third World Quarterly*, 11(1), 116–35.

Eggleston, K., Jensen, R., and Zeckhauser, R. (2002). Information and Communication Technologies, Markets and Economic Development. In *The Global Information Technology Report 2001–2002: Readiness for the Networked World*. New York: Oxford University Press and Center for International Development at Harvard University.

Elasmar, M.G. and Bennett, K. (2003). The Cultural Imperialism Paradigm Revisited: Origin and Evolution. In M.G. Elasmar (ed.), *The Impact of International Television: A Paradigm Shift*. Mahwah: NJ, Lawrence Earlbaum Associates, pp. 1–16.

Eminova, E. (2005). Raising new questions about an old tradition. *Open Society News*, Summer-Fall, 12–13.

ERRC. (2008). Official Site of the European Roma Right Centre (EERC). <www.errc.org/About_index.php>, accessed May 5, 2008.

Escobar, A. (1992). Reflections on Development: Grassroots Approaches an Alternative Politics in the Third World, *Futures*, 24(5), 11–36.

Escobar, A. (1995). *Encountering Development: The Making of and Unmaking of the Third World*. Princeton: Princeton University Press.

Escobar, A. (2000). Place, Power, and Networks in Globalization and Post-development. In K. Wilkins (ed.), *Redeveloping Communication for Social Change*. Lanham, MD: Rowman and Littlefield Publisher, pp. 163–73.

Escobar, A. and Alvarez Sonia, E. (1992). *The Making of Social Movements in Latin America: Identity, Strategy, and Democracy*. Boulder, CO: Westview Press.

Fagerlined, I. and Saha, L.J. (1989). *Education and National Development*. Oxford: Pergamon Press.

Fair, J.E. (1989). 29 Years of Theory and Research on Media and Development: The Dominant Paradigm Impact. *Gazette*, 44, 129–50.

Fair, J.E. and Shah, H. (1997). Continuities and Discontinuities in Communication and Development Research since 1958. *The Journal of International Communication*, 4(2), 3–23.

Fanon, F. (1963). *The Wretched of the Earth*. New York: Grove Press.

Farrington, J. and Bebbington, A. (1993). *Reluctant Partners? Non-Governmental Organizations, the State and Sustainable Agricultural Development*. New York: Routledge.

Fernandez-Armesto, F. (2006). *Pathfinders: A Global History of Exploration*. London: Norton.

Figueroa, M.E., Kincaid, D.L., Rani, M., and Lewis, G. (2002). Communication for Social Change: An Integrated Model for Measuring the Process and its Outcomes. The Communication Initiative Webpage <www.comminit.com/en/node/1273>, accessed December 4, 2008.

Foucault, M. (1987). *The History of Sexuality. Vol. 1: An Introduction*. New York: Random House.

Frank, A.G. (1969). *Latin America: Underdevelopment or Revolution*. New York: Yale University Press.

Frank, A.G. (1972). *Dependent Accumulation and Underdevelopment*. London: Macmillan.

Fraser, A. (1992). *The Gypsies*. Oxford: Blackwell.

Frau-Meigs, D. (2004). On Research and the Role of NGOs in the WSIS Process. *The Massachusetts Institute of Technology: Information Technologies and International Development*, 1, 103–7.

Frederick, H.H. (1993). *Global Communication and International Relations*. Belmont, CA: Wadsworth Publishing Company.

Freire, P. (1970). *Pedagogy of the Oppressed*, (M.B. Ramos, Trans.). New York: Continuum.

Freire, P. (1983). *Pedagogy of the Oppressed*. New York: Continuum.

Friend, J., Searle, B., and Suppes, P. (eds) (1980). *Radio Mathematics in Nicaragua*. Stanford, CA: Stanford University Press.

Funk, K. (1999). Information Networking as an Instrument of Sustainable Development: Connectivity, Content and (Co-) Capacity Building. *Social Science Computer Review*, 17(1), 107–14.

Gallagher, M. (2005). Beijing's Legacy for Gender and Media. *Media Development* (3).

Gallagher, M. (2008). Feminist Issues in the Global Media System. In K. Sarikakis and L.R. Shade (eds), *Feminist Interventions in International Communication*. Boulder, CO: Rowman & Littlefield, pp. 7–31.

Galli, R.E. (1976). The United Nations Development Program, "Development," and Multinational Corporations. *Latin American Perspectives*, 3(4), 65–85.

Garbacz, C. and Thompson Jr, H.G. (2007). Demand for Telecommunication Service in Developing Countries. *Telecommunications Policy*, 31(5), 276–89.

Gerbner, G. Gross, L., Morgan, M., Signorielli, N., and Shanahan, J. (2002). Growing Up With Television: Cultivation Processes. In J. Bryant and D. Zillmann (eds), *Media Effects: Advances in Theory and Research*. Mahwah, NJ: Lawrence Erlbaum Associates, pp. 43–68.

Gilbert, D.T. (1991). How Mental Systems Believe. *American Psychologist*, 46, 107–19.

Giddens, A. (1984). *The Constitution of Society: Outline of a Theory of Structuration*. Berkeley: University of California Press.

Global Envision (2007). Reducing the Global Digital Divide in Sub-Saharan Africa. <www.globalenvision.org/library/7/1406/>, accessed January 8, 2008.

Global Internet Liberty Campaign (2000). *Bridging the Digital Divide: Internet Access in Central and Eastern Europe*. Global Internet Liberty Campaign.

Goldston, J.A. (2005). Advancing Romani Rights in the Czech Republic and Euorpe. *Open Society News*, Summer-Fall, 5–6.

Graham, S. (2002). Bridging the Digital Divides: Urban Polarization and Information and Communications Technologies (ICTS). *Urban Studies*, 39(1), 33–56.

Gramsci, A. (2002). *The Antonio Gramsci Reader: Selected Writings 1916–1935*. New York: New York University Press.

Granqvist, M. (2005). Assessing the ICT Development: A Critical Perspective. In O. Hemer and T. Tufle (eds), *Media and Global Change*. London: Verso, pp. 285–96.

Grant, J.P. (1978). *Disparity Reduction Rates of Social Indicators*. Overseas Development Council, Monograph No. 11.

Grant, P.S. and Wood, C. (2004). *Blockbusters and Trade Wars: Popular Culture in a Globalized World*. Vancouver, BC: Douglas and McIntyre.

Gumucio-Dagrón, A. (1991).The Overmarketing of Social Marketing. <www.comminit.com/es/node/72068>, accessed May 11, 2007.

Gunn, C. (2004). *Third-Sector Development: Making Up for the Market*. Ithaca: Cornell University Press.

Hancock, S. (ed.) (1984). *Technology Transfer and Communication*. Paris: UNESCO.

Haqqani, A.B. (ed.) (2005). *The Role of Information and Communication Technologies in Global Development: Analyses and Policy Recommendations*. United Nations ICT Task Force. New York: United Nations Press.

Harcourt, W. and Mumtaz, K. (2002). Fleshy Politics: Women's Bodies, Politics and Globalization. *Development*, 45(1), 36–41.

Harrison, L. (2000). *Underdevelopment is a State of Mind*. New York: Madison Books.

Harvey, D. (2003). *The New Imperialism*. New York: Oxford University Press.

Hemer, O. and Tufte, T. (eds) (2005). *Media and Glocal Change: Rethinking Communication for Development*. Buenos Aires: Clasco.

Hills, J. (2002). *The Struggle for Control of Global Communication*. Urbana: University of Illinois Press.

Hochschild, A. (1989). *The Second Shift*. New York: Avon Books.

Hogg, R., Cahn, P., Katabira, E., Lange, J., Samuel, N., O'Shaughnessy, M., Vella, S., Wainberg, M., and Montaner, J. (2002). Time to Act: Global Apathy Towards HIV/AIDS Is a Crime Against Humanity. *Lancet*, 9347, 1710–11.

Holmes, D.E. (1972). Some Unrecognized Assumptions in Research on the Diffusion of Innovations. *Rural Sociology*, 37(3), 463–9.

Hooks, b. (1994). *Teaching to Transgress*. New York: Routledge.

Hoover, J. (2007). *Persistence Pays: The Challenges and Rewards of One NGO's Health Promotion Outreach among Roma Drug Users*. Sofia, Bulgaria: The Initiative of Health Foundation (IHF) Publication. <www.soros.org/initiatives/health/focus/roma/articles_publications/publications/persistence_20070930>, accessed February 23, 2008.

Hornik, R. and McAnany, E. (2001). Theories and Evidence: Mass Media Effects and Fertility Change. *Communication Theory*, 11(4), 454–71.

Houston, R. (1993). Predicting Discontinuance in Diffusion: An Elaboration of Expectancy Value Theory. Unpublished Master's Thesis, Tallahassee: Florida State University.

Houston, R. and Heald, G.R. (1995). Using Logistic Functions to Predict the Discontinuation of Interactive Media Innovations in International Develoment Projects. Paper presented at the 12th Annual Intercultura/International Communication Conference, Miami, FL.

Hudson, M. (1999). Understanding Information Media in the Age of Neoliberalism: The Contributions of Herbert Schiller. *Progressive Librarian*. 16, 11 December 2007.

Huesca, R. (2003a). Communication as Process. In. A. Gumocio-Dagrón, and T. Tufte (eds), *Anthology: Historical and Contemporary Readings*. South Orange, NJ: Communication For Social Change Consortium, pp. 566–77.

Huesca, R. (2003b). Participartory Approaches to Communication Development. In B. Mody (ed.), *International and Development Communication*. Thousand Oaks, CA: Sage, pp. 209–26.

Huntington, S. (1996). *The Clash of Civilizations and the Remaking of World Order*. New York: Simon and Schuster.

Huws, U. (2008). Women, Participation and Democracy in the Information Society. In K. Sarikakis and L.R. Shade (eds), *Feminist Interventions in International Communication*. Boulder, CO: Rowman and Littlefield, pp. 45–56.

Inagaki, N. (2007). Communicating the Impact of Communication for Development: Recent Trends in Empirical Research. World Bank Working Paper no. 120, Washington DC: World Bank.

InfoDev.org (2002). Sector Strategy Paper for the Global Information and Communications Department of the World Bank, (April). <www.infodev.org/library/working.htm>.

Inglehart, R. (1977). *The Silent Revolution*. Princeton: Princeton University Press.

Inglehart, R. (1990). *Culture Shift in Advanced Industrial Society*. Princeton: Princeton University Press.

Inkeles, A. and Smith, D.H. (1974). *Becoming Modern: Individual Change in Six Developing Countries*. Cambridge: Harvard University Press.

International Labour Organization (2001). *World Employment Report: Life at Work in the Information Economy*. Geneva: ILO.

International Network for Cultural Diversity (INCD) (2003). *Newsletter*, *4(1)*, Ottawa: Canada Council.

International Telecommunication Union (2005). <www.itu.int/wsis/index. html>.

Internet World Stats (2008). Internet Usage Statistics: The Internet Big Picture. <www.internetworldstats.com/stat.htm>.

Iriye, A. (1999). A Century of NGO's. *Diplomatic History*, 23, 421–35.

Jackson, M.H. (1996). The Meaning of Communication Technology: The Technology- Context Scheme. In B. Burleson (ed.), *Communication Yearbook 19*. Thousand Oaks, CA: Sage Publications, pp. 229–68.

Jackson, M.H., Poole, M.S., and Kuhn, T. (2002). The Social Construction of Technology and Studies of the Workplace. In L. Lievrouw and S. Livingstone (eds), *The Handbook of New Media*. London: Sage.

Jacobson, T.L. and Storey, J.D. (2004). Development Communication and Participation: Applying Habermas to a Case Study of Population Programs in Nepal. *Communication Theory*, 14(2), 99–121.

Jana, S., Banerjee, B., Saha, A., and Dutta M. (1999). Creating an Enabling Environment: Lessons Learnt from the Sonagachi Project, India. *Research for Sex Work*, 2(1), 22–4.

Jana, S., Basu, I, Rotheram-Borus, M.J., and Newman, P. (2004). The Sonagachi Project: A Sustainable Community Intervention Program. *AIDS Education and Prevention*, 16(5), 405–14.

Joseph, A. (2004). Working, Watching and Waiting: Women and Issues of Access, Employment, and Decision-Making in the Media in India. In K. Ross and C.M. Byerly (eds), *Women and Media: International Perspectives*. Oxford: Blackwell, pp. 132–56.

Kabacheiva, P. (2005). A Community Grapples with Desegregation in Bulgaria. *Open Society News*, Summer-Fall, 14–16.

Kalathil, S. (2001). The Internet in Asia: Broadband or Broad Bans?, *Foreign Service Journal*, 78(2), February, 21–36.

Kalathil, S. and Boas, T.C. (2001). The Internet and State Control in Authoritarian Regimes: China, Cuba, and the Counterrevolution. Carnegie Endowment for International Peace, Global Policy Program, Working Papers, no. 21, (July).

Kalb, J. (2006). The Institutional Ecology of NGOs: Applying *Hansmann* to International Development. *Texas International Law Journal*, 41, 298–310.

Karlyn, A. (2001). The Impact of a Targeted Radio Campaign to Prevent STIs and HIV/AIDS in Mozambique. *AIDS Education and Prevention*, 13(5), 438–51.

Kauffman, R.J. and Techatassanasoontorn, A.A. (2005). Is There a Global Digital Divide for Digital Wirelss Phone Technologies?, *Journal of the Association for Information Systems*, 6(12), 338–82.

Kayman, M.A. (2004). The State of English As a Global Language: Communicating Culture. *Textual Practice*, 18(1), 1–22.

Kelsey, J. (2005). Why Culture Activists Should be Concerned about Trade Agreements. *INCD Newsletter*, 6(10), 2–6.

Kenny, C. (2002). *The Costs and Benefits of the ICTs for Direct Poverty Alleviation*. Washington, DC: World Bank.

Kimberly, J.R. (1981). Managerial Innovation. In P. Nystrom and W.H. Starbuck (eds), *Handbook of Organizational Design*. New York: Oxford University Press.

Kumar, M.S.V. (1986). Introducing Technological Innovations for Education in a Developing Country: Implications for Planning. Unpublished doctoral dissertation. Amherst: University of Massachusettes.

Laclau, E. and Moufe, C. (1987). Post-Marxism Without Apologies, *New Left Review*, 166, 79–106.

Lapeyre, F. (2004). The Outcome and Impact of the Main International Commissions on Development Issues. Working paper no. 30. Policy Integration Department, World Commission on the Social Dimension of Globalization, International Labour Office, Geneva.

Latour, B. (1987). *Science in Action: How to Follow Scientists and Engineers through Society*. Cambridge, MA: Harvard University Press.

Latour, B. (2005). *Reassembling the Social: An Introduction to Actor-Network Theory*. Oxford: Clarendon Press.

Law, J. (2002). *Aircraft Stories: Decentering the Object in Technoscience*. Durham, NC: Duke University Press.

Lazarsfeld, P.F., Berelson, B., and Gaudet, H. (1944). *The People's Choice*. New York: Duell, Sloan and Pearce.

Lazreg, M. (2002). Development: Feminist Theory's Cul-de-sac. In K. Saunders (ed.), *Feminist Post-Development Thought*. London: Zed Books, pp. 123–45.

LeBaron, M. and Pillay, V. (2007). *Conflict across Cultures: A Unique Experience of Bridging Differences*. Boston: Intercultural Press.

Lee, R. (2002). Globalization and Mass Society Theory. *International Review of Sociology*, 12(1), 45–61.

Leonardi, P.M. (2008). Indeterminacy and the Discourse of Inevitability in International Technology Management. *Academy of Management Review*, 33(4), 975–84.

Lerner, D. (1958). *The Passing of Traditional Society: Modernizing the Middle East*. Glencoe, IL: The Free Press.

Lind, A. (2003). Feminist Post-Development Thought: "Women in Development" and the Gendered Paradoxes of Survival in Bolivia. *Women's Studies Quarterly*, 31(3–4), 227–46.

Lipset, S. (1959). Some Social Requisites of Democracy: Economic Development and Political Legitimacy. *American Political Science Review*, 53(1), 69–105.

Luthra, R. (1991). Contraceptive Social Marketing in the Third World: A Case Study of Multiple Transfer. *Gazette*, 47, 159–76.

MacBride, S. (1980). *Many Voices, One World*. New York: Unipub.

Maitland, D. (1984). *The Missing Link*. Geneva: ITU Press.

Mamidipudi, A. and Gajjala, R. (2008). Juxtaposing Handloom Weaving and Modernity: Bulding Theory Through Praxis. *Development in Practice*. 18(2), 235–44.

Martens, K. (2003). Examining the (Non-) Status of NGOs. *Indiana Journal of Global Legal Studies*, 10(2), 1–24.

Martín Barbero, J. (2002). *La educación desde la communicación*. Buenos Aires: L Grupo Editorial Norma.

Marx, K. and Engels, F. (1848). *The Communist Manifesto*. Oxford: Oxford University Press, 1992.

Mayo, J.K. (1989). Unkept Promises: Educational Broadcasting in the Third World. Paper Presented to the Intercultural/Development Division of the International Communication Association at its 1989 Annual Convention.

McChesney, R. (2001). Global Media, Neoliberalism, and Imperialism. *Monthly Review*, 52, 1–19.

McChesney, R (2005). *The Future of Media: Resistance and Reform in the 21st Century*. New York: Seven Stories Press.

McGinn, N.F. (1996). Education, Democratization, and Globalization: A Challenge to Comparative Education. *Comparative Education Review*, 40, 341–58.

McLaughlin, L. (2008). Women, Information and the Corporatization of Develoment. In K. Sarikakis and L.R. Shade (eds), *Feminist Interventions in International Communication*. Boulder, CO: Rowman and Littlefield, pp. 224–40.

McNair, S. (2000). The Emerging Policy Agenda. In *Schooling for Tomorrow: Learning to Bridge the Digital Divide*. Paris: Organization for Economic Cooperation and Development, pp. 9–20.

McNamara, K.S. (2003). Information and Communication Technologies, Poverty, and Development: Learning from Experience. A Background Paper for the infoDev Annual Symposium December 9–10, 2003 Geneva, Switzerland. Washington, DC: The World Bank.

McPhail, T. (1981). *Electronic Colonialism: The Future of International Broadcasting and Communication*. Newbury Park: Sage, (with Forward by Everett Rogers).

McPhail, T. (1989). Inquiry in International Communication. In M. Asante and B. Gudykunst (eds), *Handbook of International and Intercultural Communication*. Newbury Park, CA: Sage Publications, pp. 47–66.

McPhail, T. (1994). Television and Development Communication: A Canadian Case Study. In A. Moemeka (ed.), *Communicating for Development: A Pan-Disciplinary Perspective*. Albany, NY: State University of New York Press, pp. 191–218.

McPhail, T. (2006). *Global Communication: Theories, Stakeholders, and Trends* (2nd ed.). Oxford: Blackwell.

McPhail, T. and Judge, S. (1983). Direct Broadcast Satellites: The Demise of Public and Commercial Policy Objectives. In I. Singh (ed.), *Telecommunications in the Year 2000: National and International Perspectives*. Norwood, NJ: Ablex, pp. 72–9.

McPhail, T. and McPhail, B. (1987). The International Politics of Telecommunications: Resolving the North-South Dilemma. *International Journal*, 42, 289–319.

McPhail, T. and McPhail, B. (1990). *Communication: The Canadian Experience*. Toronto: Copp Clark Pitman.

Meehan, E.R. (2008). Audience Commodity. In W. Donsbach (ed.), *The International Encyclopedia of Communication*, vol. 8, Oxford: Wiley-Blackwell.

Mefalopulos, P. (2002). Empowerment Communication. In A. Gumocio-Dagrón and T. Tufte (eds), *Anthology: Historical and Contemporary Readings*. South Orange, NJ: Communication for Social Change Consortium, p. 836.

Melkote, S.R. and Steeves, H.L. (2001). *Communication for Development in the Third World: Theory and Practice for Empowerment*. New Delhi: Sage Publications.

Mies, M. and Shiva, V. (1993). *Ecofeminism*. Halifax: Fernwood Publications.

Miller, A. (2001). Reaching Across the Divide: The Challenges of Using the Internet to Bridge Disparities in Access to Information. *First Monday*, 6(10), October, 8–16.

Mitchell, P. and Chaman-Ruiz, K. (2007). *Communication-Based Assessment for Bank Operations*. Washington, DC: The World Bank.

Mody, B. (1985). First World Technologies in Third World Contexts, In E.R. Rogers and F. Gall (eds), *The Media Revolution in America and in Western Europe*, vol. 2. Norwood, NJ: Ablex, pp. 134–49.

Mody, B. (1997). Communication and Development: Beyond Panaceas. *The Journal of International Communication*, 4(2), 1–2.

Mody, B. (ed.) (2003). *International and Development Communication.* Thousand Oaks. CA: Sage.

Moemeka, A.A. (1994). *Communicating for Development.* Albany, NY: State University of New York Press.

Mohanty, C.T. (1991). Under Western Eyes. In C.T. Mohanty, A. Russo, and L.M. Torres (eds), *Third World Women and the Politics of Feminism.* Bloomington and Indianapolis: Indiana University Press.

Morales-Gómez, D. and Melesse, M. (1998). Utilising Information and Communication Technologies for Development: The Social Dimensions. *Information Technology for Development,* 8(1), 3–13.

Mosco, V., McKercher, C., and Stevens, A. (2008). Convergences: Elements of a Feminist Political Economy of Labor and Communication. In K. Sarikakis and L.R. Shade (eds), *Feminist Interventions in International Communication.* Boulder, CO: Rowman and Littlefield, pp. 207–23.

Murdock, G. (2006). Notes From the Number One Country: Herbert Schiller on Culture, Commerce and American Power. *International Journal of Cultural Policy,* 12(2), 209–27.

Murphy, C.N. (2006). *The United Nations Development Programme: A Better Way?* Cambridge: Cambridge University Press.

Myers, M. (2002). Institutional Review of Educational Radio Dramas. Report for Centers for Disease Control and Prevention. Atlanta, Georgia.

Nariman, H. (1993). *Soap Operas for Social Change: Toward a Methodology for Entertainment-Education Television.* Connecticut: Praeger.

Nath, M. (2000). Women's Health and HIV: Experience from a Sex Workers' Project in India. In C. Sweetman (ed.), *Gender in the 21st century.* London: Oxfam, pp. 100–7.

National Office for the Information Economy (2002). *The Current State of Play: Australia's Scorecard.* Commonwealth of Australia: National Office for the Information Economy, April.

Navas-Sabater, J., Dymond, A., and Junutumen, N. (2002). *Telecommunications and Information Services for the Poor.* Washington, DC: World Bank.

Noronha, F. (2003). Community Radio: Singing New Tunes in South Asia. *Economic and Political Weekly,* 38(22), 168–72.

Nussbaum, M.C. (2000). *Women and Human Development: The Capabilities Approach.* Cambridge: Cambridge University Press.

Open Society Institute (2006). About Us. <www.soros.org/about/bios/a_soros>, accessed December 3, 2006.

Open Society Institute Initiatives (2006). Roma Initiative: Building Global Alliance for Open Society. <www.soros.org/initiatives/roma>, accessed December 7, 2006.

Open Society News (2005). The Decade of Roma Inclusion: Challenging Centuries of Discrimination. *Open Society News*, Summer-Fall. <www.soros.org/resources/articles_publications/publications/osn_20051011/osnroma_20051011.pdf>, accessed September 12, 2006.

Organization for Economic Cooperation and Development (2001). *Understanding the Digital Divide*. Paris: Organization for Economic Cooperation and Development.

Organization for Economic Cooperation and Development (2002). *Measuring the Information Economy*. Paris: Organization for Economic Cooperation and Development.

Orlikowski, W. (1992). The Duality of Technology: Rethinking the Concept of Technology in Organizations, *Organization Science*, 3(3), 398–427.

Orlikowski, W.J. and Iacono, C.S. (2001). Research Commentary: Desperately Seeking the "IT" in IT Research: A Call to Theorizing the IT Artifact. *Information Systems Research*, 12(2), 121–34.

OSI/EU Monitoring and Advocacy Program (2007). *Monitoring Reports: Equal Access to Quality Education for Roma. Volume 2:Croatia, Macedonia, Montenegro, Slovakia*. Budapest, Hungary: OSI Publications. <www.soros.org/initiatives/roma/articles_publications/publications/equal_20071217/equal_20071218.pdf>, accessed March 12, 2008.

Ottaway, M. (2002). Nation Building. *Foreign Policy*, 132, 16–24.

Otto, D. (1996). Nongovernmental Organizations in the United Nations System: The Emerging Role of International Civil Society. *Human Rights Quarterly*, 18(1), 107–31.

Oza, R. (2001). Showcasing India: Gender, Geography, and Globalization. *Signs*, 26(4), 1067–94.

Parenti, M. (2006). *The Culture Struggle*. New York: Seven Stories Press.

Parmar, I. (2002). American Foundations and the Development of International Knowledge Networks. *Global Networks*, 2, 13–30.

Peters, T. (2003). Bridging the Digital Divide. *Global Issues*, 8(3), 3–7.

Petersone, B. (2007). Integrated Approach to Development Communication: A Public Relations Framework for Social Changes. Paper Presented at the Annual Meeting of the International Communication Association, San Francisco.

Petrova, D. (2005). Marginalization of Roma in Russia: Less Noticed but No Less Oppressive. *Open Society News*, Summer-Fall, 18–19.

Pigato, M. (2001). Information and Communication Technology, Poverty and Development in Sub-Saharan Africa and South Asia. Africa Region Working Papers Series no. 20, Washington, DC: World Bank.

Popper, K. (1945). *The Open Society and Its Enemies.* London: Routledge.

Porras, L.E. (2008). Moving from *Cantaleta* to *Encato* or Challenging the Modernization Posture in Communication for Development and Social Change: A Columbian Case Study of the Everyday Work of Development Communicators. Unpublished PhD dissertation. Eugene: University of Oregon.

Porroveccio, M. (2007). Lost in the WTO Shuffle: Publics, Counterpublics and the Individual. *Western Journal of Communication*, 71(3), 235–56.

Portas, A. (1974). Modernity and Development: A Critique. *Studies in Comparative International Development*, 9, Spring, 247–9.

Poster, M. (2004). The Information Empire. *Comparative Literature Studies*, 41(3), 317–34.

Postma, W. (1994). NGO Partnership and Institutional Development: Making it Real, Making it Intentional. *Canadian Journal of African Studies*, 28, 447–71.

Pye, L (ed.) (1963). *Communications and Political Development.* Princeton: Princeton University Press.

Quebral, N.C. (2006). Development Communication in the Agricultural Context. *Asian Journal of Communication*, 16(1), 100–7.

Raley, R. (2004). eEmpires. *Cultural Critique*, 57, 111–50.

Regan, L.S. and Porter, N. (2008). Empire and Sweatshop Girlhoods: The Two Faces of the Global Culture Industry. In K. Sarkikakis and L.R. Shade (eds), *Feminist Interventions in International Communication*. Boulder, CO: Rowman and Littlefield, pp. 241–57.

Rice, M.F. (2001). The Digital Divide and Race in the United States. *Politics, Adminstration, and Change*, 36, July-December, 20–31.

Rishi, W.R. (1976). *Roma.* Patiala, India: Punjabi University.

Robertson, R. (1992). *Globalization: Social Theory and Global Culture.* London: Sage.

Robinson, W.I. (2006). Reification and Theoreticism in the Study of Globalisation, Imperialism and Hegemony: Response to Kiely, Pozo-Martin and Valladao. *Cambridge Review of International Affairs*, 529–33.

Rodriguez. C. (2001a). Shattering Butterflies and Amazons: Symbolic Constructions of Women in Colombian Development Discourse. *Communication Theory*, 11(4), 472–94.

Rodriguez, C. (2001b). *Fissures in the Mediascape: An International Study of Citizen's Media*. Cresskill, NJ: Hampton Press.

Rodriguez, F. and Wilson, III, E. (2000). Are Poor Countries Losing the Information Revolution?, InfoDev Working Paper. Washington, DC, World Bank Group.

Rogers, E.M. (1962). *The Diffusion of Innovations*. New York: The Free Press.

Rogers, E.M. (1976). *Communication and Development: Critical Perspectives*. Beverly Hills: Sage.

Rogers, E.M. (1994). *A History of Communication Study: A Bibliographical Approach*. New York: The Free Press.

Rogers, E.M. and Kincaid, D.L. (1981). *Communication Networks: A Paradigm for New Research*. New York: Free Press.

Rogers, E.M. and Vaughan, P. (2000). A Stage Model of Communication Effects: Evidence from an Entertainment Education Radio Soap Opera in Tanzania. *Journal of Health Communication*, 5(3), 203–27.

Rogers, E.M., Ratzan, S.C., and Payne J.G. (2001). Health Literacy: A Non-issue in the 2000 Presidential Election. *American Behavioral Scientist*, 44(12), 2172–95.

Rogers, E.M., Vaughan, P.W., Swalehe, R.M.A., Rao, N., Svenkerud, P., and Sood, S. (1999). Effects of an Entertainment-Education Radio Soap Opera on Family Planning Behavior in Tanzania. *Studies in Family Planning*, 30(3), 193–211.

Romani Organization (2008). History of the Roma. <www.romani.org/local/romhist.html>, accessed April 27, 2008.

Rorke, B. and Wilkens, A. (eds) (2006). Roma Inclusion: Lessons Learned from OSI's Roma Programming. <www.soros.org/initiatives/roma/articles_publications/publications/inclusion_20060605>, accessed July 26, 2006.

Rostow, W.W. (1960). *The Stages of Economic Growth: A Non-Communist Manifesto*. Cambridge: Cambridge University Press.

Rothkop, D. (1997). In Praise of Cultural Imperialism? Effects of Globalization on Culture. *Foreign Policy*, 107, 38–53.

Roy, P., Waisanen, F., and Rogers, E. (1969). *The Impact of Communication on Rural Development: An Investigation in Costa Rica and India*. Paris: UNESCO.

Sachs, J. (2000). Today's World is Divided not by Ideology but by Technology. *The Economist*, 26 July, 99.

Sagna, O. (2000). *Information and Communications Technologies and Social Development in Senegal: An Overview*. United Nations Institute for Social Development, Research Project of Information Technologies and Social Development.

Sahay, S. and Avgerou, C. (2002). Introducing the Special Issue on Information and Communication Technologies in Developing Countries. *The Information Society*, 18, 73–6.

Said, E.W. (1978). *Orientalism*. New York: Random House.

Saunders, K. (ed.) (2002). *Feminist Post-Development Thought*. London, UK: Zed Books.

Schiller, H. (1976). *Communication and Cultural Domination*. White Plains: International Arts and Sciences Press.

Schiller, H.I. (2001). Not Yet the Post Imperialist Era. In M.G. Durham and D. Kellner (eds), *Media and Cultural Studies: Keyworks*. Malden, MA: Blackwell, pp. 318–33.

Schramm, W. (1964). *Mass Media and National Development: The Role of Information in Developing Countries*. California: Stanford University Press.

Schramm, W. (1977). *Big Media, Little Media*. Beverly Hills and London: Sage.

Schuurman, F. (ed.) (1993). *Beyond the Impasse: New Directions in Development Theory*. London: Zed Books.

Sciadis, G. (2003). *Monitoring the Digital Divide . . . and Beyond*. Montreal, Canada: Orbicom.

Sein, M. and Harindranath, G. (2004). Conceptualising the ICT Artefact: Towards Understanding the Role of ICT in National Development. *The Information Society*, 20(1), 15–24.

Sen, A. (1994). Freedoms and Needs. *The New Republic*, October 17.

Servaes, J. (1994). Advocacy Strategies for Development Communication. *The Journal of Development Communication*, 5(2), 1–16.

Servaes, J. (1995). Participatory Communication (Research) From a Freirean Perspective. Paper Presented at IAMCR Conference Portoroz, Slovenia, June.

Servaes, J. and Arnst, R. (1999). Principles of Participatory Communication Research: Its Strengths (!) and Weaknesses (?). In T. Jacobson and J. Servaes (eds), *Theoretical Approaches to Participatory Communication*. Cresskill, NJ: Hampton Press, pp. 107–30.

Servaes, J. and Malikhao, P. (1991). Concepts: The Theoretical Underpinnings of the Approaches to Development Communication. UNFPA/UNESCO Project. Integrated Approaches to Development Communication: A Study and Training Package. Paris: UNFPA/UNESCO.

Servaes, J., Jacobson, T., and White, S. (eds) (1996). *Participatory Communication for Social Change*. Thousand Oaks, CA: Sage.

Shade, L.R. and Porter, N. (2008). Empire and Sweatshop Girlhoods: The Two Faces of the Global Culture Industry. In K. Sarikakis and L.R.

Shade (eds), *Feminist Interventions in International Communication*. Boulder, CO: Rowman and Littlefield, pp. 241–58.

Shandra, J.M. (2007). International NGOs and Deforestation. *Social Science Quarterly*, 88, 665–72.

Sharan, M. and Valente, T. (2002). Spousal Communication and Family Adoption: Effects of a Radio Serial in Nepal. *International Family Planning Perspectives*, 28(1), 16–25.

Sharma, M. (2006). Applying a Freirian Model for Development and Evaluation of Community-Based Rehabilitation Programs. *Asia Pacific Disability Rehabilitation Journal*, 17, 42–49.

Shiva, V. (1991). *Stolen Harvest: The Hijacking of the Global Food Supply*. Cambridge, MA: South End Press.

Shome, R. and Hedge, R.S. (2002). Postcolonial Approaches to Communication: Charting the Terrain, Engaging the Intersections. *Communication Theory*, 12(3), 249–70.

Simmons, P.J. (1998). Learning to Live with NGOs. *Foreign Policy*, 112, 82–96.

Singh, J.P. (2007). Culture or Commerce? A Comparative Assessment of International Interactions and Developing Countries at UNESCO, WTO, and Beyond. *International Studies Perspectives*, 8(1), 36–53.

Singhal, A. (2007). Popular Media and Social Change: Lessons from Peru, Mexico, and South Africa. *Brown Journal of World Affairs*, 13(2), 259–69.

Singhal, A. and Rogers, E. (1999). *Entertainment Education: A Communication Strategy for Social Change*. Mahwah, NJ: Lawrence Erlbaum Associates.

Singhal, A., Cody, M.C., Rogers, E. and Sabido, M. (eds) (2003). *Entertainment-Education and Social Change: History, Research and Practice*. NJ: Lawrence Erlbaum Associates.

So, A. (1990). Social Change and Development: Modernization, Dependency, and World-System Theories. Newbury Park, CA, Sage.

Soros, G. (1994). The Theory of Reflexivity. Speech delivered on April 26 to the MIT Department of Economics World Economy Laboratory Conference, Washington, DC. <www.geocities.com/ecocorner/intelarea/gs1.html>, accessed May 24. 2008.

Soros, G. (2000). *Open Society: Reforming Global Capitalism*. New York: Public Affairs.

Soros, G. (2002). *Globalizacion*. Barcelona, Spain: Planeta.

Soros, G. (2003). *The Alchemy of Finance*. Hoboken, NJ: John Wiley and Sons.

Soros, G. (2006). *The age of Fallibility: Consequences of the War on Terror*. New York: Public Affairs.

Soros, G. and Walker, P.A. (2003). *The Alchemy of Finance.* Hoboken, NJ: Wiley and Sons.

Sosale, S. (2002). Towards a Critical Genealogy of Communication, Development, and Social Change. Paper presented at the annual conference of the AEJMC.

Sproull, L. and Kiesler, S. (1991). *Connections: A New Way of Working in Networked Organizations.* Cambrige, MA: MIT Press.

Sreberny, A. (2005). Gender Empowerment and Communication: Looking Backwards and Forwards. *International Social Science Journal,* 57(2), 285–300.

Stacey, R.D. (1996). *Complexity and Creativity in Organizations.* San Francisco, CA: Berret-Koehler Publications.

Staudt, K. (1985). *Women, Foreign Assistance and Advocacy Administration.* New York: Praeger.

Steeves, H.L. (2001). Liberation, Feminism and Development Communication. *Communication Theory,* 11(4), 397–414.

Steeves, H.L. and Wasko, J. (2002). Feminist Theory and Political Economy: Towards a Friendly Alliance. In E. Meehan and E. Riordan (eds), *Sex and Money: Intersections of Feminism and Political Economy in Media,* Minneapolis: University of Minnesota Press, pp. 16–29.

Stiglitz, J. (2002). Participation and Development: Perspectives from the Comprehensive Development Paradigm. *Review of Development Economics,* 6(2), 163–82.

Stover, W.J. (1984). *Information Technology in the Third World: Can IT Lead to Humane National Development?* Boulder, CO: Westview Press.

Streeten, P. (1979). Development Ideas in Historical Perspective. In K. Hill (ed.), *Towards a New Strategy for Development.* New York: Pergamon Press, pp. 21–52.

Suppes, P., Searle, B., and Friend, J. (eds). (1978). *The Radio Mathematics Project: Nicaragua 1976–1977.* Stanford, CA, Stanford University, Institute for Communication Research.

Swann, W., Giuliano, T., and Wegner, D. (1982). Where Leading Questions Can Lead: The Power of Conjecture in Social Interaction. *Journal of Personality and Social Psychology,* 42, 1025–35.

Szalvai, E. (2008). Emerging Forms of Globalization Dialectics: Interlocalization, a New Praxis of Power and Culture in Commercial Media and Development Communication. PhD Dissertation. Bowling Green State University, Ohio.

Tandon, R. (1985). Participatory Research: Issues and Prospects. In *Farmer's Assistance Board Response to Asian People's Struggle for Social Transformation.* Manila: Farmer's Assistance Board.

Thomas, P. (1994). Participatory Development Communication: Philosophical Premises. In A. Gumocio-Dagrón and T. Tufte (eds), *Anthology: Historical and Contemporary Readings*. South Orange, NJ: Communication for Social Change Consortium, pp. 475–81.

Thussu, D.K. (2000). *International Communication: Continuity and Change*. New York: Oxford University Press.

Tomaselli, K., McLennan-Dodd, V., and Shepperson, A. (2005). Research To Do, Results To Sell: Enabling Subjects and Researchers. *Society in Transition*, 36(1), 24–37.

Truman, H. (1949). *Inaugural Address of January 20, 1949*. Washington DC: Government Printing Office.

Tufte, T. (2004). Entertainment-Education in HIV/AIDS Communication: Beyond Marketing, Towards Empowerment. In C. von Feilitzen and U. Carlsson (eds), *Yearbook 2003: Promote or Protect?* The UNESCO International Clearinghouse on Children, Youth and Media. Nordicom, Göteborg University.

UNESCO (2005). *Convention on the Protection and Promotion of the Diversity of Cultural Expressions*. Paris: UNESCO.

UNESCO (2007). *UNESCO's Contribution to the to the UN Secretary General's Fifth Annual Progress Report on the Implementation of the Brussels Programme of Action for the Least Developed Countries (LDCs) for the Decade 2001–2010*. New York: United Nations.

UNICEF (2008). Meena Communication Initiative. <www.unicef.org/rosa/media_2479.htm>, accessed August 29, 2008.

United Nations (2000a). *United Nations Millennium Declaration*. New York: United Nations.

United Nations (2000b). *Report of the Meeting of the High-Level Panel of Experts on Information and Communication Technology*. New York: United Nations, April, 17–20.

United Nations (2007). *The Least Developed Countries Report 2007: Overview by the Secretary-General of UNCTAD*. New York: United Nations.

United Nations Association, United States of America, and the Business Council for the United Nations (2003). <www.unausa.org/site/pp.asp?c=fvKRI8MPJpF&b=373983>.

United Nations Development Programme (1999). *Human Development Report*. New York: Oxford University Press.

United Nations Development Programme (2000). *Driving Information and Communications Technology for Development: A UNDP Agenda for Action 2000–2001*. New York: United Nations Development Programme, October.

United Nations Development Programme (2001). *Human Development Report 2001*. New York: Oxford University Press.

United Nations Development Programme (2005). *Human Development Report 2005: International Cooperation at a Crossroads. Aid, Trade and Security in an Unequal World*. New York: United Nations.

United Nations Development Programme (2006). *Communication for Empowerment: Developing Media Strategies in Support of Vulnerable Groups: Practical Guidance Note*. New York: United Nations, Bureau for Development Policy, Democratic Governance Group.

United Nations Development Programme (2007). *The Millennium Development Goals Report: 2007*. New York: United Nations.

United Nations Industrial Development Organization (2002). *UNIDO Initiative on Technology Transfer for WSSD: Assessing Needs – Promoting Actions*. <www.unido.org/userfiles/ hartmany/WSSD_UNIDO intech transfer.pdf>.

United Nations, Secretary General, SG/SM/9760 (2005). Secretary-General Reiterates Determination to Build Global, Inclusive Information Society, in Message to Ceremony Launching Digital Solidarity Fund in Geneva. United Nations Information Service, March 15.

United Nations, Secretary General, SG/SM/11577 (2008). Narrowing Digital Divide Crucial Part of Achieving Global Anti-Poverty Goals. New York, United Nations, Department of Public Information, News and Media Division, May 16.

Van Tuijl, P. (2000). Entering the Global Dealing Room: Reflections on a Rights-Based Framework for NGOs in International Development. *Third World Quarterly*, 21, 617–26.

Vaughan, P., Regis, A., and St Catherine, E. (2000). Effects of an Entertainment-Education Radio Soap Opera on Family Planning and HIV Prevention in St. Lucia. *International Family Planning Perspectives*, 26(4), 148–57.

Vaughan, P., Rogers, E.M., Singhal, A., and Swalehe, R.M. (2000). Entertainment-Education and HIV/AIDS Prevention: A Field Experiment in Tanzania, *Journal of Health Communication*, 5(Suppl.), 81–100.

Wallerstein, I. (1983). *Historical Capitalism*. London: Verso.

Wang, W. (2008). A Critical Interrogation of Cultural Globalisation and Hybridity: Considering Chinese Martial Arts Films as an Example. *The Journal of International Communication*, 14(1), 46–64.

Wangwacharakul, Vute (no date). Technological Transfer: Thailand's Perspective. <www.unfcc.int/program/sd/technology/techdo/thaicp. pdf>.

Waters, M. (1995). *Globalization*. New York: Routledge.

Watson, K. (ed.) (1984). *Dependency and Interdependence in Education: International Perspectives*. London: Croom, Helm.

Waverman, L., Meschi, M., and Fuss, M. (2005). *The Impact of Telecoms on Economic Growth in Developing Countries*. Vodafone Policy Paper Series, 2, London, (March).

Weiler, H.N. (1978). Education and Development: From the Age of Innocence to the Age of Skepticism, *Comparative Education*, 14(3), 179–98.

Weiner, T. (2008). *Legacy of Ashes: The History of the CIA*. New York: Anchor.

West, H.G. and Fair, J.E. (1993). Development Communication and Popular Resistance in Africa: An Examination of the Struggle over Tradition and Modernity through Media. *African Studies Review*, 36(1), 91–114.

White, R.A. (2004). Is Empowerment the Answer? Current Theory and Research in Development Communication. In A. Gumocio-Dagrón and T. Tufte (eds), *Anthology: Historical and Contemporary Readings*. South Orange NJ: Communication for Social Change Consortium, pp. 830–31.

Wilkins, K.G. (1999). Development Discourse on Gender and Communication in Strategies for Social Change. *Journal of Communication*. 49(1), 46–68.

Wilkins, K.G. (2005). Out of Focus: Gender Visibilities in Development. In O. Hemer and T. Tufte (eds), *Media and Glocal Change*. Sweden: Nordicom.

Wilkins, K.G. and Mody, B. (2001). Reshaping Development Communication: Developing Communication and Communicating Development. *Communication Theory*, 11(4), 385–96.

Wilkens, A. and Rostas, J. (2005). Time for Europe to Erase a Critical Democratic Deficit. *Open Society News*, Summer-Fall, 3–4. <www.soros.org/initiatives/roma/news>, accessed January 12, 2006.

Wilkin, K. and Waters, J. (2000). Current Discourse on New Technologies in Development Communication. *Media Development*, 1, 57–60.

Winner, L. (1977). *Autonomous Technology: Technics-Out-of-Control as a Theme in Political Thought*. Cambridge, MA: MIT Press.

Winner, L. (1986). *The Whale and the Reactor: A Search for Limits in an Age of High Technology*. Chicago: University of Chicago Press.

Wilson, E. (2006). *The Information Revolution and Developing Countries*. Cambridge, MA: MIT Press.

World Economic Forum (2000). From the Global Divide to the Global Digital Opportunity: Proposals Submitted to the G-8 Kyushu-Okinawa Summit.

Yapa, L. (1991). Theories of Development: The Solution as the Problem. *Research and Exploration*, 3, 263–75.

Yong Jin, D. (2007). Reinterpretation of Cultural Imperialism: Emerging Domestic Market Vs Continuing US Dominance. *Media, Culture and Society*, 29(5), 753–71.

Zaharopoulos, T. (2003). Perceived Foreign Influence and Television Viewing in Greece. In M.G. Elasmar (ed.), *The Impact of International Television: A Paradigm Shift*. Mahwah, NJ: Lawrence Earlbaum Associates, pp. 39–56.

Index